D1282628

COMMUNICATION
ETHICS
LITERACY

Dialogue & Difference

Second Edition

RONALD C. ARNETT
DUQUESNE UNIVERSITY

JANIE M. HARDEN FRITZ
DUQUESNE UNIVERSITY

LEEANNE M. BELL MCMANUS
STEVENSON UNIVERSITY

Kendall Hunt
publishing company

Cover image courtesy of Millie Arnett

Kendall Hunt
publishing company

www.kendallhunt.com
Send all inquiries to:
4050 Westmark Drive
Dubuque, IA 52004-1840

Previously published by SAGE Publications, Inc.
Copyright © 2017, 2018 by Kendall Hunt Publishing Company

ISBN 978-1-5249-3633-4

Published in the United States of America

Table of Contents

Preface

[T]he ethical relation cannot be reduced either to an act of self-affirmation or to one of selflessness, but instead emerges in the presence of the other . . . in the view of dialogic philosophy, communication avoids reducing recognition of the other to a kind of mimetic re-cognition of the other in which we view the other solely in terms of our own precognitions and thus assimilate them into what we already know (or think we know) about their point of view. Rather, communication is a process of opening to the other. (Lipari, 2004, pp. 130–131)

It is impossible for one voice to . . . approach a complete version of reality that is fully representative of all human and cultural activities. (Jackson, 2000, p. 49)

Communication Ethics Literacy: Dialogue and Difference begins and ends with a consistent refrain—we live in a time of rival understandings of the "good," an era defined by competing narrative and virtue structures. Perhaps our one communication ethics agreement is that contention is now normative; it is no longer a communicative surprise. The reality of difference as the defining characteristic of this historical moment makes the study of communication ethics necessary in order to live and work with others effectively. This work considers the study and practice of communication ethics a pragmatic necessity. Difference presupposes multiple views of the good, and communication ethics literacy assumes the importance of understanding and learning from difference, from the Other. We use the term "Other" in a philosophical sense to refer to any human being embedded within a set of assumptions about right and wrong, good and bad, appropriate and inappropriate ways of engaging human life grounded within and definitive of what Alasdair MacIntyre (1998) refers to as a tradition with whom we may come into contact. In this sense the Other points to our general responsibility to the entire human community (Appiah, 2006). At the same time, we recognize that human life is lived one conversation at a time, within constraints of particular settings and concerns.

Although the subject of this book is communication ethics, we find it important to focus briefly on the broader term, "ethics," and its associated term, "morality." Both terms deal generally with principles of right and wrong and how human beings should conduct themselves according to these principles. These terms have been formally defined by various schools of philosophical thought. Ethics in the *Cambridge Dictionary of Philosophy* is "the philosophical study of morality" (Audi, 1999, p. 284), the "general study of right action . . . [concerning] the principles of right and wrong that govern our choices and pursuits" (p. 286). For others, ethics deals with making decisions about the right course of action to take in life contexts. Jürgen Habermas (1979), for example, addresses ethics as procedural, as dealing with communicative conduct appropriate for determining public courses of action. In this book, we consider "ethics" as practices that enact or support a good, a central value or set of values associated with human life and conduct. In this sense, ethics lies at the heart of communicative practices, a point we will return to over and over in this book. In Chapter 3, we address various definitions of communication ethics, each of which points to a particular underlying good.

Communication as a discipline has historically assumed the importance of the audience, the Other, the speaker, and the message. Communication ethics follows this classic assumption into an even more demanding era, a time without common public agreement. Throughout human history, disputes about the good have been engaged through various means, including wars of weapons and of words. In this sense, our moment is not new; again, we meet the perennial question of how to work out our differences in productive ways. What may be new is a greater willingness to learn from alternative points of view and new ways of framing previous unchallenged perspectives on human history, ideas, and action. Communication ethics enters the conversation with pragmatic importance as the core message of this era becomes increasingly understood as difference, different views of what is and is not the good. Sorting through differing views of the good defines this historical moment. We, along with other scholars, use the term "postmodernity" as a marker of this time of narrative and virtue contention, a time of explicit and recognized disagreement about the shared stories that give our lives meaning. In the first chapter, we will explain the term postmodernity and its relevance to communication ethics in this historical moment.

Struggles in the Middle East, clashes among and within religious groups, arguments over human sexuality, appropriate responses to ongoing terrorist threats, concerns about school safety, and other life-and-death issues meet questions about new technologies and human security—from uncertainty of job longevity and Social Security to identity theft. One is no longer surprised to discover that a "friend" thinks "so differently than I do." Difference and loss of common public agreement on the good give identity to this historical moment. Communication ethics literacy makes a pragmatic entrance into the conversation of difference, and the table of participants continues to expand.

The Pragmatic

We live in a moment in which public and private rules for engagement with one another are no longer in place, and common spaces and places of agreement are not the normative background for communicative life. This moment, however, is not a time for lament, but, on the contrary, an occasion for rejoicing if one wants to learn or has been on the outside of what a dominant group attempted to claim as universal when it was actually empowering only a select few. This moment of contention about the good disrupts what Hannah Arendt called the life of the "parvenu," the person wanting acceptance, only to have those in power offering constant denial based upon expectations that the seeking person could never meet. The joy of this learning moment is not that such local sanctuaries are no more; the communicative joy rests with knowledge that such sanctuaries are no longer defensible with universal claims of rightness. Learning from difference takes on both pragmatic and, in some cases, a liberating reality.

The contrasting position to an ongoing commitment to learning is the demand that life not change. The communicative result is a refusal to learn. This action forfeits the possibility of leadership in a century defined by learning how to negotiate difference. As this book, *Communication Ethics Literacy: Dialogue and Difference,* suggests: Let us expect the different, learn from the unknown, and not take for granted that the Other holds dear the same sense of the good that gives our individual and collective communicative lives meaning. Pragmatic communication ethics action begins with learning, withholding the impulse to tell until one understands the context, the topic, and the persons. Learning is the pragmatic good of communication ethics in an era of narrative and virtue contention.

A Minimalist Era

This era of difference necessitates the pragmatic communicative move of connecting communication ethics to literacy, foregoing the desire to "tell" or to prescribe as the initial communicative gesture. Imagine a college student from the United States, Liz, meeting her roommate, Yuan, from China, for the first time. During a discussion of their families, Yuan mentions that she would never contradict her mother about family matters. Liz, surprised, states that she often disagrees with her mother about such issues and tells Yuan that she should be more assertive with her mother, as well. Yuan drops the subject and moves to another topic, thinking that Liz does not have proper respect for her mother. What if Liz had asked Yuan about what it means to be a "good daughter" in her culture instead of moving immediately to a position of telling?

The first principle of communication ethics is learning, ever wary of lament that masks narcissism and/or a refusal to learn. Learning is the pragmatic communicative action in a moment in which clarity does not reign. This era offers multiple views of the good, sorted out without the benefit of assuring light. We must now navigate varying shades of the dark, ranging from dusk to midnight. Simply put, if we are in the dark in an area that we do not know well, it is prudent to learn what is before us before we run off with confidence, or we are likely to collide with something in our ill-considered movement. In places that are familiar, telling and quick running can work, but if the communicative terrain becomes more diverse and less familiar, then learning must supersede telling. In the face of learning, the imposition of telling looks like a communicative act akin to running without direction in the dark with an accompanying screech that cries out for the return of the familiar, an "existential stipulation" demanding a reality that one can control.

This book works at a minimal level of "telling," minimizing the impulse to proclaim the details of normative communicative ethics in an era in which normative more aptly coincides with difference. We credit the insight of Sissela Bok (2002) and Christians and Traber (1997) for providing an opportunity for talking about ethics from a minimalist perspective. For instance, some of the classes we teach are composed primarily of nontraditional students, adult learners seeking a college degree. We ask for a minimal agreement—the program and the classes gather all of us together around one public good: learning. We do not ask for a maximal sense of agreement that takes us into the "why" of learning. Why a student learns—for love of knowledge, career advancement, or boredom—is not our business. We operate by agreement on a minimal sense of the good—learning. Our expectation for Ph.D. students, in contrast to our hopes for our nontraditional and traditional undergraduate students, involves more of a maximal understanding of the good, requiring more love of the learning itself, greater commitment to the particular mission and goals of the institution, and unique scholarly contributions to the ongoing story of the disciplinary enterprise. Nevertheless, even with Ph.D. students there is multiplicity of goods from different ideas, theories, professional/ vocational goals, and type of educational commitment.

Following the insight of Bok, we recognize this era as a time of "minimal" agreement as opposed to "maximal" agreement, in which only a few basic agreements about the good are discernible. Minimal agreement can actually invite productive communication among persons with different understandings of the good and makes learning about the Other an absolute necessity. Each chapter in *Communication Ethics Literacy: Dialogue and Difference* underscores a minimal set of communication ethics coordinates, a minimal understanding of the good. One could understand each chapter as working at the macro, rather than micro, level of communication ethics, aiming for a broad discussion of approaches and theories with a focus upon context and application rather than prescriptions for specific situations. Communication ethics in such a moment of difference begins not with abstract advice giving, but with learning about the different, the unexpected, and the unknown. Bok's distinction between minimal and maximal agreement keeps us from confusing concern for the "particular" with the micro level. Concern for the particular requires that we work at a minimal level of telling, giving space for the unique navigating of communication ethics in real life between persons and in communities and organizations.

The rationale for this minimalist approach is two-fold. First, the wisdom of Bok seems irrefutable in this historical moment. If we live in a time of disagreement, finding a minimal set of ethical agreements is more likely than identifying a maximal set of ethical agreements. Second, we seek to move communication ethics discussion away from its use as an ideological weapon that justifies the worst of provinciality by permitting unreflective confidence in pronouncements of "this is right" and "that is wrong." We offer a more modest option—communication ethics literacy—encouraging learning from and about differing understandings and enactments of the good. At first blush, this move seems to decrease the power of communication ethics; however, in actuality, it moves communication ethics literacy into a privileged communicative position, with the aim of meeting and learning differing understandings of the good in a time of normative disagreement.

Kwame Anthony Appiah (2006), in *Cosmopolitanism: Ethics in a World of Strangers*, adds another voice to the issue of universal and particular goods and the importance of minimalist, or what he calls "thin," agreement. His framing of the issue of ethics within an intercultural context reminds us that both the larger human community and our local, particular allegiances are vital in this moment. His work offers additional insight into engaging similarity and difference in understandings of the good within and across cultural boundaries. His work reminds us, as does the work of Bok, Christians and Traber, and Taylor, that ethical decision making does involve judgments of good and bad, better and worse, with regard to courses of action that one could engage at either the private or the public level.

Judgment is important in any communication schema. However, in a time defined by difference, the first impulse cannot be judgment. In this historical moment, judgment loses its privileged status to learning, which makes any later judgment walk alongside the privileged voice of our time, difference. When we judge we do so with recognition that we have taken a value-laden step, one that we cannot, with assurance, assume guides all others. One of the leading ethics scholars, Alasdair MacIntyre (1989), frames the dilemma of our time with the questions: *Whose Justice? Which Rationality?*

Alasdair MacIntyre (1989, 2016) addresses the issue of making judgments among claims and options for action within and among differing virtue-laden traditions. Our project acknowledges this task as necessary for meaningful human existence; however, the first communicative step that we suggest, also framed by MacIntyre, is the mandate to learn about and from different traditions. We acknowledge that traditions with radically incommensurable claims about the nature of the world, human existence, and the good will find the task of "translation" and negotiating of goods and decisions about communicative ethical action to be more difficult, and that traditions sharing some minimal commitment to a set of goods will find that task less daunting. As an example, one which we use later in this work, consider Gandhi's suggestion to Martin Buber that Buber engage in nonviolent resistance in the face of Nazi terror. Buber recognized that there was insufficient shared narrative ground to permit such engagement. If one of the parties in discourse does not agree on the value of conversation or even on the right of the other party to exist, there is little opportunity for shared learning. In such cases, dialogue is simply not possible. Such is one of the reasons that this work assumes a pragmatic stance on dialogue—it cannot, nor should, be demanded. The heart of a dialogic ethic rests in an irony—there must be a commitment to honor the dialogic interweaving of the demands of a given historical moment and the "type" of communication appropriate and necessary. We cannot impose dialogue on all situations any more than we can impose our friendship upon an unwilling recipient.

This work, *Communication Ethics Literacy: Dialogue and Difference,* attends to the privileged voice of our time—difference—with a pragmatic communication ethics admission. Learning is the keystone to communication ethics literacy in an era that acknowledges its heartbeat as a composite of multiple disparate and dissonant rhythms. This project highlights a minimal "ought" of learning—the importance of knowing one's own ground and the ground of others informs continuing conversations about understandings of the good. We offer this work for situations in which there is at least some minimal shared ground that permits a space for continuing conversation, with the implication that decisions among and between competing goods from different traditions or variations within a given tradition must take place in order for the work of human living to continue, and all begin with one initial demand in this historical moment—learn from the different.

A Narrow Ridge

This book adheres to Buber's (1948) notion of the "narrow ridge," which necessitates walking between extreme positions (Friedman, 1976). *Communication Ethics Literacy: Dialogue and Difference* seeks to avoid contrasting pitfalls that reside on opposing sides of the same narrow ridge. These pitfalls represent dual temptations—first, of a relativism that undermines temporal clarity, and, second, of an objectivism (Bernstein, 1983) that embraces a "bad faith" (Sartre, 1953, pp. 86–116) confidence that gives the illusion of standing above history and telling, rendering "the truth" for others.

Adhering to the insight of Richard Bernstein (1983), this work places communication ethics *Between Objectivism and Relativism.* We acknowledge the public presence of multiple competing goods, and we assume the importance of the first principle of communication ethics—learning that seeks to attend to the face of another, negotiate difference, and locate minimal agreement—permitting persons to function in the public sphere with those of differing maximal positions. Of course, such learning is not easy; this moment calls us to know the why and the how of our communication ethics actions in order to provide a public communication ethics map of the rationale for our decision making, recognizing that another moment may call for new consideration of action. Communication ethics works within the realm of temporal decision making, not answers for all time. Communication ethics is responsive to the demands and needs of the context, persons, and topics that shape our lives together.

We live in a time of disagreement that calls us to learn about and to negotiate difference, moving us to connect communication ethics with a communication model opposed to demand and open to learning—dialogue. Dialogue takes on pragmatic currency when it begins with attentiveness to the historical moment and the narrative content that shapes one's own communication ethics and that of another. Dialogic ethics lives in a communicative realm ever skeptical of demand, ever attentive to learning, ever wary of the impulse to stand above history and proclaim "the truth" with an air of unquestioned authority. Communication ethics does not live within the demand of "my way or the highway" or within the blaming demand of "it was entirely your fault." Dialogue that rejects the norm of demand invites learning and also works as a general communicative method, as outlined further in this book. The method of dialogue is, however, only a pointing, never a dictating, never a demand.

Dialogic ethics begins with modesty, not unabated self-assurance. Dialogic ethics begins with invitation, not demand. Dialogic ethics begins with difference, not commonality. Dialogic ethics begins with the assumption that ethics used as a weapon and dialogue used as a weapon turn upon themselves, becoming counterfeit communicative actions in an era that cries for learning over the rush to blame. Communication ethics literacy with a dialogic leaning/impulse begins with a pragmatic "why" to learn about differing "hows," communication ethics, or goods in action. Simply put, there is much that we do not share in common with one another, which moves us, first and foremost, from trying to impose ourselves on another to trying to learn from the differences that meet us. Our communication ethics burden begins with learning and ends with communicative action tempered by the conviction that negotiation of temporal agreement is not a resolution, but simply a juncture taking us to the next moment of questioning or of contending goods in a time that makes communication ethics literacy necessary.

This work assumes that James Chesebro (1997) was correct when he predicted the following:

> As we enter the twenty-first century, we should anticipate that a host of diverse ethical systems will be proposed, and that each of these proposals will make us reconsider our established and habitual symbol-using practices. This process will be challenging, perhaps maddening, but it may also move us closer to our goal of enhancing the quality of life for each of us. (p. 145)

The quality of our lives together rests within a pragmatic hope that learning about the new will temper our short-sighted self-protective impulses to reject whatever is in contrast with what we already know and do.

Communication Ethics Literacy: Dialogue and Difference takes Chesebro's prediction into book form, counting this historical moment as an opportunity to enhance communicative life for each of us. The narrow ridge before us requires a communication ethic that matters and a communication ethic wary of "the" answer. Each communication ethic comes with a heart-felt desire to protect and promote a given sense of the good, just as this project protects and promotes learning as the first principle of communication ethics in an era of narrative and virtue contention.

Learning, as a mantra of this moment, suggests the retreat of common agreement, forbidding us to take communication ethics for granted. In the words of Kenneth Andersen (2003), this is no longer the time of the unchallenged "free rider":

> Many aspects of what we are talking about are problematic. One of them is the issue of the free rider—the person who takes advantage of the fact that we live by the rules and they do not. But, we have many opportunities to deal with this. We can establish and enforce laws. But more importantly we create a culture, a set of practices and norms. Perhaps a society should be best known for the laws it does not need to enact. (p. 20)

Andersen, a disciplinary champion who acted as a protector and promoter of the good of the study and practice of communication ethics, understood that there is no "free rider" who can take communication ethics for granted. Using the notion of a "responsible rider" requires understanding the joy of riding a horse in unknown terrain, where only increased riding in unfamiliar areas can offer skill for such a task. Only then can one begin to sense the demands and the rewards of communication ethics in this moment of difference. Responsible riders learn from what free riders simply complain about when the trip is not to their liking. Communication ethics gives up the demand for the perfect journey. *Communication Ethics Literacy: Dialogue and Difference* forgoes the demand for a perfect journey and outlines an understanding of communication ethics literacy tied to understanding of the "good" we protect and promote and the "good" protected and promoted by those we meet.

Communication Ethics Praxis in an Era of Difference

Communication Ethics Literacy: Dialogue and Difference has three sections: (1) Communication Ethics Approaches, (2) Communication Ethics in Contexts, and (3) The Pragmatics of Communication Ethics. The first section, Communication Ethics Approaches, consists of five chapters that outline the importance of communication ethics in this moment in time, the history of communication ethics, and the specific approach of this work—dialogic ethics with learning as the first principle of this form of communication ethics. The second section examines contextual approaches to the field of communication. This section, Communication Ethics in Contexts, offers chapters that integrate communication ethics and public discourse, interpersonal communication, organizational communication, intercultural communication, business and professional communication, integrated marketing communication, health care communication, and mediated communication. The third section examines the implications of communication ethics literacy for engaging this historical moment, recognizing the importance of difference, learning, and dialogue.

At the end of each chapter, we draw upon Victor Hugo's (1833/1976) classic novel, *Les Misérables*, to illustrate the main points of each chapter. This novel serves as a "humanities case study" for engagement and application of what we refer to throughout the book as "metaphors of communication ethics praxis." We use the term "metaphor" following the philosopher Ricoeur (1975/2000). In this sense, the term "metaphor" offers direct admission that our conceptualization rests within "fuzzy clarity." Communication ethics does not live in precise definitions of right and wrong; from its beginnings with Aristotle, communication ethics attends to nuance—not only what is good, but what is the right amount at the right time in the right place—knowing full well that the right answer requires us to make a judgment each time. Communication ethics remains tied, from its very conception, to learning, adaptation, and change.

Communication ethics has historically begun with the "oughts" of telling the Other what the good life should be. At its worst, communication ethics found a home in the self-assurance of hegemonic proclamations of imperialism and colonialism; it can be used as a weapon. This book begins with a more modest and demanding "ought"—learn, and, when one must tell, do so without forgetting that this era finds its identity in difference.

Acknowledgments

We would like to thank Duquesne University, the Spiritan community, and the Department of Communication & Rhetorical Studies. We offer thanks and gratitude to graduate assistants Michael Kearney and Susan Mancino—your insights and recommendations for each chapter made this book far better. We are deeply thankful to Paul Carty and Angela M. Willenbring, our editors at Kendall Hunt, for ongoing support, encouragement, and wisdom. We are thankful for the gracious scholarly support from Patricia Doherty Yoder and Ronald Wolfe; this book is one of a number of projects made possible by the Patricia Doherty Yoder and Ronald Wolfe Endowed Chair in Communication Ethics.

Ronald C. Arnett is grateful to family, departmental colleagues, the generosity of Patricia Doherty Yoder and Ronald Wolfe, and the field of communication, which has supplied ongoing opportunities for productive learning and labor over the years.

Janie Harden Fritz thanks her wonderful coauthors, departmental colleagues, and husband, Carl, for constant support and encouragement. She particularly acknowledges her brother, Bobby Robert McNeal Harden, and Robert E. and Timmy F. Harden, her nephews, who remind her regularly of the "good" of relationship.

Leeanne M. Bell McManus thanks her husband, Mark; daughters, Isabella and Elouise; and parents, Gary and Darlene Bell, for their constant support, guidance, and encouragement. She also thanks her colleagues, Ronald C. Arnett and Janie Harden Fritz, for giving her the opportunity to write and learn with them.

We dedicate this book to Donald Clark Edwards (1941–2006), colleague, friend, and champion.

About the Authors

Ronald C. Arnett (Ph.D., Ohio University, 1978) is chair and professor of the Department of Communication & Rhetorical Studies, the Patricia Doherty Yoder and Ronald Wolfe Endowed Chair in Communication Ethics at Duquesne University, and the Henry Koren, C.S.Sp., Endowed Chair for Scholarly Excellence (2010–2015). He is the author/coauthor of eleven books and co-editor of six books. His most recent books are *Levinas's Rhetorical Demand: The Unending Obligation of Communication Ethics* (2017, Southern Illinois University Press) and *Corporate Communication Crisis Leadership: Ethics and Advocacy* (2017, Business Expert Press). He is the recipient of eight book awards, including the 2017 Top Book award from the National Communication Association's Communication Ethics Division and 2017 Distinguished Book award from the National Communication Association's Philosophy of Communication Division for his book *Levinas's Rhetorical Demand: The Unending Obligation of Communication Ethics* and the 2013 Top Book Award for *Communication Ethics in Dark Times: Hannah Arendt's Rhetoric of Warning and Hope* from the Communication Ethics Division of the National Communication Association. In 2017, he was named Distinguished Scholar by the National Communication Association. He is the recipient of the 2013 Presidential Award for Excellence in Scholarship from Duquesne University and is the recipient of the 2005 Scholar of the Year Award from the Religious Communication Association. Dr. Arnett was named both Centennial Scholar of Communication and Centennial Scholar of Philosophy of Communication by the Eastern Communication Association in 2009. Dr. Arnett has served multiple terms as editor of the *Journal of Communication and Religion* and is the former editor of the *Review of Communication*. He is the Executive Director of the Pennsylvania Communication Association and former Executive Director of the Eastern Communication Association.

Janie Harden Fritz (Ph.D., University of Wisconsin-Madison, 1993) is professor and co-director of the B. A., M.A., and Ph.D. programs in the Department of Communication & Rhetorical Studies. Her research focuses on communicative practices that constitute, sever, and restore the ties that bind persons to the institutions of which they are a part. She is the author of *Professional Civility: Communicative Virtue at Work* (Peter Lang, 2013, which received the 2013 Clifford G. Christians Ethics Research Award from the Carl Couch Center for Social and Internet Research and the 2014 Everett Lee Hunt Award from the Eastern

Communication Association), coeditor (with S. Alyssa Groom) of *Communication Ethics and Crisis: Negotiating Differences in Public and Private Spheres* (2012, Fairleigh Dickinson University Press), and coeditor (with Becky L. Omdahl) of *Problematic Relationships in the Workplace* (Peter Lang Press, 2006) and *Problematic Relationships in the Workplace, Volume 2* (Peter Lang, 2012). Her most recent work focuses on the intersection of professional civility and leadership practices. Her work has been published in a number of scholarly journals. She is a past president of the Pennsylvania Communication Association, the Eastern Communication Association, and the Religious Communication Association, and she currently serves as the executive director of the Religious Communication Association. She has received numerous several awards for teaching, scholarship, and service, including the Eugene P. Beard Award for Leadership in Ethics from Duquesne University and the National Communication Association Communication Ethics Division's Teacher of the Year Award.

Leeanne M. Bell McManus (Ph.D., Duquesne University, 2007) is a professor in the Business Communication department at Stevenson University. She has co-authored two books, *Conflict between Persons: The Origins of Leadership* (with Ronald C. Arnett and Amanda G. McKendree, now in its second edition) and *Event Planning: Communicating Theory and Practice* (with Chip Rouse and Stephanie Verni). She has published excerpts in *Integrated Marketing Communication: Creating Spaces for Engagement* (with Chip Rouse), *Exploring Communication Ethics: Interviews with Influential Scholars in the Field* (with Ronald C. Arnett and Pat Arneson) and *The Encyclopedia of Social Identity*. Dr. Bell McManus has also published in *Atlantic Journal of Communication, Choice: Current Reviews for Academic Libraries, Communication Annual: Journal of the Pennsylvania Communication Association, Communication Education, Journal of the Association for Communication Administration,* and *Review of Communication*. She is a member of the National Communication Association, the Eastern Communication Association and the Southern Communication Association. She is the past president of the Communication Ethics Division of the National Communication Association and president of the Eastern Communication Association. She teaches and conducts research in communication ethics, event planning, conflict, leadership, instructional communication and interpersonal communication.

Communication Ethics

A Pragmatic Necessity

There is an interesting consequence here: when we shift the burden of the moral test in communicative ethics from consensus to the idea of an ongoing moral conversation, we begin to ask not what all would or could agree to as a result of practical discourses to be morally permissible or impermissible, but what would be allowed and perhaps even necessary from the standpoint of continuing and sustaining the practice of the moral conversation among us. The emphasis now is less on *rational agreement*, but more on sustaining those normative practices and moral relationships within which reasoned agreement *as a way of life* can flourish and continue. (Benhabib, 1992, p. 38)

In this historical moment, a time of narrative and virtue contention, communication ethics has significant pragmatic currency as we meet a diversity of ideas and communicators. One of the defining givens of communication today is that there is little consensus, or public agreement, about what is right and wrong. Such a moment propels communication ethics to the forefront of communicative importance as we negotiate difference together. This era of disagreement, labeled with the term "postmodernity," highlights the fact that our confidence in one universal sense of the "good" is no longer normative, no longer the accepted reality. We begin with a simple assumption: we cannot assume that any given person—not even a neighbor—protects and promotes the same goods as we do. The clashing of goods or views of what should be "ethical" defines our time. After reading this chapter, you will be able to demonstrate the following learning objectives:

- Describe the importance of ethical communication
- Identify the good in various situations
- Analyze this historical moment to find opportunities for learning

Introduction

We live in a time when disillusionment more often than the hope of Truth promised by the Enlightenment defines us. Each day in an era of narrative and virtue contention is another clash of competing goods. Recognizing this clashing of goods leads to the insight that the first pragmatic mandate for communication ethics is learning about and from diversity. This book protects and promotes learning with reference to competing goods, making communication ethics central in an age defined more by difference than commonality. To begin discussion of communication ethics with an emphasis upon difference ties learning to communication ethics literacy as a pragmatic alternative to prescriptive telling about "the right" and "the wrong" that aligns solely with one's own ideas of the good irrespective of another's position.

This chapter connects the study of communication ethics to communicative practices with attention to the following four metaphors of communication ethics praxis:

1. **The good**—describes a central value or set of values manifested in communicative practices that we seek to protect and promote in our discourse together.
2. **Historical moment**—announces a question relevant to human existence that we must engage; our manner of engaging this question announces the good we seek to protect and promote. We may agree on a given question announced by a historical moment and find significant disagreement on what communicative action should follow.
3. **Postmodernity**—identifies our current historical moment and announces narrative and virtue contention as normative.
4. **Learning**—is the communication ethics good of this era; we begin with learning our own framework for what is good to be and to do, and then we learn about the framework of others, meeting the different or strange with a pragmatic desire to learn, not necessarily to agree.

▶

▶ **Student Application: Contending Goods**

In most colleges and universities, there is a rule within the school's handbook against plagiarizing. This rule reflects what some would consider an individualist model of learning and personal responsibility. Many instructors elaborate on these ideas in their syllabi. The act of avoiding plagiarism protects the **good** of original ideas, doing one's own work, and academic integrity. Plagiarism is akin to stealing, and most people believe that stealing is wrong, accepting the need for punishment for those who steal. In this **historical moment**, with global connectivity via laptops, tablets, and smartphones, the Internet offers ever-increasing convenience for plagiarism. Students can now purchase papers quickly over the Internet and claim them as their own. Plagiarism in **postmodernity**, a time of narrative and virtue contention, takes on a new form when agreement on the wrongness of "idea theft" is no longer as common as many once assumed. The doing of communication ethics in such an era requires one to ask, "What is the good we seek to protect and promote?" In the case of plagiarism, educational institutions seek to protect and promote the good of doing one's own work, keeping personal responsibility for **learning**, not assignment completion, as primary.

The Good

The good is the valued center of a given communication ethic—what is most important and held in highest regard finds protection and promotion in our communicative practices. Goods are often associated with what is right and appropriate for humans to be and to do. The question for us is what living a "good life" or being "a good person" looks like in a time of narrative and virtue disagreement. Does a "good life" involve concern for others who have less? For example, such a view of the good life might include contributing to Habitat for Humanity or changing social structures of inequality because they are unjust, as civil rights workers did in the middle of the 20th century to end racial segregation.

In the first example, the good takes the form of helping others through giving; in the second example, the good is a particular form of justice enacted through the way society is arranged. Yet another perspective might understand the good life as attending to

© Rob Hainer/Shutterstock.com

one's own wants and needs, permitting others to attend to their wants and needs without interference. In this case, the good connects with independence and autonomy. The notion of the good has many definitions and levels of application in a time identified with diversity and change.

Questions about the good are not new, just more contentious today as we recognize the many options before us. Philosophers have explored questions related to the good for millennia. Religious traditions, academic disciplines, and the scientific enterprise all rest on some conception of the good. Some goods reach across traditions, but many do not translate from one tradition to another; they come into conflict with one another when citizens seek to take action in an increasingly fragmented society. Goods are often in conflict in this postmodern era of difference. Even the idea of the nature of goods themselves is the focus of discussion today. We may view given goods as handed down to us from a particular tradition; in many cases, the tradition recognizes those goods as preexistent. The application of those goods requires negotiation and enactment through discourse. Some scholars argue, however, that the very nature and existence of goods are not preexistent but generated, negotiated, and actualized through discourse; the issues of this moment, not tradition, are most important. This work chooses to resist wading into that debate, but moves differently, connecting communication ethics to a pragmatic question: What good does a person, group, institution, society, culture, or other social formation seek to protect and promote?

Our position is that every communication ethic carries or reflects two sorts of related goods. The first is a substantive good that one wants to protect and promote. The second is a set of communicative practices that assures active protection and promotion of a given good. This first good gains substance through a belief or virtue system, which is an encompassing framework that works as a standard or guide and that organizes and directs contributing or smaller goods. Charles Taylor (1989) calls this encompassing good a "hypergood" or a "superordinate good." For example, one person may have a philosophy of life in which service to others is the greatest good. Goods that contribute to that greater good might include the good of volunteering to assist others in need, the good of sending money to different philanthropies, and the good of providing support to political figures who advocate for these causes. Another person may have a philosophy of life in which the good rests in career success. Related goods that work to support that greatest good might include status and recognition by others. Within this framework, a high salary becomes a contributing good because it is a marker of recognition or status.

In each case, one seeks actively to protect and promote a particular hypergood and its supporting goods with communicative practices. For example, the communicative action of offering career advice to unemployed persons seeking work gives life to—protects and promotes—the good of serving others through the supporting good of assisting a person in need to find a job. This second sense of the good, focused on communicative practices, guides this work; we protect and promote goods through our communicative practices in our personal and professional time together. Communication ethics literacy is the sorting out and discernment of goods that we protect and promote.

Our task in this book is akin to that of Paulo Freire (1972) in his dialogic literacy campaigns. Freire worked with the assumption that anyone could learn to read and that literacy was and is possible for all. We work with an assumption that communication ethics literacy is teachable—one watches the communicative practices of a given person, organization, or group and asks one simple question: What good do the communicative practices protect and promote? In the pattern of communicative practices, one begins to discern or to read the good someone protects and promotes. Communication ethics literacy requires one to watch and to learn—dialogue begins with attending to what is before us, not what we demand the moment or our partner in discourse to provide for us.

Protection and Promotion of Goods: On Our Watch

Learning takes center stage when we cannot agree on one universal view of the good. This disagreement defines "fragmentation," the reality of differing views of the good held by groups of persons and individuals. In *Sources of the Self: The Making of the Modern Identity*, Taylor (1989) discusses the historical roots of the modern tendency to associate the notion of the good with the notion of the self, which Alasdair MacIntyre (1984) terms "emotivism" (pp. 10–11), rather than recognizing a larger story or narrative within which one is situated as a source of the good. The issue of the good is the value-laden heart of communication ethics that provides the pulse for communicative life together, and when that good rests with small bands of persons or individuals alone, the term fragmentation defines the historical moral moment. Fragmentation, constructively engaged, opens the door to learning from difference, the necessity of dialogue, and the pragmatic recognition of the first communicative gesture of communication ethics as learning before telling.

Perhaps the defining good of this historical moment is difference, requiring a unique communication ethics effort in the protection and promotion of a given good, since it is unlikely that one view will align with another view on each issue. A dialogic communication ethic begins with a simple, but demanding, requirement. One must learn about the goods of self and others that we and others seek to protect and promote. We must acknowledge the goods of another, even if we do not agree. In addition, when we meet another who pursues goods we want to protect and promote, we take on an obligation of communication ethics assistance.

The communicative means of protecting and promoting a given good—the communication ethics method—must undergo change in the way it applies to current circumstances in order for that good to endure throughout time. Our understanding of a given good may change, as well, but even when a particular understanding of a good remains stable, the communicative manner of protecting and promoting it must adapt to a new moment. Each new moment requires a renewed application of the good, which manifests differently at different historical moments and in response to reconfigured situations. When goods that we support vanish, we fall short "on our watch" for communication ethics. For without what Michael Hyde (2001) calls champions willing to step out for a given good, those goods vanish. Protection requires adaptation—a willingness to be open to new manifestations of the old and a willingness to admit when an idea's time is past and its currency has runs its course. For example, when the champion is Don Quixote, such a person simply falls out of place and out of time, fighting windmills misunderstood as opponents, and the good begins to die. The good lives with the quality of its champions, for communication ethics does not live in the abstract, but in the give and take of life before us. We begin with a basic assumption: If you care about a given good, then your showing up to engage the communicative practices of that good makes all the difference. Communication ethics does not live in codes or principles, but in the willingness of communicators to show up for the communicative task of protecting and promoting a given good.

This section assumes the importance of showing up to protect and promote a given good—a communicator willing to engage an active sense of taking one's watch. For a good to have communicative significance, communicators must take the responsibility to assume watch over a given sense of the good. Goods live and die in communication ethics by the communicative actions of persons. Whether one begins with the classical philosophical assumptions of Plato's cave within which great ideas emerge, with engagement of Aristotle's polis, or from the standpoint of contemporary social constructionist theory, a given good needs communicators to bring the idea and/or practice into action. Taking one's watch begins with a simple assertion—showing up and participating is a given in communication ethics.

Communicative Absence

The fundamental requirement for classroom learning, whether in face-to-face or mediated environments, is showing up. Absence from classroom discussion or from the public conversation about ideas takes away our opportunity to texture and nuance understanding. One needs not only to be present, but to engage a public presence, which Scott Myers and his colleagues (2016) describe as classroom citizenship behavior (CCB). Myers and his colleagues measure CCB with a 23-item instrument centered around three major behaviors: involvement, affiliation, and courtesy. They stress not only being physically present but students' being actively engaged in a manner that constructively assists their own learning and that of others.

Warren Buffett suggests that those who show up and assist the public work environment reflect three major qualities: intelligence, energy, and integrity (Schwantes, 2018). The order of those terms does not reflect their importance. Integrity is essential. The question is: When this person works, does this person assist the mission of the organization and all those connected with it? Integrity matters. Something happens when we show up—the ideas become embodied, understood more richly and deeply. Absence hurts learning; it impoverishes engagement with ideas and masks our responsibility. Even the act of skipping a class has an impact on communication ethics; each time we do not show up for a given responsibility, we lose a chance to practice a simple act that makes communication ethics possible—showing up.

Beyond the mere physical sense of absence is the absence of reflection. Aristotle's stress on deliberation remains central to communication ethics today. We need reflection and deliberation to identify the good needed for a given moment and situation. Both the reading of a given good and the communicating of it in action require communication ethics literacy.

The absence of reflection is the loss of the ability to deliberate, to reflect upon the implications of a given good. Without recognizing and reflecting on the good or set of goods that drives communicative practices, one cannot assess the ethical consequences of communication. Communicating without recognizing the ethical consequences of what we say and do as communicators reflects an absence with major consequences—where was the discussion of communication ethics in major historical junctures that found a solution, only to plant the seeds of an even greater problem? Such is the legacy of the Treaty of Versailles that concluded World War I and promptly put in motion the inevitability of another world war. Contemporary events from tragedies in high schools to questions about national policies require us to ask: "Where was the deliberation prior to the tragedy? Where was a modest beginning of communication ethics in action?"

On college and university campuses, leaders must show up and ask: "Where is the discussion of ethics in education when cheating, falsifying grades, and plagiarizing occur?" There is no easy answer to issues like these; the beginning of communication ethics emerges not with answers, but with showing up to figure out, together, what might work in a given situation. Routine incidents such as school violence, corporate negligence, plagiarism, student misconduct, and terrorism serve as catalysts for thinking about communication ethics and related issues of the good.

Problems in schools, government agencies, corporations, and communities also find their way to relationships with family and friends, workplaces, places of worship, and neighborhoods. The problems we encounter will not always be of great magnitude, but they will contribute, despite their potentially limited scope, to the formation of what Aristotle called habitudes, which are practices that make you who you are and that propel you toward one decision rather than another. Recognizing that these practices reflect some good reminds us of a Bob Dylan song that emerged in the late 1970s: "Gotta Serve Somebody." We would alter his wording thus: You've got to enact some good. Human beings can no more escape being bound to some sense of the good than we can escape experiencing the world through our physical bodies and their situatedness in space around us (Taylor, 1989). In similar fashion, our lives orient toward a given set of goods. The goal of communication ethics literacy begins with active learning that counters unreflective engagement of a given good that often goes unnoticed in our communicative practices.

From Unreflective Communication Ethics Practices to Literacy

Ideally, communication ethics might begin with a well-thought-out ethical position. More often in our everyday lives, we communicate without thinking that our communication arises from a set of commitments to a given ethical position or good with inevitable consequences and implications. Our practices habituate without reflection; we generally communicate what we have learned from family and friends, and we become accustomed to talking without deliberation upon our thoughts and practices.

© Chinnapong/Shutterstock.com

Communication ethics literacy moves us away from unreflective engagement of the good, recognizing the necessity of reflective engagement and learning in a time of normative difference. Communication ethics literacy assists in reflection upon the good or goods that self and others seek to protect and promote. Emphasis upon communication ethics literacy shifts discussion of ethics from the position of weapon and condemnation to questions about learning and deliberation. Those whom we considered to be our "enemies" seek to protect and promote ethics in contrast with our own. The question is not who is and who is not ethical, but what set of ethics we and others seek to protect and promote and why. We must justify why we accept some positions and discard others.

Diversity moves ethical decision making to a public communicative mapping of a sense of the good and away from the personal use of ethics as a weapon for meeting difference. Tammy Swenson-Lepper (2012) argues that diversity, comfort, and expectations are central considerations in any contemporary communication ethic. She justifies her position with recognition that Caucasians are quickly becoming a minority. By the year 2050, Hispanics will make up 24% of the workplace, and the white non-Hispanic part of the workplace will move from 70% to 51.4% (p. 1). Diversity engagement is not an abstract expectation but central to career development and excellence.

In places of narrative and virtue agreement, there is no need for reflection on the connection of communicative practices to a shared understanding of the good. Our current moment, however, demands questioning of the unreflectively assumed. Indicators of disagreement and challenges to assumed background meanings began to surface more consistently and publicly since the Middle Ages, and, today, multiple competing goods make it problematic to call anyone to account for violation of a common good; the key is to link a given good to a particular narrative structure, not to a common universal appeal.

A communication ethics literacy position is pragmatic: (1) we will not agree with everyone on what is good; (2) all communication has an ethical dimension; (3) the commonality of ethical differences requires one to learn to read what good a given communication ethic seeks to protect and promote. This position recognizes that we practice communication ethics whether or not we know what we do when we communicate. We live in a multiplicity of goods, whether known or unreflectively engaged.

Multiplicity of Goods

Alasdair MacIntyre (2016) suggests that we find ourselves in a realm of perpetual disagreement about the good or goods that should unite us and guide us. His understanding of the good rests in external criteria, narratives that shape persons. Narratives consist of practices that announce the particularity of a given good or set of goods. The fact that "emotivism," decision making by personal preference, is now rampant rests with an inability to understand narrative practices that announce a good or goods that do not align with my own personal preference (p. 17). Groups, societies, and cultures dwell with goods that do not always coincide with "me" or "my"—the privileged demands of a single person.

Communication ethics in our age begins with the reality of challenges that we encounter when we come across what appear to be different understandings of the good. Such differences in our daily living point to the existence of radically different understandings of what is good and right held by different people, who, as stated earlier, may not reflect on the connection between an underlying good and engaged communicative practices. As a common example, imagine two friends, Lelisia and Jael, shopping for clothes. Jael tries on a jacket that Lelisia believes does not look good on Jael. Lelisia then faces at least two communicative choices, each of which protects and promotes a different underlying good:

1. "I think I will tell her what I really think of that jacket. Friends should always be honest."
2. "If Jael is happy with that jacket, I am glad. I'll just tell her that I like the color. It's better to let this issue alone for now. Friends should not hurt each other's feelings over trivial matters."

Now imagine a typical workplace. Felicia discovers that Bill has been disclosing company secrets to a rival organization, a practice that violates company policy. Felicia must decide what communicative action to take. Each action protects and promotes a different good:

1. "I have a responsibility to report this violation of the organization's code of ethics, but I might be perceived as a troublemaker by my colleagues and bosses. I will go ahead and tell and take the risk. Protecting the organization is more important than being liked."
2. "It is not my responsibility to interfere in someone's private choice about how to act in this company. I know what Bill is doing is a violation of company policy, but it is not my business. Individual privacy is more important than company policy."

In each scenario, multiple goods compete for allegiance. Each communicative choice derives from an understanding of what is good to do and to say. In our public sphere, similar conflicts among goods and/or between goods and practices of the good emerge. Take school violence, for instance. In some cases of school violence, those committing the acts may deny or place little importance on the good of education or the good of the well-being of others. A greater good of self-expression or belonging to a more esteemed group than that represented by classmates in school takes precedence. On the other hand, consider this scenario: You log onto a social media platform and read a close friend's post that is condescending and very judgmental about another friend. As you scroll down, it becomes clear that the communicative practices are inconsistent with the good of caring for a friend. Perhaps your friend simply has not given the comments much thought, or perhaps your friend does not realize the power of the words. In either case, the damage occurs—though not without the possibility of restoration through the communicative process of forgiveness (Waldron & Kelley, 2008). Linda Lauren (2016), in the *Huffington Post*, discusses the need for respect on social media. She discusses the importance of seeing "beyond ourselves" (para. 2) and reflecting on our word choice. The multiplicity of goods requires us to show up and to take the time and energy to learn and reflect upon the goods at hand—such is the charge of communication ethics, which asks us to be attentive to how communication ethics works hand in hand with a given historical moment, not just our own demands for how the world should be.

Historical Moment: Mapping Communication Ethics

A historical moment announces itself by the questions that require our attention; how we answer those questions shapes our lives and offers us identity. A brief, general historical outline provides an intellectual genealogy of some of these ideas of the good as they emerge as questions in given historical moments. Tracing the development of ideas of the good allows one to make use of the resources for engaging visions of the good developed over time in response to both common and changing human conditions. In different historical moments, questions arise that propel thinkers to explore answers to these perennial questions.

MacIntyre (1998) displays the connections among the good, shifting historical moments, and the questions that arise in junctures of change in *A Short History of Ethics*. In this work, MacIntyre takes a historical perspective that helps us understand that ideas about the good are situated; they do not live in the abstract, but in real life and genuine human questions. In addition, as he works his way through this project, he announces the questions of given historical moments that shaped ethical theory, its change, and its application. Melissa Cook's (2005) research moved MacIntyre's history of ethics into discussion of communication ethics implications between persons. Cook outlines how views of the good respond differently to particular concerns in given historical moments. This responsiveness does not necessarily mean that the good changes radically across all historical periods, but rather that our understanding and application of a given sense of a good finds shape in circumstance and human engagement. Cook followed MacIntyre's project chapter by chapter, tracing the progress of ethics from the notion of unreflective practices to commitments central to the polis to increasing focus upon the individual.

Answers to ethical questions given in a particular historical moment provide the raw materials from which thinkers of the future may address moments of their own age. For example, if we review philosophers from different eras, we see different views of the good. Aristotle, from the classical era, found the good in the polis or city state. Thomas Aquinas, from the medieval era, found the good in God, and Adam Smith, from the modern era, placed the good in individual accumulation. Learning how these different sources of the good give rise to different understandings of the world and human life together helps us understand the complex nature of our current age. Differing historical moments announce different questions and different goods or views of the good; in communication ethics, both the good itself and its enactment are central to the how and why of communication ethics in a given moment. To understand communication ethics within a given historical moment, we offer the image of a map, a map with general indicators rather than specific details, one without the clarity and precision that makes navigating a predictable enterprise.

A communication ethics map in this historical moment is temporal, open to change, ever requiring discernment of a given communicative path toward the good. As we attempt to discern what map should guide our lives, we discover that some maps may be unduly inviting and others too demanding. In everyday life, we find ourselves in the presence of multiple maps of the good. An ethical map provides a plausibility structure within which we live our lives. We question a map of the good when it does not seem to be a helpful guide for life. If I fall into a river that I did not know was there because the map did not indicate its presence, I may ask, "Did I read the map wrong?" or "Is the map wrong?" Alternatively, I may ask a larger question: "What is this map intended to show? Was it meant, perhaps, only to display roads and not rivers?"

An ethical map is a guide, but not an answer, for us. The map is more like a public record of what is "said" to a given question in a given historical moment. Ultimately, in communication ethics, we engage some form of a map that shifts as we meet others in the ongoing demands of life before us.

Communication ethics finds application in a specific time and place with specific people, not in the pristine region of theory found within the pages of a book. Communication ethics finds application in a place where maps both guide and, at times, give way to people who, through their courage, chart new territory. Sissela Bok (1979) states that justification for a lie is possible when one can provide a public accounting of why the lie occurs. For example, when Nazi officers appeared at the door of persons hiding members of the Jewish community and asked, "Are there any Jews here?" the reply of "no," considered a lie from a strict representational view of truth, saved human lives. The higher good of human life justified the answer. This textured read from Bok frames Dietrich Bonhoeffer (2005), the 20th century theologian and German Lutheran pastor who lost his life during WWII contending against the Nazis and opposing Adolf Hitler. His courage suggests that ethics has both manifest and deep significance. Communication ethics involves an encounter, a sharing between persons, the uniting of communities in a public account of an ethical map that makes public commitments to the good, shaping identities of persons, communities, and institutions. Communication ethics lives in the good that we as communicators seek to protect and promote. Bok would suggest that in a time of ethical contention and difference, offering a public map for decisions takes on pragmatic urgency when one's view of the good will affect others.

We could identify the 21st century with a continuing echo that is getting louder, stating repeatedly, "What is the ethical position from which you work, and how is it communicated?" This question rests in the recognition that a given good guiding our public and private lives in everyday communicative practices requires learning and public accounting. Communication ethics literacy in an era of narrative and virtue contention moves us from unreflective communicative practices to learning and public accountability.

Postmodernity

Postmodernity, a term coined by Arnold Toynbee in the 1950s (Peters, 1995) and brought to public visibility by Daniel Bell (1973), is not an actual era, but more akin to a condition (Lyotard, 1984), a juncture, a moment in which we recognize that we hold something quite odd in common—the inability to agree with one another. Postmodernity is a time period extending from the middle years of the 20th century through today; a related term, postmodernism, describes the condition of postmodernity as characterized by new forms in architecture and literature and by challenges to the assumption that there is only one form of rationality and that progress is the most important good (Best & Kellner, 1991). The architecture of Robert Venturi (Jameson, 1984) and the philosophy of Jean-François Lyotard (1984), for example, frame a moment that calls into question universal rationality, or, in this case, the possibility of one communication ethic. In short, postmodernity is a juncture in human history that challenges the assumption that there is only one form of reasoning and one understanding of the right and good. Umberto Eco (2005) describes postmodernity in "hypertextual" terms (p. 25). He outlines an existential fact that all epochs or eras are co-present, sometimes with one more powerful or influential than another. Postmodernity is not an era after modernity, but rather a juncture of recognition that all historical eras are co-present and, at times, conflict with one another.

This postmodern moment is an opportunity for those wanting to learn from difference. Such learning is a necessary accompaniment to the rejection of modernist assumptions that we live in a world of objective and universal truth. Forgotten all too often in discussions of postmodernity is that the era does not reject materialist, scientific, and other understandings of the world—it simply recognizes that other understandings exist. All eras are co-present in this juncture called postmodernity, inviting an ongoing debate about truth, methods for its identification, and, in this case, the appropriate understanding of communication ethics. The defining feature of postmodernity is lack of agreement, not the total eclipse of features of previous eras.

Postmodernity and Communication Ethics

The movement from one view of truth to competing understandings of truth takes us from communication ethics as prescription to communication ethics as learning, giving pragmatic rebirth to creative engagement with the questions of our time. Postmodernity offers a world in which many goods manifest themselves in one moment. Each of these goods gives rise to particular, situated communicative practices. We need to recognize the ground of the good upon which we walk, that to which we are indebted, in order to engage other persons who situate ethical decision making upon different ground. We need to understand our ground, the good to which we are committed, in order to offer an account of our understanding of the good in conversation with others often committed to a different set of goods. It is for this collage of difference that we consider postmodernity to be the initiating force for the study of communication ethics, calling forth reconsideration and rebirth of situated goods and their expression in communicative interaction. This postmodern "renaissance of learning" presupposes learning as the responsible act for engaging the 21st century; it is the return of a hero (Hyde, 2004) in the garb of a learner embedded within narrative limits. The hero engaged in communication ethics is the learner, one who meets difference without forgetting the limits of one's own situation and particular commitments to the good.

Any discussion of the good in this historical moment must take account of what MacIntyre (1984, 2006) refers to as narrative contention: There is no universal conception of the good finding agreement today. We can find clear, agreed-upon guidelines in given activities, games, and organizations marked by openly articulated rules to follow. Yet, we need not look far to find other activities, games, and organizations working with differing rules. For example, some businesses require employees to dress formally, but others permit greater flexibility in choice of attire. Even offering advice for what to wear takes on increasing complexity in this era of difference. Life begins to move from a universal view of existence to something closer to a game. As MacIntyre (1984) states, if you are not playing by the rules, you are not playing the game. In an age where rules from one game to another are not clear, the protection and promotion of a given good takes a rhetorical/persuasive turn, acknowledging a communication ethics bias that guides conversational life together. We live in a rhetorical moment of contending views of the good. Communication ethics takes up the challenge of uniting the notion of the good with a story of a given virtue structure that situates our talk and requires our protection and promotion with the ever-lingering knowledge that change of our position may be the end decision.

Postmodernity and the Rhetorical Turn

Postmodernity, identified by multiple scholars, necessitates a "rhetorical turn" (Schrag, 1986; Simons, 1990). Calvin Schrag's suggestion is that our engagement with communication has a persuasive consequence not only for ourselves but also for others. Additionally, communication ethics takes a rhetorical turn for the 21st century. Every message is persuasive and value laden. The rhetorical turn is recognition that we persuade not with information but with value-laden content that frames information. Communication information understood as situated invites a different understanding and framing with value-laden possibilities and limits. Michael Crichton, a well-known author whose views on science and public policies have clear and, at times, controversial ethical implications, has written multiple books that remind us that only at our own peril do we disassociate information from ethical consequences. Experimentation in *Jurassic Park* (1991) has ethical consequences for those eaten by dinosaurs. His novel *Timeline* (1999) revisits the theme of time travel in which one recognizes the influence that a different ethical position has on information and historical outcomes. *Next* (2006) outlines the challenges faced by a DNA researcher who wrestles with ethical questions related to responsibility, human identity, and the accountability of science to the human community. The value dimension of information matters—the ethical import of that information matters.

Anatole Rapoport (1967), considered the premier social scientist of the holocaust, reminds us that a major value commitment of the Nazis was efficiency. What was problematic in this case was not efficiency, but the ethical framework underlying the Nazi version of efficiency, which led to pride in the ability

to transport people in cattle cars with down-to-the-minute predictability to final deadly destinations. The ethical framework of the statement "We are on time" had obvious consequences not only for those losing lives, but also in a rupture of the human spirit that ripples throughout the West. That moment announced the public disruption of our faith in a universal commitment to truth defined by scientific progress, the worldview of the late 19th and 20th centuries carrying the assumption that all problems would find solutions through science, reason, and rationality. We recognized, again, the power of the message of the sophists long ago—do not equate truth with any given community. Every ethical position lives in a given situation, ground, and bias. Postmodernity does not tell us what is ethical. It requires that we know what our ethical position is, learn that of others, and figure out how to communicate our own position and negotiate the difference that we encounter.

The good life takes on rhetorical argumentative power when there is no consensus about what the good life is or should be. Robert Bellah and colleagues address this question in *Habits of the Heart* (1985). Through interviews with ordinary people, they discovered that persons found it difficult to articulate why they held to a particular understanding of the good life. In many cases, people struggled with defining what a good life was for them. In other cases, people could state the elements that made their lives worthwhile, such as a happy family and a good job, but not why those elements are worthwhile from a perspective beyond their own preference. Taylor (1989) traces the rise of this perspective in his history of the idea of the self, or the "modern identity." He describes the movement from identifying the good as emerging from a framework outside of human experience, such as a religious perspective, to the idea of "nature" and, eventually, to within human experience, such that values emerge from the individual. MacIntyre's (1998) treatment of the history of ethics and his work on different views of justice and rationality (1989) address this same issue. Jürgen Habermas (1984, 1987) offers further texture to the conversation in his treatment of discourse ethics. He facilitates communication grounded in good reasons, insisting that each person have an equal opportunity to participate in public conversation, and that "interests" be transparent in discourse. In each case, we hear a call for a new understanding of what it means to have "ground" under our feet, to have public evidence for the ethical ground we stand on and the positions we embrace and advocate.

This call suggests that the persuasive power of positions exists both in their articulation and in lived action—the good gathers influence through an account of its substance and validity and by its ability to bear the weight of a life. In Walter Fisher's (1987) terms, a persuasive account of the good has narrative fidelity; in other words, it represents the way human beings attempt to engage life with the recognition that we do not always live up to this good. Fisher reminds us that we need to be able to articulate and offer a public account of the good in which we believe and that propels our communicative action in public and private life. Bellah privileges the pragmatic necessity of rhetoric in the education curriculum as we meet and engage difference together. Rhetoric is the educational center of the *Good Society* (Bellah, Madsen, Sullivan, Swidler, & Tipton, 1991). Communication ethics in a time of disagreement finds temporal ground—a place to stand for the moment, recognizing that this ground of agreement may shift later—in the dialectical tension between identifying communication ethics positions as necessary for guiding a life and recognizing their necessarily persuasive nature. Acknowledging that our learning requires a dialogic openness to listening to another's point of view invites a space for finding common ground in postmodernity.

Finding Common Centers in Postmodernity

Aristotle (1948) stated repeatedly that human beings are political creatures—we interact to coordinate our social lives. Without our social nature, the connection of communication and ethics would be unnecessary. However, in this juncture, we live in a puzzling moment in which the obvious is often muddied or unclear. Robert Putnam's *Bowling Alone* (2000) captured national attention because it brought before us the error of our moment, the temptation of assuming that we can function without regard for others. Our assumptions about the world make up the ground upon which we stand, the tradition that enriches our conversation with others. In this book, we deliberately employ the pronoun "we." Usually, the use of "we" in this book will refer to us as authors, but in this case, we embrace the reader because we live in a time when bowling alone is our collective communicative temptation. It is the moral cul-de-sac (Arnett, 1998) of our time. Life is social and points to the reason that we differentiate a human being from a feral child (Newton, 2002). Humans need to interact with others to learn from them. We do not give ourselves identity; we inherit our identities from others—from persons, events, and ideas.

George Herbert Mead (1962), in his understanding of the "generalized other," argues that the shaping of who we are never stops; others continue their influence upon us. In the field of communication, Julia Wood (1992) follows this assumption with her emphasis on the web of human interaction. Seyla Benhabib (1992) states that today there are "particular" persons who shape who we are, even when they no longer walk this earth. Mead, Wood, Benhabib, and Aristotle all agree with Putnam (2000): We can act as if we bowl alone, but we deceive ourselves in the act. Again, this book assumes that "absence" is a significant error and curtails our ability to live within the confines, constraints, and opportunities of this moment. Communication ethics is about filling the void of absence with insight into different ideas and perspectives; it is about showing up and engaging what is before us.

Of course, some sense of shared values is necessary to live with others. We need a "minimalist" set or small number of shared goods to coordinate human life. Bok (2002) makes this case for ethical living in a time of difference. A pragmatic view of communication ethics requires that a given community locate minimal virtues that permit life together to continue, despite disagreement on deeply held convictions about the good and despite human failure to achieve any good consistently. These minimal virtues define "common sense" for a community. This common sense manifests the good through human action, embracing the local, not the universal, and is ever modest about the utility of a given sense of the good outside a given community. "Common sense" for ethical communicative behavior does not necessarily cut across all communities. When we engage in communication with another person from another community, opportunities for learning emerge, because communication reflects and often articulates differing ethical positions, identifying potentially different underlying "common sense" understandings of the good. From these varied positions, we can identify a minimal set of shared underlying goods.

The minimal assumption that shapes the ground of this book is that common sense is no longer common or universal, making learning and dialogue keys to communication ethics in the 21st century. Common sense rests within shared communicative practices that protect and promote a given good. The loss of the universal, however, does not mean that all disbelieve in universals. Benhabib (1992), Fisher (1987), and Habermas (1984, 1987) all argue for universals. Their work argues for a position in a postmodern rhetoric of contention over what is right. In this book, we take a pragmatic stance, one that listens both to their arguments and to those of others. Right now, it is clear there is no consensus; however, at the end of 21st century, this argument might look quite different, with universals once again driving the conversation.

In this historical moment, we accept the reality of a loss of consensus, a loss of agreed upon common sense. We can no longer look to universals with complete assurance; such a reality suggests a loss of what Martin Buber (1958) called a "common center." Instead, we must find temporal common centers that bring us together today and move us away from an illusion of self-sufficiency (Buber, 1958). One example of coming together around a common project with a minimalist sense of the common good is the nonprofit organization Habitat for Humanity. This organization assumes the good of human dwelling within a place owned and cared for by a particular person or family. It also assumes the good of cooperative engagement in offering assistance to others. The moral practice of constructing a dwelling place connects seamlessly to the eventual moral good of inhabiting a home that is part of a larger community, moving the person or family into connections with others in that geographical location. The interconnected practices of homebuilding and home dwelling share grounding in a good assumed by Habitat for Humanity. The notion of dwelling is central in the finding of common centers; this insight comes from the work of Michael J. Hyde (2004) in communication and Emmanuel Levinas (1969) in philosophy, who considered ethics to be the first philosophy and, we suggest, the first principle of humanness. A given good has temporal ground of a common center that brings people together.

Another example of a common center in postmodernity is the resurgence of "third places" (Oldenburg, 2001) such as coffee shops and bookstores. These third places are locations outside of work or the home where people gather to connect with others around common interests and activities. Within the physical walls of a bookstore, one encounters many others who adhere to competing views of the good, but who share an interest in reading and learning. While one person shops for books on Catholic perspectives on marriage, another may seek a secular volume on relational health for gay couples. Yet another person seeks information about planning an estate sale. The bookstore stays in business as it makes a place for multiple goods, many of which are in competition. Whatever the temporal common centers might be, they offer a place of sanctuary, a place to find some commonality with the additional opportunity to reach out and learn from difference, from those who do not claim the same common sense as we do. The communication ethics mantra moves to learning, no longer resting in the taken-for-granted.

Learning

This era places before us a pragmatic demand—to learn about our own sense of the good and the reality of difference manifested in the beliefs and actions of others. Learning requires understanding a position or framework for viewing the world and how our viewing shapes our understanding of any given set of data or facts. The intimate link of communication ethics to learning is a pragmatic recognition that to engage our own and others' perspectives about the world, we must know where we stand and learn about the ground of others. We have a commitment to a minimalist understanding of keeping the conversation going in the public square (Rorty, 1979). Our first line of communication ethics defense is not violence, silence, or political action, but learning/understanding about difference. It is important here to acknowledge that in order to learn, "telling" of some sort must take place, but without a relentless monologic chant that dictates what another should or should not believe or do. Lisbeth Lipari, in her book *Listening, Thinking, Being: Toward an Ethics of Attunement* (2014), outlines the limits of telling, speaking as if one is a sovereign, which collapses into Gemma Corradi Fiumara's notion of "narcissistic isolation" (p. 187; Corradi Fiumara, 1990, p. 163). Instead of attending to others, we often attend to ourselves alone, but others enrich us. To fail to work with and understand others is to diminish oneself.

We see that communication ethics and its associated sense of the good are temporally, geographically, and culturally situated, shaped by a given time period, place, and culture. We see the classical period as attaching communication ethics to the city-state and the medieval world attaching communication ethics to faith. The Renaissance united communication ethics to the person of creativity, and modernity attached it to universal rationality inherent in every person and manifested, ironically, in allegiance to corporate structures. Postmodernity is a moment in which we openly acknowledge that all of these locations for communication ethics have emerged in the human community. The location of the good protected and promoted, whether city-state, faith, creativity, or rationality, changes, but the importance of learning common sense practices around that given good has not wavered. We have a responsibility to acknowledge the situated bias in our communicative knowing and action.

Communication ethics literacy is a call for learning that invites human flourishing in a postmodern era of difference. Communication ethics literacy requires attentiveness to learning, to the pragmatic celebration of difference and what is possible in the meeting of what we would not request. Communication ethics begins by meeting this historical moment, not a fictional one that we wish for or demand, just the one before us. We bear a responsibility to engage communication ethics literacy. As Kenneth Andersen (2003) outlined in his Carroll Arnold address,

> Because we recognize that ethical issues are a dimension of all elements in communication in everything from choosing to communicate to refusing to listen, from the appeals offered and arguments chosen to the audience targeted, information presented and words chosen, we have a unique opportunity to transmit that understanding and the awesome responsibility that goes with that understanding. (p. 16)

The study of communication ethics as situated within an understanding of the good shaped by differing historical moments acknowledges that in today's postmodern moment, multiple goods compete for allegiance and that learning and dialogue are keys to communication ethics in this historical moment. As we seek to understand the ground that situates our own understanding of the good and that of others, we engage the pragmatic heart of communication ethics in an age of difference—we begin to privilege learning.

COMMUNICATION ETHICS: REFLECTION AND ACTION

1. Describe different understandings of what it means to live a good life based on the perspectives of several different people you met in the past month.
2. During the past week, in what contexts did you encounter "routine disagreement" about what is good to do or to be?
3. Is it possible to hold strongly to a belief or viewpoint while learning from a different viewpoint? How do you balance or reconcile the goods of conviction and learning, two goods that appear, at first glance, opposed to one another? Give an example.
4. When you find yourself in disagreement with another person about something you believe in strongly, is it easy or difficult to listen to the other person's perspective? What makes it easier or more difficult to listen to a point of view different from your own?
5. The terms "pluralism," "multiculturalism," "difference," and "diversity" are potential defining characteristics of the cultural and social makeup of the United States in this historical moment. Working with three other persons, locate articles from the academic and popular press literature that address these terms. How are they similar? How are they different? How do these terms relate to communication ethics as discussed in this chapter?

ENGAGING COMMUNICATION ETHICS THROUGH LITERATURE: *LES MISÉRABLES*

The historical moment of the major action in the setting of *Les Misérables* spans the years 1815 until about 1848. Shifting political allegiances and events characterize this time period in France. After the French Revolution of 1789 and subsequent political struggles,

including the restoration and subsequent deposition of King Charles X, conditions for the poor (as depicted in the novel) were desperate. From the standpoint of our historical moment, laws were harsh. The story is about Jean Valjean, a man sent to 20 years of hard labor in prison for stealing a loaf of bread to feed his starving family. After his release from prison, Valjean finds himself in need of lodging. He stops at a house where a bishop (Bishop Myriel, also known as Monseigneur Bienvenu) serves in a small town. The bishop welcomes him when others turn him away and sets him on a road to a better life of virtue and service to others by giving him the household's silver candlesticks after the police catch Valjean stealing the silverware. When Valjean returns them to the bishop, the response is one that frees Valjean from the arms of the authorities and puts a claim on him for a lifetime: "Thank you for bringing him back. He did not steal, but he did forget to take the candlesticks along with the silverware. I wanted him to have both."

Jean Valjean, by a fortuitous series of circumstances, becomes a rich entrepreneur and mayor of a town to which he brings prosperity and improvement. However, Valjean gives up his freedom after the arrest of another man mistaken for him. The real Valjean confesses his identity at the trial so an innocent man will not suffer because of him. Valjean returns to the town, knowing that he has little time to lose, for the authorities, who had let him leave the courtroom after the trial, will surely be coming for him. Valjean is anxious to fulfill the promise he had made to a dying woman, Fantine, to find her child, Cosette, left in the care of the Thénardiers, an unkind, greedy innkeeper and his wife. When Valjean confesses to save the innocent man, the exacting and suspicious officer Javert finds grounds for Valjean's arrest. Upholding justice to the letter of the law, Javert arrests Valjean, and Fantine dies. Rescued by an endangered sailor after falling deliberately into the sea, Valjean escapes, searching for and eventually finding Cosette. Thought dead by almost everyone else, Valjean finds himself pursued yet again by Javert.

Cosette grows up, educated in a convent in which the two take refuge after a narrow escape from Javert and his officers. Upon their departure from the convent when Cosette is a young woman, Valjean risks his freedom once again by saving the life of Marius, a young man with whom Cosette has fallen in love and who is fighting in the insurrection of 1847. The apprehended Valjean carries the unconscious Marius from the sewers of Paris, jeopardizing his own safety. After permitting Valjean to take Marius home, Javert unexpectedly sets Valjean free, but, unable to live with the contradiction between his commitment to law and authority and his own action of freeing Valjean, Javert ends his own life.

Les Misérables takes us to the heartbreak and joy of competing goods. At the end of each of the following chapters in this book, we will connect the story to key ideas in each chapter. Les Misérables is an ongoing interplay of goods that shaped and transformed lives set in a particular historical moment, just as goods shape and transform our lives today. Communication ethics literacy is the reading and the doing of how people protect and promote differing goods in a time of narrative and virtue contention, even through the physical items they give away, like candlesticks, which carry with them an ethical good that reshapes a life.

Communication Ethics

History and Definitions

> What ought I, or what ought we, to do? But the 'ought' has a different sense once we are no longer asking about rights and duties that everyone ascribes to one another from an inclusive we-perspective, but instead are concerned with our own life from the first-person perspective and ask what is best 'for me' or 'for us' in the long run and all things considered. Such ethical questions regarding our own weal and woe arise in the context of a *particular* life history or a *unique* form of life. They are wedded to questions of identity: how we should understand ourselves, who we are and want to be. Obviously there is no answer to such questions that would be independent of the given context and thus would bind all persons in the same way. (Habermas, 2003, p. 3)

The relationship between communication ethics and the "ought" has historical and contemporary currency. Our contemporary political landscape, for example, provides a host of opportunities to consider how politicians ought to negotiate with each other in public settings. This chapter outlines a number of communication ethics positions that protect and promote a given "good" that one "ought" to put into practice if one hopes to work within a given communication ethic. Practicing the good protected and promoted by a given communication ethic places one within that communication ethic, just as failing to practice that good places one outside a given communication ethic, which leads us to the basic assumption of this chapter—there is more than one communication ethic. When a communicator seeks to protect and promote a given good, the beginning ground for a communication ethic takes shape. Today, we recognize a multiplicity of oughts, with limited agreement about what particular rights and duties should guide our communicative lives with one another. After reading this chapter, you will be able to demonstrate the following learning objectives:

- Define communication ethics
- Explain the importance of a multiplicity of communication ethics
- Differentiate competing narratives

Introduction

Communication ethics in a postmodern moment of narrative and virtue contention assumes that multiple "goods" compete for allegiance in the public sphere. This chapter addresses definitions that shape our discipline's understanding of communication ethics and point to the reality of multiple views of the good. Examination of multiple definitions of communication ethics highlights the underlying goods that each definition attempts to protect and promote, with implications for learning in this moment. Stephen J. Hartnett (2017), in his National Communication Association (NCA) presidential address, discussed the many opportunities for the discipline of communication in an age of globalization. He advocated a new form of cosmopolitanism that is situated in an ethic of civic engagement and social justice. Collaborating with education programs, research programs, and service experiences, the discipline of communication will build pathways of connectivity. From the beginning of the field of communication to now, theory and practice define our discipline, and, in the case of communication ethics, philosophical knowing of theory and application co-inform one another in the practice of communication ethics and in the invitation to communication ethics literacy.

The extension of Hartnett's work suggests a definition of communication ethics that considers the communicative action of the good as situated within the intersection of philosophy of communication and applied communication. We build upon the importance of the conception of narrative as framed by Alasdair MacIntyre (1984, 2016), Stanley Hauerwas (1981), and Walter Fisher (1987, 2006) and the insights of previous and ongoing scholarship in the discipline of communication. Our particular approach to communication ethics rests within the interplay of philosophy of communication and applied communication; we understand a communication ethic to arise from an understanding of the good situated within a given narrative structure. ▶

▶ This chapter connects the study of communication ethics to communicative practices with attention to the following four metaphors of communication ethics praxis:

1. **Multiplicity of communication ethics**—we cannot assume that each good that we seek to protect and promote and that shapes the heart of a given communication ethic finds support from others.

2. **Philosophy of communication**—having a "why" for the doing, for communicative action, is pragmatic in an era defined by difference. To understand what one does and to discern the communicative action of another opens the door to communication ethics assessment and change; a communication ethic finds shape in the ongoing conversation of "why" in interplay with the demands of a given historical moment.

3. **Applied communication**—the "how" of communicative doing tests any philosophy or theory and ultimately is the laboratory of communication ethics. Communication ethics does not live in the abstract, but, in the words of Willie Nelson, understands the necessity of being "on the road again," making a difference through action. Application is the place where communication ethics comes to life.

4. **Narrative**—a story agreed upon by a group of people that provides limits within which we dwell as embedded communicative agents. Communication ethics philosophy and application are foreground issues for this chapter, but it is the background narratives of what groups of persons know and do that put limits and shed light on the knowing and doing of communication ethics. Narratives can and do change from the actions of communicative agents and shifts in the historical moment—narratives change, ideologies resist alteration from the outside, and stories sometimes fail to move people to the point of active support.

Student Application: Finding Narrative Ground

Entering college may be the first time students meet life away from home for an extended period of time. As one encounters new roommates, classmates, and instructors, **multiplicity of communication ethics** is an ongoing reality. People vary in the way they treat friends and roommates and how they choose to spend their time. One learns that people disagree about the right and the wrong. A **philosophy of communication** gives an understanding of the importance of difference in purposes and goals among fraternities, sororities, and service groups and how those goals emerge in communicative action. **Applied communication** moves philosophy of communication into action as one joins organizations on campus for what they do, such as engaging in community service or promoting a particular tradition. We commit to organizations because of the **narrative** structures they follow. These narrative structures, the practices and beliefs that define the narrative, shape and guide the organization's action and our actions throughout life, thereby having a hand in the shaping of who we are as persons.

Multiplicity of Communication Ethics

Multiple definitions of communication ethics have emerged in the field of communication, with one major point of consistency across the definitions: each definition points toward an articulation of a given good. Each underlying good produces and shapes a unique communication ethic. Each definition assumes an understanding of a good that underlies communication ethics practices. The next section situates our discussion of this definition within the recent historical development of the study of communication ethics. Communication ethics assumes the importance of others, highlighting the consequences of questions about how to engage competing views of the good. This commitment to others begins as we acknowledge those who came before us and who contributed to and continue the ongoing story of communication ethics in our field. We participate in an ongoing disciplinary story about communication ethics, revealing the power of change in a narrative tied to the study of what we considered and consider good and how these goods live, protected and promoted through various understandings of communication ethics.

History of Communication Ethics

As our historical roots make clear, the connection between communication and ethics is long-standing, from Aristotle's *Nicomachean Ethics* (1962) to many contemporary treatments of communication ethics (Arnett, 1987; Arnett, Arneson, & Bell, 2006; Chesebro, 1969; Christians & Traber, 1997; Johannesen, Valde, & Whedbee, 2008; Neher & Sandin, 2007). The formal study of communication ethics at the national level of the discipline commenced with Kenneth Andersen, Vice President of the Speech Communication Association (SCA) (now the National Communication Association, or NCA), when he declared the 1983 theme of the Speech Communication Association annual convention to be "Communication Ethics and Values." His presidential address in 1984, titled "A Code of Ethics for Speech Communication," started the recognition of communication ethics as an important field of study.

Andersen's work led to the institutionalization of the area of communication ethics, initiated by James A. Jaksa in 1984. Jaksa as chair, Ken Andersen as vice chair, Richard Johannesen as vice chair elect, Vernon Jensen as secretary, and Ronald C. Arnett as newsletter editor were the inaugural officers of the communication ethics commission of SCA (Andersen, 2000). Clifford Christians was a central part of the original group that brought communication ethics to a national forum, and his publications assisted the maturation of communication ethics scholarship (2008b, 2011b, 2017).

In 1990, Jaksa, along with Michael S. Pritchard, championed the first National Conference on Communication Ethics. Jaksa and Pritchard helped shape what is now the Communication Ethics Division of NCA. At that time, along with Andersen, Vernon Jensen was one of the few instructors working with communication ethics in the context of a Ph.D. program. Other scholars, such as Josina Makau (Makau & Marty, 2001), revolutionized our understanding of argument with an emphasis on ethics and cooperative communicative engagement. Julia Wood (1994, 1996, 2004), throughout her work, reminds us repeatedly of the particularity of persons and the pragmatic necessity of respectfulness. The work of Wood finds kinship in the ongoing projects of Michael Hyde (2001, 2005, 2010, 2012, 2016), from his work on the call of conscience to his examination of the life-giving importance of acknowledgment to his delineation of limits of perfection. Hyde, the University Distinguished Professor of Communication Ethics in the Department of Communication at Wake Forest University, is doing philosophy of communication and applied communication ethics, offering a model for outstanding work in communication ethics for this historical moment.

Perhaps the leading communication ethics scholar has been Richard Johannesen. His book *Ethics in Human Communication*, now in multiple editions, represents an encyclopedic tradition of human communication ethics (Johannesen, Valde, & Whedbee, 2008). Following Johannesen's lead, we provide definitions of ethics from the scholars we have discussed. It is informative to recognize some of the underlying goods that have emerged consistently across the discipline: responsibility, choice, and discernment. These goods are important in a time in which confidence in universal principles has proven to be inadequate and there is ever-increasing recognition of competing narrative structures. With the multiplicity of choices before us, it is even more important today to privilege the study of communication ethics. The next section addresses definitions of communication ethics.

Defining Communication Ethics Across the Discipline

The following definitions of communication ethics highlight differing facets of the broad domain of this term and arise from particular goods. Jensen (1991), in the foreword to *Conversations on Communication Ethics*, recognizes the

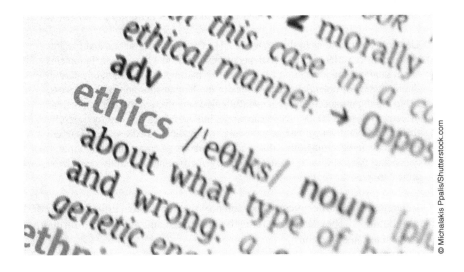

© Michalakis Ppalis/Shutterstock.com

multiplicity of goods arising in the study of communication ethics: "We grapple with the tension between relativistic and absolute ethics, between ends and means, between the 'is' and the 'ought' and between private and public goods" (p. xi). Jensen reminds us to protect and promote the good of tension, ever wary of answers that emerge without any counter claim.

Jaksa and Pritchard (1994), in *Communication Ethics: Methods of Analysis*, state, "As a normative study, ethics is concerned with determining what values are worthy of our acceptance" (p. 4), protecting and promoting the good of careful discernment.

Makau and Arnett (1997), in *Communication Ethics in an Age of Diversity*, state:

> Particularly noteworthy in this regard is the evidence of postmodern influences on the majority of the essays. Many of the authors challenge enlightenment approaches to ethical issues, calling for the abandonment of abstract ideological frameworks. Emotions receive acknowledgment and serious attention in many of the chapters. The chapters also share a recognition that fruitful scholarship on communication ethics integrates theory and *praxis*. (pp. x–xi)

Makau and Arnett highlight protecting and promoting the good of the continuing public search for that which is ethical while being attentive to changes in the historical moment.

Jensen (1997), in *Ethical Issues in the Communication Process*, defines ethics as "the moral responsibility to choose, intentionally and voluntarily, oughtness in values like rightness, goodness, truthfulness, justice, and virtue, which may in a communicative transaction significantly affect ourselves and others" (p. 4). Jensen highlights the importance of protecting and promoting the good of choice, a central question in the West and in the disciplinary tradition of communication.

Johannesen and colleagues (2008) state, in *Ethics in Human Communication*:

> Our primary intentions in this book are: (1) to provide information and insights concerning a variety of potential perspectives for making ethical judgments about human communication; (2) to sensitize participants in communication to the inherency of potential ethical issues in the human communication process; (3) to highlight the complexities and difficulties involved in making evaluations of communication ethics; (4) to encourage individuals to develop thoughtfully their own workable approach to assessing communication ethics; and (5) to aid individuals in becoming more discerning evaluators of communication through enhancing their ability to make specifically focused and carefully considered ethical judgments. (p. xi)

Johannesen and colleagues protect and promote the good of information-based ethical judgments. They keep before us the difference among ethics, information, and unsubstantiated opinion.

Makau (2002), in the preface to *Moral Engagement in Public Life: Theorists for Contemporary Ethics*, states:

> So called universal principles have proven inadequate (and often counterproductive) to resolution of many, if not most, "real world" moral challenges. Similarly, pursuit of value neutrality has proven to be both fruitless and undesirable, particularly given the demonstrable role of power in human relations and social structures. Disregarding the key role of the heart in ethical deliberation and action, traditional paradigms have undermined the very foundations of spirituality and other critical resources for ethical interaction. (p. ix)

Makau emphasizes protecting and promoting the good of the "heart" in moments of ethical ambiguity. She points to the importance of care for another, recognizing that communication ethics does not rest in information alone. There is a good in attentiveness to another.

Together, these definitions highlight a number of significant points with the caveat that communicating ethically is not easy—it is a struggle to discern worthwhile values and requires reflection, care, and choice. Communication ethics is sensitive to historical situatedness and is not value-neutral. It involves searching for direction and recognition of diversity of values/virtues; the search is dialogic, open to others while still standing on one's ground within a given narrative.

Communication ethics matters because decisions hold implications for human lives. According to Susan Petrilli (2016), attentiveness to others is far greater than formal and technical action. Reducing ethics to technical action is akin to "linguistic alienation" (p. 274); the attempt to place all ethics within the boundaries of rules actually limits responsibility and the call to human action. Communication ethics requires continual deliberation; it is not for the faint of heart or for those satisfied with easy answers. The previous definitions point in the direction of our understanding of communication ethics: the need to learn one's own standpoint on the good and the standpoint of others. Communication ethics lies within the tension of competing goods or, as discussed by Buber (1948), a "unity of contraries" of guidance and responsiveness to change when called forth by other persons, ideas, or the historical situation.

The following section situates our definition of communication ethics within a pragmatically modest spirit. The key is not to say what "is" communication ethics today, but, rather, to offer a view of communication ethics that publicly discloses the why and the how of what we consider one of the major questions of our time: "What is the good that a given communication ethic seeks to protect and promote?" Such a question makes communication ethics literacy the pragmatic necessity of our time.

Situating Our Definition of Communication Ethics

We live in a time of constant disagreement about which virtues and narratives do and should guide us. Argument is not new; however, argument over what is good has become the defining issue of the 21st century. We live in an era of recognized difference. We no longer have public consensus on what counts as virtuous behavior and what is good for human beings to be and to do. For the study of communication ethics, this historical moment has profound implications. Should digital communication technologies such as the Internet be subject to government regulation, or should they be free to everyone? Should the United States have an "open door" immigration policy, or should it prohibit certain groups of people from entering? The conflicting goods involved in these questions remind us that we cannot teach or learn one specific communication ethic; such an entity is no more, if it ever really existed. We are now aware that there are multiple communication ethics. This work understands and situates the term "communication ethics" as a creative juncture between two other areas of the discipline of communication: philosophy of communication and applied communication. Communication ethics is the recognition that we take a given philosophy of communication, an understanding of the good, and apply it in interaction with others. The study of communication ethics is the study of philosophy of communication brought into engaged communicative application in the marketplace of ideas. There is no one communication ethic, but there is a way to understand, theoretically, the construction of "communication ethics," and this knowledge moves us closer to communication ethics literacy for the remainder of what will be a challenging century of change.

Philosophy of Communication

Communication as a discipline has evolved with descriptors that illustrate communication in contexts, such as public, interpersonal, small group, and organizational communication. These descriptors indicate that communication has an identifiable function within an area of human activity. Philosophy of communication seeks to provide a coherent understanding of the importance, or the "why," of communication. The term "philosophy of communication" employed in a broader sense refers to a general way of thinking about communication, or it can refer to a particular philosophy of communication.

A philosophy of communication works like an operations manual for a vehicle that explains how each part connects to the others and, at the same time, is contingent, responsive to the demands before us that we often do not expect. If one were to envision an automobile repair manual written as philosophy, it would be like the now-classic popular culture book *Zen and the Art of Motorcycle Maintenance* (Pirsig, 1974). It is not just information, but the unique manner in which that information meets us and shapes us that takes us from a branch of analytic philosophy to application in lived experience. Each time one attempts a repair, there is a *why*, not only in the significance of a given part and its function for the machine, but also in the coherence of its connection to other parts. Another example of how philosophy of communication and application work together

© sabrisy/Shutterstock.com

might be a cookbook that situates each recipe within a tradition of national or regional heritage, explaining the significance of a given dish to a culture's values and meaning structures. The value of a philosophy of communication is to connect the "why" to the "how" of the doing, keeping the "why" as primary.

The major questions that arise from philosophy of communication are why each item connects to the other, why we do what we do, and their meaningfulness to you and me. Even in the move from philosophy to philosophy of communication, one senses the increasing importance of practical application. In a book project edited by Julia Wood and Richard Gregg (1995), Arnett penned an essay titled *Defining Communication: A Practical Act*. Application is the key to our identity as students and scholars of philosophy of communication—at our best, we take philosophy into the human community. The study and practice of communication ethics brings philosophy, community, and application together, contrasted with the abstract engagement characterizing the history of philosophical ethics.

As scholars develop a philosophy of communication about any subject, they begin to develop an argumentative rationale that can propel and guide action. For instance, if Andre asks Titus, "What is baseball?," Titus can offer the following description: "Baseball is a game played by two teams. Each team consists of nine players on a diamond-shaped field. On the field, at each of the four points of the diamond, there is a base, with a player standing near each base. There is a pitcher who throws the ball to a batter on an opposing team, and there is a catcher who catches the ball thrown from the pitcher. If one of the players standing near the bases fails to catch a ball hit by the batter, the ball goes into the outfield where there are three people waiting to catch the ball." If you are from another country known for a different sport, such as soccer or cricket, you might read this description and ask the question, "Why? Why would anyone play such an odd game?" The information offered by Titus about "what" and "how" provides no philosophy of communication about the "why" of baseball. Baseball looks quite different from the vantage point of a story that gives immediate actions meaning.

From a philosophy of communication perspective, one might offer the following "why" about baseball, once known as the American pastime. It has a tradition and heritage that take us back to the beginning of cities and the industrial revolution in the United States. As this country was attempting to build its future, it created a game in which, if you got a hit as few as one out of three times

© Chris Hill/Shutterstock.com

and made it safely to a base, you were outstanding. Baseball is not a game about failure, but, more accurately, about the patience and tenacity needed for success. As a batter, you get four balls and three strikes. If you take four balls (pitches that do not fit an agreed-upon strike zone), you walk to first base. More often than not, you will strike out or ground out, knowing full well that even the most outstanding players will strike out often and get a hit only one out of every three times, which makes them a success.

As this country entered the industrial revolution, it honored a game where patience and tenacity aligned closely with success, and phrases like "the game must go on" and "play ball" would reach the hearts of many. What generated success in the early stages of the industrial revolution was having people who were fearless in the face of the idea of the unlikelihood of success—hoping for no more than one success out of three attempts. From such courage emerged a country gaining significance and power in the development of its very own industrial complexity, and each day at the ballpark, young people discovered that even if one fails two times out of three, there is still a chance to succeed.

Perhaps this is the philosophy of communication rendition of baseball, and perhaps this is why it no longer claims the status of the American pastime. We have forgotten the "why" of playing the game. We ask potential baseball players to play a game that requires skills that will take years to hone, often with a required apprenticeship in the minor leagues—and at the end of the apprenticeship, the player still may not reach a level of skill high enough to play in the major leagues. He may be good enough only to talk with a son or a daughter about the sport and teach that child the same skills, and then the most important element of baseball becomes teaching it to another. In a culture that values immediate success, in a moment when people are not willing to fail two out of three times, and in a time in which one may not have the patience to teach another, baseball no longer registers as the American pastime. From a standpoint of philosophy of communication, if one understands the value of patience and tenacity, one can understand the game of baseball where failing two out of three times makes for success.

Such is the value of the philosophy of communication. It gives life richness, depth, texture, and meaning. Without a philosophy of communication, we meet only a technical manual or a set of isolated recipes that assumes that we already know why what we are doing matters. A philosophy of communication never takes for granted why something matters. We need to understand the why: why we are taking this class, why we chose the university we did, why we show up— why we do the things we do. The philosophy of communication understanding of baseball carries the good of a story of more failure than success without quitting. A philosophy of communication understanding of communication ethics provides the "why" for communicative action, and applied communication carries the "why" into interaction with others. The "why" gives us supporting background to enter a world of "how," a world that demands implementation and needs a sense of "why" when success is not the first knock on our door. Communication ethics connected to the "how" takes us to applied communication.

Applied Communication

Applied communication as a formal area of communication study originated with the founding of the *Journal of Applied Communication Research* by Mark Hickson, III, in 1972. Kenneth Cissna, William Eadie, and Mark Hickson, III (2009), provide a historical narrative of its development in the field. Put in the terms of this chapter, they are offering a philosophy of communication that points to the "why" of importance for applied communication in the field of communication.

Applied communication grew out of a concern for making the products of communication research and scholarship relevant to human life, responsive particularly to issues of social justice and its practice. Applied communication moves theory into action. Over the years, the area of applied communication has come to embrace not only issues of social problems, but the marketplace, as well, with the aim of developing meaningful connections between social goods and marketplace practices. Cissna's (1995) edited book, *Applied Communication in the 21st Century*, was a major step in making public the first formal collection of essays addressing the nature, scope, and importance of applied communication research, highlighting the connection of theory to practice.

From its inception, the field of communication has had interest in application. There are many definitions of applied communication. For example, Seibold's (1995) definition in Cissna's edited volume states that applied communication provides "a means to answer a specific question about a specific problem in a specific setting" (p. 25). We refer to applied communication as taking communication into engagement, whether that engagement be in an organization, a small group, a hospital, an interpersonal relationship, or a family. Applied communication attempts to make a difference, and communication ethics seeks to make a difference. From the very foundation of Western civilization, we have applauded application. Aristotle would not have thought of ethics as merely a form of study but as an application of the everyday. For Aristotle, ethical understanding involved the performative study of practices within the Athenian polis.

All of us know people capable of engaging in analysis of self, others, and institutions. We hear their critiques, assessments, and evaluations repeatedly. Their critiques, assessments, and evaluations lead us to our final question: "What do you intend to do about it?" Failure to answer this question accompanies the critique of the dilettante, a person who "plays at" a given task, hobby, or endeavor but is not really serious about making a difference. For example, Morgan goes on a spring break service trip to New Orleans just for the "fun" of traveling, rather than the call to service. Morgan's goal is not to make a difference, but merely to experience Bourbon Street. Listening to the soulful music of the French Quarter, Morgan decides to purchase a saxophone upon her return. However, after Morgan realizes the number of hours needed to become proficient, her saxophone becomes a dusty object in her dorm room on which to

hang clothes. Dilettantes like Morgan gather a bit of information and then move on to gather more information, but they never gather a great deal of depth or push the information to application. Dilettantes attempt to skate on the surface rather than walking with their feet in the mud of everyday life; they try to live life unscathed. When we apply ideas in the arena of human life, there is almost a guarantee of numerous bruises and bumps along the way. The cliché of turning problems into opportunities rests within a basic adage central to applied communication: "What are you going to do about it?" One could call the person who languishes in lament "a dilettante of complaint," unable to assist self or others.

To bypass the impulse of the dilettante, the uninvolved, or the uncommitted, one must take the risk of bringing ideas to the public, to the marketplace of ideas, to the test of ideas in application. Hyde (2001) makes this public move with medical questions, now asking us to consider not postmodernity, but the "posthuman" person in our age. Additionally, Fritz and Omdahl provide two edited volumes on problematic work relationships that ask us to take communication ethics into the marketplace, raising questions about appropriate professional communication practices in this time of difference (Fritz & Omdahl, 2006; Omdahl & Fritz, 2012). Writing about professional civility, Arnett and Fritz (Arnett, 2006a; Arnett

& Fritz, 2001; Fritz, 2013) apply the story of employee–organization connection and engagement to the good of productivity and mission sensitivity through public discourse in organizational settings. The good protected and promoted by an ethic of professional civility competes with the good of unlimited self-expression and unrestrained individual freedom in organizational settings. Such work points to the uniting of philosophy of communication and applied communication in the study and practice of communication ethics.

Communication ethics is a philosophy of communication area of emphasis with a practical, applied outcome. It is the unified home of philosophy of communication and applied communication. The two coordinates of philosophy of communication and applied communication in interplay with one another provide the theoretical grounding and practical application of a communication ethic. Because there is no one communication ethic, learning and understanding propel the study of communication ethics more than prescriptive statements about communication ethics. We begin to learn about communication ethics as we understand the construction of a given communication ethic and recognize its result in the marketplace of ideas, whether in personal or professional life. Philosophy of communication and applied communication together frame a central question: "What is the good that inheres in a given philosophy of communication, and how does one apply that good in communicative practices?" In short, a communication ethic begins with content, or a good or set of goods that matters, and moves that content into application. The practices, or the "how," of application and the philosophy, or a sense of "why," frame what has become known within the discipline as a narrative.

Narrative

A narrative is a story agreed upon by a group of people. This public story explains the way the world works and the meaning of human life, including what is good for humans to be and do. A narrative provides guidelines for human action. For example, religious traditions, the scientific enterprise, and some political

philosophies constitute narratives. Narratives require agreement from a group of people who moves a story into a communicative background that offers interpretive guidance for decision making—in this case, communication ethics guidance. Walter Fisher's narrative paradigm states, "Humans are essentially storytellers" (Fisher, 1987, p. ix). Within the narrative paradigm, people are storytellers who read and evaluate the texts of both life and literature. Human communication from a narrative perspective understands people as full participants in the making and interpreting of their communication from a story-laden context (Fisher, 1987). The ethical theorist most known for narrative understanding is Alasdair MacIntyre. The notion of multiplicity of narratives that carry differing virtue structures is at the heart of a number of his books, including *After Virtue* (1984) and *Whose Justice? Which Rationality?* (1989).

A narrative is the ground that offers a sense of voice or articulateness to a good or set of goods—a narrative lives in a manner akin to what George Herbert Mead (1962) called the "Generalized Other," a location for values where one finds implications without a specific face. Communication ethics in action requires a dwelling place from which the good originates and then enters into persuasive engagement. A narrative serves as such a dwelling place, working rhetorically to protect and promote a given sense of the good. Benhabib's (1992) notion of the "particular Other" brings us to uniqueness of application; each ethical decision requires discernment of how the narrative good emerges in a given life circumstance. She works within a narrative of particularity, offering an alternative to Mead's perspective.

Postmodernity assumes a multiplicity of narratives within which persons and communities find meaning, generating rival understandings of virtues and competing views of the good. These competing narratives now take the form of "petite narratives," a term that acknowledges the existence of more than one understanding of human life and the good. Competing communication ethics situated within petite narratives give rise to the currency of rhetoric in our time, echoing the work of Richard M. Weaver (1970, 1984) and Henry Johnstone (1981), among others, who recognize the persuasive nature of language and the need to acknowledge the ethical implications of rhetorical action. We resonate with their work and add the perspective that communication ethics is rhetorical. The multiplicity of narratives, with each capable of carrying differing virtue structures, moves rhetoric into a primary position in postmodern scholarship (Hyde, 2004; Schrag, 1986).

Rhetorical Functions of Narrative

Each communication ethic is inherently persuasive, arguing implicitly and, at times, explicitly for a given understanding of the good. The study of communication ethics is the examination of competing views of the good taken into communicative action. Both the good and communicative action prompted by that good reside in narrative structures. Narrative structures find their identity through practices. Jens Erik Paulsen (2011) suggests that a narrative ethics of care begins with practices toward and with another person. According to Teresa L. Thompson (2009), the existence of people, our conceptualization of humanity, and individual identity begin within narratives that nurture their development and change. Indeed, moral and ethical decision making and our understanding of the good dwell within narrative structures.

The multiplicity of communication ethics places this area of study within the domain of persuasion. Communication ethics is not universally normative—that is, a given communication ethic does not guide action for everyone; each communication ethic lives within narrative structures or communities of discourse that argue for the importance and value of a given set of communicative goods. Additionally, this book assumes that a given ethic reflects a particular bias about the manner in which we "should" understand and engage others. Differing ethical positions among different narratives, whether Marxist, capitalist, Christian, atheistic, Buddhist, or humanistic, are differing/competing views of the good. Of course, there are some shared understandings of the good across these traditions, but for this historical moment, it is wise to learn from the differences. It has been, is, and will be the differences, not our commonalities, that present us with communication ethics demands and challenges. A particular communication ethics position resides within and emanates from a particular narrative that carries ideas and practices that shape a philosophical and pragmatic view of the good, and not all views will conform to our own position.

Each of us meets others in everyday discourse, a discourse that has rhetorical implications because it emerges from a sense of the good and influences self and others. We suggest that the study of communication ethics implies the question, "What is the narrative ground that shapes a philosophy of the good and sanctions given practices in application of that good?" The world in which we live brings us example after example of a basic fact: philosophies of the good matter, and their implementation matters—the "why" and the "how" unite in importance in the study and practice of communication ethics. Philosophies and application strategies derive from the narrative that nourishes them. For instance, consider struggles in the Middle East, conflicts that arise from competing understandings of who has the right to particular segments of land and which human beings have a right to be in a certain place or even to exist at all. The continuing presence of terrorism shows us competing ways of understanding the world and making a given good manifest in the world. The introduction of large retail stores to small communities and the varied effects on those who dwell in that community show us the competing goods of low prices for many, on the one hand, and uniqueness of small businesses and traditional livelihoods on the other, as well as other goods that rest in such a context. Persons living in rural and urban areas face different life circumstances, which lead to different rankings of various goods, including laws governing land use, noise, and recreational possibilities. Each of these goods springs from a narrative or tradition about the good life.

Competing Narratives

A given communication ethic both unites and divides people. To understand communication ethics and to engage in communication ethics literacy in this moment requires basic rhetorical skills. First, one must discern the narrative, the story-housed content out of which a given ethic finds shape. Second, one must again discern the goods (virtues and communicative social practices) within a given narrative that shapes or constitutes the "ethical." Third, one must understand that any "web of goods" lives within a particular timeframe. When we meet others in our life circumstances, we communicate from this "temporal narrative ground." We engage a communication ethic in foreground communicative action that simultaneously points to a particular narrative background that nurtures a given virtue structure, framing the good of that narrative. Because our communication ethics action comes from an understanding of the good, it is persuasive—rhetorical and attentive to the temporal nature and unique particularity of application.

This chapter begins and ends with the emphasis on oughtness, the central communication ethics engine. The notion of ought finds life in the ideas and practices promoted and protected as "good" by a given narrative, which manifests the ought of a given communication ethics action. Differing narratives function as differing grounds for differing oughts, taking communication ethics into a pragmatic rhetorical turn that seeks both to understand and to persuade how to engage a given view of the good within a unique set of historical constraints, not the least of which are context and persons.

Narrative content shapes communication ethics with a rhetorical turn that has evaluative and persuasive consequences. Narratives frame the "oughtness" that arises from a given sense of the good. Jensen (1997) expresses this position well:

> Oughtness does battle over *values*. We struggle to understand right and wrong, good and bad, true and false, just and unjust, virtuous and corrupt. In dealing with these ends, we assume that we seek the right, good, the true, the just, and the virtuous rather than their opposites. (p. 5)

Multiple views of oughtness guide multiple understandings of the good, resulting in a multiplicity of communication ethics. George Yancy's work (2012, 2013, 2015, 2016, 2018) frames the clashing of narrative structures and the necessity of learning from them in order to counter racist philosophical assumptions. He talks about African-American philosophy as positioned to reconfigure unexamined assumptions (2015). Such philosophy is not only a counter voice to unreflective whiteness, but to the unknowing presuppositions of totality.

The oughtness of differing goods rests within a narrative that unites a philosophy of communication, a sense of "why," with communicative practices of applied communication, the doing of the "how." It is the oughtness that gives a persuasive tone to a communication ethic. The good persuades the communicator, and then the communicator takes that good, or a particular understanding of that good, into persuasive engagement with others who reciprocate with their own articulation of a good that may or may not be consistent with the original communicator's good. Communication ethics is the intersection of philosophy of communication and applied communication responsive to narrative ground and the historical moment of application, requiring a rhetorical turn that seeks to protect and promote a given sense of the good that must fend against other goods in a time of challenge and change.

COMMUNICATION ETHICS: REFLECTION AND ACTION

1. Using the notion of narrative in this chapter, describe the narrative or narratives that guide your life. For some, a religious or faith-informed perspective may provide this narrative framework. Others may identify their narrative "ground" as emerging from a political or philosophical system that describes the way the world works or should work. What narrative(s) inform(s) and guide(s) your sense of the good in life?
2. How does this narrative inform your life as you make everyday decisions about how to communicate with others? For example, consider conversations you have with your friends. What guides you as you consider ideas you hope to put into words, the words you choose to use, and how you listen to what they have to say?
3. Think about the people you have encountered so far in your higher education experience. How many different narratives can you identify? Is it easy or difficult to identify these commitments? Do persons committed to a given narrative communicate in particular ways? Identify the "narrative vocabulary" of a narrative of your choice.
4. How is a narrative the home or starting place of a communication ethic?

ENGAGING COMMUNICATION ETHICS THROUGH LITERATURE: *LES MISÉRABLES*

Multiplicity of communication ethics reveals itself in *Les Misérables* by the contrasting communicative practices and underlying commitment to differing goods on the part of Jean Valjean and the Thénardiers, the innkeepers with whom Cosette lodges and who mistreat her. The Thénardiers were, like many in that era, just trying to survive; they ran an inn and made a living by their wits, seeking to gain as much as possible from lodgers and taking advantage of every opportunity to gain more. When Fantine makes arrangements for them to take care of her child, the Thénardiers find many opportunities to write, demanding more and more money for Cosette's purported needs, which they spend on themselves and their own daughters.

In contrast, Jean Valjean's communication with others throughout the novel illustrates the good of care for others. This "why" prompts his communicative actions, which test the strength of this "theory" in lived experience. Valjean demonstrates the good that Bishop Myriel encouraged him to follow through a variety of communicative practices. He risks revealing his identity as an ex-convict to save a man trapped under a cart; he speaks kindly to Fantine, a woman persecuted and scorned by others because of her trade as a prostitute and her child born out of wedlock. He does not reveal to Marius that it is he, Valjean, who saved Marius's life, in order to avoid burdening the young man with such knowledge. The narrative within which Valjean stands finds life through his communicative interactions with others, and these practices of the good anchor Jean Valjean within a new narrative offered him by the bishop. He discovers the meaning and shape of a narrative of care for others through communicative practices and the meeting of others in need. Valjean's experience reminds us that we need not begin with a given narrative, but may encounter the communicative practices that eventually give a narrative life and provide a home for a sense of a given good.

Approaches to Communication Ethics

The Pragmatic Good of Theory

How can one, in fact, do full justice to the words used in court: 'The truth, the whole truth, and nothing but the truth'? These words mock our clumsy efforts to remember and convey our experiences. The 'whole truth' has seemed so obviously unattainable to some as to cause them to despair of human communication in general. They see so many barriers to prevent us from obtaining truthful knowledge, let alone communicating it; so many pitfalls in conveying what we mean. (Bok, 1979, p. 4)

With accusations of "fake news" spreading in current political discourse, deciphering the accuracy of information has become a challenge. "Fake news" has no basis in fact but creates the illusion that the information is factual. Theory acts as a roadmap for understanding information and frames how a particular part of the world works. The previous chapter discussed the reality of multiple definitions of communication ethics, concluding with an emphasis on narrative and its organic connection to the study of communication ethics. This chapter examines communication ethics approaches from the field of communication that set the stage for our particular framing of dialogic ethics. Each of the approaches seeks to protect and promote a given understanding of the good with implications for the study and practice of communication ethics. After reading this chapter, you will be able to demonstrate the following learning objectives:

- Identify various approaches to communication ethics
- Apply various communication ethics approaches attentive to diverse social settings
- Formulate criteria for communicative action that can withstand scrutiny from alternative perspectives

Introduction

A comprehensive examination of the disciplinary study of communication ethics begins with a major conceptual framing of the theoretical diversity of communication ethics articulated by James Chesebro (1969). Additional conceptual essays by Ronald C. Arnett (1987) and Ronald C. Arnett, Pat Arneson, and Leeanne M. Bell (2006) build upon the theoretical ground-breaking work from Chesebro's 1969 insights. The diversity of theoretical approaches to communication ethics shapes the heart of two reports on communication ethics pedagogy, which continue a like conversation, announcing a multiplicity of communication ethics perspectives in the curriculum and in everyday life (Ballard et al., 2014; Swenson-Lepper et al., 2015).

Chesebro (1969) outlined the following theoretical ways of understanding communication ethics: (1) universal-humanitarian ethics, (2) democratic ethics, (3) codes and procedures, and (4) contextual ethics. In the language of this book, Chesebro was the first in the field to point to communication ethics literacy and away from a prescriptive telling about the ethical. Arnett (1987) used those same conceptual frameworks, adding narrative ethics, and then, with Arneson and Bell (Arnett, Arneson, & Bell, 2006), added dialogic ethics. These six conceptual frameworks announce a given good that each approach seeks to protect and promote. We offer a brief summary of these six conceptual approaches to communication ethics in this chapter and add a seventh approach, discussing the sense of the "good" that each approach asks us to protect and promote.

This chapter connects the study of communication ethics to communicative practices with attention to the following seven metaphors of communication ethics praxis:

1. **Democratic communication ethics**—a public communication ethics process for discussion of ideas, customs, and rights, protecting and promoting the good of collaborative decision making.
2. **Universal-humanitarian communication ethics**—assumes one guiding communicative ethical principle of reason from the Enlightenment, protecting and promoting the ability of the human to discern the good through a rational process.

▶

3. **Codes, procedures, and standards in communication ethics**—defines communication ethics guidelines to evaluate appropriate ethical conduct, protecting and promoting the good of corporately agreed-upon practices and regulations.

4. **Contextual communication ethics**—recognizes communication ethics variations across differing cultures, persons, and settings when applying communication ethics principles, protecting and promoting the good of the particular.

5. **Narrative communication ethics**—assumes that a communication ethic begins with persons' lives guided by stories about the way the world is or should be, protecting and promoting the good residing within given narratives. Recent discussion on virtue ethics includes recognition of public virtues that guide the coordinates of a narrative ethic.

6. **Dialogic communication ethics**—acknowledges communication ethics as attentive to the emergent, not owned by either party in the conversation, responsive to multiple goods that give rise to and emerge in ongoing conversations, protecting and promoting the good of learning.

7. **Standpoint communication ethics**—suggests that the ground upon which one stands and meets the Other shapes one's perspective through differences in gender, race, ethnicity, affectivity, and culture.

Student Application: Choice Making

College students face a number of choices. Some choices are easy—What should I wear today? When should I take a break for lunch and/or dinner?—but some choices are considerably more difficult. Should I stay here or transfer to another institution? What is the right major? What campus clubs or social groups are worthy of my time and energy? Whom should I date? Where do I want to work and live after college? One may meet the challenges of running for president of a campus organization, participating in **democratic communication ethics**. Sometimes choices seem so natural to us that we cannot imagine another alternative, following what one might call a **universal-humanitarian communication ethic** that makes the liberty of self and others an irrefutable good. Other choices come from attention to **codes, procedures, and standards in communication ethics** that tell us it is not right to do something like plagiarize an essay because such action violates the educational institution's code of conduct. Additionally, a **contextual communication ethic** suggests that the situation in which we find ourselves should guide our choice of what to say or do. For example, we may skip a class on Thursday night in order to help a friend study for a statistics test that she has to pass on Friday morning. Depending on the instructor's attendance policy, we may choose not to reveal the details related to our absence. With knowledge of a sense of "why" in place, we make decisions based on **narratives** from our family traditions or religious backgrounds. We may find ourselves learning and making choices in conversation with roommates, classmates, friends, and instructors through a **dialogic communication ethic**, attending to what emerges between oneself and another, surprised by the revelation. For example, in conversation with another, students may find themselves reconsidering a major issue or opportunity they had initially rejected, finding an emergent answer transforming

▶ their thinking in unexpected ways. **Standpoint theory** helps us recognize the different perspectives that exist in various living spaces. Roommates might view study hours differently with some people playing music or having the TV volume on low while others like no background noise at all. Dirty dishes in the sink might be offensive to some but a sign of being busy to others. Parents might still enforce a curfew while students might argue for more independence while trying to study for exams. The choices we make highlight our ethical views.

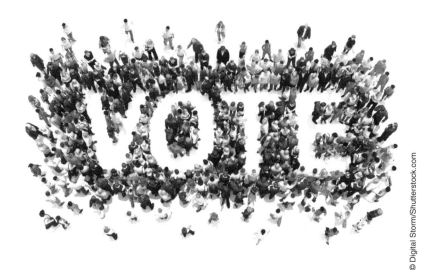

© Digital Storm/Shutterstock.com

Democratic Communication Ethics

Democratic communication ethics defines a public process for contention about ideas, customs, and rights, protecting and promoting the good of public decision making. The metaphors of "public" and "decision" mark democratic communication ethics. As Ronald C. Arnett (1987) suggests, "Democratic communication ethics are based on a public 'process' ethic, an open airing of diverse opinions and control by majority vote" (p. 46). He elaborates further: "The democratic ethic in the field of communication is a 'public' process for forging public mass collaboration on ideas, customs, and rights" (p. 48).

Within the discipline of communication, the democratic approach is the most well-known method for engaging communication ethics and has been central since its Athenian inception, where the practice of ancient Greek rhetoric provided a foundation for public participation. The discussion of democratic communication ethics has classical roots; however, for our discipline, much of the connection between communication ethics and democracy emerged during major democratic "stress points" in American history. The entry of the United States in 1941 into the Second World War, accompanied by the growth of communication departments in higher education, connected to questions about democracy and free speech (Cohen, 1994; Rogers, 1997). In that historical moment, one could not disassociate "democratic" from the notion of "ethical"—the good of "one person, one vote" reflected a commitment to popular justice uniting democracy and ethics (Commager, 1950).

In the World War II moment, conventional wisdom connected the terms "ethics" and "democracy" in opposition to forms of government such as totalitarianism (Alpers, 2002)—such a connection reflected an "enthymematic agreement" of innate connection for citizens of the United States. In other words, these terms interconnected to such a degree that by saying one term, everyone assumed that the other followed, whether stated explicitly or not. The term "communication" also connoted the notion of democracy, an assumption that led communication scholars to examine the propaganda techniques used by Nazi Germany and autocratic techniques employed by mid-twentieth century Japan (Cohen, 1994; Rogers, 1997). World War II was fought not just to free people, but to make sure free discourse was possible. The legacy of World War II remained with us for an extended period in the persons of well-known figures in the field of communication who fought for freedom of discourse during World War II and after. For instance, arguably the most well-known proponent of free speech was Franklin Haiman, who served in World War II along with Paul Boase and others too numerous to mention. They fought on behalf of their country on the battlefield of arms and in the academy, linking communication and democratic principles.

In the historical moment of World War II, the terms communication, democracy, and ethics interconnected as part of an understood conceptual background, forming a pragmatic unity. To say that someone was not democratic implied that the person was not ethical. An emphasis on public speaking and group discussion in secondary and postsecondary contexts reflected this concern for responsible democratic participation through preparation for public participation and citizenship required by a democratic society grounded in the good of communicative participation in public life (Cohen, 1994; Gehrke, 2009).

Ideas about communication ethics tied to notions of democratic ethics shaped public speaking and later work in interpersonal and organizational communication. Interpersonal freedom of expression assumed that efforts to limit expression and democratic participation were equivalent to ethical misconduct. The connection to organizational communication rests with the call for democratic participation in the shaping of organizational structures (Deetz, 1992). One can even go so far as to say the whole area of applied communication, including public relations and advertising, exhibits a pragmatic and market-driven democratic ethic. Advertising's connection rests in the drive to get as many products out as possible for people to examine to see which one they want to buy, working with a pragmatic contention that the best products rise to the top in the marketplace of commodities, akin to the best ideas rising to the top in the marketplace of ideas.

In the field of communication, a democratic ethic appears with Karl Wallace's (1955) now classic essay about habits of communication in a democratic society. His work defines a democratic ethic by articulating four habits or procedures to follow to ensure democratic communication: (1) the habit of search—openness to new ideas; (2) the habit of justice—seeking factual accuracy; (3) the habit of preferring public to private motivations—putting concern for the public good over concern for private preference; (4) the habit for respect for dissent—democracy finds renewal through learning from difference. In the last century, several public figures serve to illustrate concern for democratic ethics, from Susan B. Anthony's promotion of women's voices in the public sphere to Martin Luther King, Jr.'s leadership in the civil rights movement. In the field of communication, this ethic endures with the work of many scholars and in the national discipline's establishment of an award in honor of Karl Wallace—the Karl R. Wallace Memorial Award, which offers support to scholarship in rhetoric or public discourse.

Universal-Humanitarian Communication Ethics

A universal-humanitarian approach to communication ethics assumes a commitment to the Enlightenment ideal of rationality as the central guiding ethical principle, a rationality considered an essential part of human nature that requires protection and promotion for the good of human beings through adherence to rational principles. Universal-humanitarian communication ethics requires

> a select intelligentsia [intellectual members of society] to announce "principles" that should guide communication behavior. However, the principles are *not created* by the intelligentsia; instead, they are universal, *a priori* (pre-existing) principles announced, supported, and, if necessary, fought for by an "enlightened" and "insightful" minority. (Arnett, 1987, p. 48)

Gifted intellectuals who have the ability and responsibility to discern preexisting goods reveal them to society.

Immanuel Kant is the representative ethical theorist for universal-humanitarian ethics. His approach stems from the Enlightenment assumption that all human beings possess rational governing principles as part of their cognitive makeup. Ethical principles are inborn and universal and exist as "ideals" or principles inherent and applicable to everyone everywhere. The humanitarian element of this approach directs our attention to valuing adherence to rational principles as a duty or obligation of being part of the human community.

The assumption of *a priori* universals plays its way out in multiple configurations, including a utilitarian perspective, which refers to decision making that seeks to do the greatest good for the greatest number of people. In order to discern this greatest good, the utilitarian perspective, like the universal-humanitarian approach, presupposes the universal grounding of rationality that makes such discernment and choice possible. The question, "What is the greatest good for the greatest number of people?" presupposes an Enlightenment ideal that we can discern the correct answer. Although Kant's universal-humanitarian ethic contrasts with a utilitarian ethic, we highlight their implicit connection by noting the assumed *a priori* good underlying each, consistent with the observations of Taylor (1989) of such assumed goods. The social utility approach of William S. Howells (1986) anchors the good in the value system of a particular culture rather than *a priori* principles.

Universal-humanitarian ethics offers a realm of certainty in application of ethical principles stemming from a sense of order in life and the universe that is preexistent, or already given. In every situation requiring an ethical response, tried-and-true principles exist that govern that situation. Kant advises us to consider the wisdom of a given ethical principle by asking, "Can this principle be universalized such that it would make sense for human life?" For example, imagine that June is aware that coworker Paul has failed to complete a report. June's boss, Gertrude, asks her about the report. According to universal-humanitarian ethics, June should reason as follows when considering whether to tell the truth or to lie: "If everyone lied, the very idea of language as representing reality would make no logical sense—it would be meaningless. Therefore, I cannot believe that everyone should lie; therefore, I have a duty to tell the truth." This reasoning will lead June to recognize that her duty is to tell the truth, in every situation, without exception. In this specific case, therefore, she must tell the truth, not protect her coworker, because the universal principle of truth-telling applies to every case.

A universal-humanitarian communication ethic does not attend to the messiness of particulars, but to the principles that prescribe or dictate one's duty. The good is one's universal duty tied to a given domain of human life and experience (such as telling the truth); one's communicative behavior protects and promotes that good. Challenges arise when more than one perceived duty emerges in a situation, when rival goods compete for our allegiance. For instance, the impulse to protect a person may conflict with the universal duty to tell the truth.

In the field of communication ethics, there are several thoughtful champions of universal-humanitarian/Enlightenment approaches. Christopher Johnstone (1981) provides an exemplar of a universalistic communication ethic. He argues eloquently for a commitment to beauty, choice, and reasoning situated within the public context to help us understand the complexity of the human soul. He calls us to universal principles that inspired great documents and, at times, heroic action in the West.

Codes, Procedures, and Standards in Communication Ethics

Codes, procedures, and standards define communication ethics guidelines for evaluating conduct, which protects and promotes the good of corporately agreed-upon regulations. Codes, procedures, and standards frame communication conceptually

Code of Ethics

© moomsabuy/Shutterstock.com

and behaviorally according to guidelines defined by institutional groups. These guidelines are the "guardians of appropriate ethical conduct" (Arnett, 1987, p. 50). This perspective outlines value codes to guide discourse:

> Standards and codes are important to most organizations in crisis and in beginning identity formation, as long as they are not taken too legalistically. The value of codes lies more in their ability to promote discussion than in the total regulation of behavior. (p. 51)

Organizations develop written codes of conduct to assure common agreement on appropriate conduct. Professional groups, such as lawyers and physicians, adhere to defined codes of conduct; some of these professional codes are ancient, such as the Hippocratic oath that binds physicians to "do no harm" to those for whom they provide medical care.

This approach defines many codes of ethics in organizations. Within the field of communication, Kenneth Andersen is central to this ongoing effort to make public the expectations for academic communication professionals. Andersen was instrumental in the development of The National Communication Association (NCA) Code of Professional Responsibilities for the Communication Scholar/Teacher. The 2017 revision stresses ethics and integrity in teaching, research, and publication, outlining responsibilities of writers, editors, and reviewers (National Communication Association, 2017). The action metaphors from the 1999 statement comprise the suggestions for each of the academic activities outlined in the 2017 code, without the same explicit public pronouncements representative of the 1999 document:

The National Communication Association believes that responsible behavior is a hallmark of professionalism in communication. We believe that responsible behavior is guided by values such as integrity, fairness, ethical and social responsibility, equality of opportunity, confidentiality, honesty and openness, respect for self and others, freedom and safety. (as cited in Andersen, 2000, p. 138)

These guidelines support values that the profession, through committee approval, considers central to its teaching, research, publication activities, professional relationships with colleagues, students, members of the community, and to society as a whole.

In the marketplace, both the Public Relations Society of America (PRSA) and the American Advertising Federation (AAF) define codes of conduct for their members that consist of guidelines for professional behavior. The Public Relations Society of America's code emphasizes responsible advocacy in the public sphere. Advocacy, honesty, expertise, independence, loyalty, and fairness are the six goods put forth by PRSA. The American Advertising Federation code includes truthfulness in representing attributes and prices of products, "taste and decency" in advertising, and competence of spokespersons who provide testimonials for a given product. Communication ethics as codes, procedures, and standards rests on the centrality of corporately sanctioned public proclamation of communicative action that regulates professional behavior and requires periodic revisiting.

Contextual Communication Ethics

A contextual approach to communication ethics recognizes variations in culture, persons, and communication settings when applying communication ethics principles, protecting and promoting the good of the particular context and the good residing in that context. A contextual communication ethic encompasses and "justifies different communication standards for different audiences, cultures, and relationships" (Arnett, 1987, p. 52). A contextual approach asks questions about the situatedness of the particular, seeking to identify the good appropriate for the individual case.

An example of contextual communication ethics would be differences in appropriateness of eye contact across cultures—directness in eye contact in one culture protects the communicative goods of honesty and direct connection. The goods of privacy and distance find protection and promotion through the communicative practice of reduced eye contact in other cultures. Likewise, goods of hierarchy, freedom, authority, distance, and social harmony appear in the varied communication practices of different cultures, as intercultural research reveals (Hall, 2005). Culture is contextual host to the practice of ethics; concern for the good and its enactment are integral to culture. Particular cultures manifest particular ethical practices, many of which, at the surface level, go unshared between and among cultures (Appiah, 2006, 2010). Therefore, consideration of culture holds significant implications for the study and practice of communication ethics.

In organizational settings, the good of a particular institution defines its mission statement (Arnett & Fritz, 2001); the context of a particular organization calls forth practices that support that good. Through socialization of new employees, the good of an organization's culture finds support in the organization's day-to-day operations. In education, teachers, administrators, and all those committed to ethical care on the campus must resist forgetting our obligation to one another. We must "resist permitting our disappointments with education to eclipse the face of the Other, missing the revelatory and an immemorial responsibility that has no end, only partial and temporal resolutions" (Arnett, 2016, p. 15). Additionally, in an interpersonal context of close friendship, revealing personal information serves the good of connection and intimacy proper to that context. In a professional setting—for example, a place of employment—self-disclosure of intimate information can damage the goods of task and professional distance. In these two contexts, understood as personal and as professional, different amounts and types of self-disclosure protect and promote different goods in the engagement of communication ethics. Fritz's (2013) work explains how professional civility, marked by public discourse practices, protects and promotes the goods of productivity (work), place (the organization), and persons (employees and others associated with the organization).

Matthew Seeger's (1997) work represents a thorough treatment of communication ethics in organizational contexts. His model, based on Karl Weick's organizational sense making theory, incorporates a number of issues relevant to organizations and their internal and external publics, including employer-employee relations, whistle blowing, and democracy in the workplace. Seeger's application of Weick's work provides a focus on organizational responsiveness to the environment through the process of enactment, which refers to the way in which organizational members construct and make sense of events around them. Charles Conrad's (1993) edited volume, *The Ethical Nexus*, addresses a broad spectrum of issues related to organization communication ethics, highlighting a number of contexts calling for responsive ethical organizational decision making.

In each of these examples, the specific context frames appropriate communicative action that protects and promotes a given sense of the good. This view of communication ethics presupposes a high degree of influence associated with a given context. Simply put, the context takes on more persuasive or instructional power than the communicative agent. This view of communication ethics begins with knowledge of the context aligned with the communicative necessity to be responsive to the needs of that context in a specific situation.

Narrative Communication Ethics

Walter Fisher's (1987) work on the narrative paradigm for human communication offers a story-centered approach in which the good emerges through the action of a given story and the characters who live the practices of a given narrative structure. A narrative suggests appropriate lines of action, or instantiations of the good for lived experience: "Narrative or story provides a community with a . . . context for action and rhetoric of practice" (Arnett, 1987, p. 53). For example, the Old Testament story of Exodus, featuring a nation enslaved by another in which the enslaved nation leaves the oppressing nation in search of a new home, illustrates goods of freedom and deliverance. These goods emerged within the narrative and now provide the basis for other oppressed groups' hopes and eventual movement in search of freedom (e.g., Selby, 2001).

Fisher's work builds upon a number of sources, with the insight of Alasdair MacIntyre as key; MacIntyre (1984, 2016) offers an understanding of virtues derived from different narratives or traditions throughout culture and history. MacIntyre (1984) is also central to Bellah and colleagues' books *Habits of the Heart* (Bellah, Madsen, Sullivan, Swidler, & Tipton, 1985) and *The Good Society* (Bellah, Madsen, Sullivan, Swidler, & Tipton, 1991), which address the dangers of losing a narrative from which actions gather their meaning. A virtue ethics approach emerging from the field of communication studies has roots in Arnett's (1987) work on narrative communication ethics, his explication of a Buberian understanding of dialogue (Arnett, 1986), and Arnett and Arneson's (1999) work on dialogic civility (Fritz, 2018). From this perspective, virtues are embedded in and draw their substance from goods within a given narrative.

The goods manifested in a narrative structure or tradition offer guidelines for living and for evaluating one's own life and that of others. We see the power of narrative in human response to stories, which are narrative in form but less encompassing than the more comprehensive structures of a particular tradition. Human beings respond to stories and to the goods they manifest. Stories display attributes of the cultures of which they are a part, and some, like the Cinderella story (e.g., Alidou, 2002), emerge in multiple locations, displaying goods shared across cultures. The work of Christians and Traber (1997) on universal minimalist ethics identifies a small number of protonorms or goods valued in all cultures—for example, telling the truth, doing no harm to the innocent, and respect for persons. Like Sissela Bok (1979), Christians and Traber look for narrative agreement that might bring us together around a minimalist set of values. Narrative communication ethics recognizes the story-laden nature of human experience, framing guidelines appropriate to "characters" in a given story.

Postmodernity challenged a "metanarrative ethics" that identifies one transcendent good or set of transcendent goods invariant across time and place, represented by Kant's universal ethics. However, postmodernity announced the presence of multiple and competing petite narratives. The recognition of many narratives, as opposed to a metanarrative, understands multiple senses of "ground," each of which gives rise to a communication ethic that seeks to protect and promote a given sense of the good. Recognizing a multiplicity of petite narratives permits narrative ethics to guide without claiming universal validity. Each narrative frames a good and holds implications for action and evaluation of that action; behavior of persons in the narrative should be consistent with the good articulated by the narrative. Religiously grounded and politically grounded communication ethics—for that matter, all story-laden communication ethics—can be understood as narrative ethics. The narrative perspective offers the possibility of seeking temporal agreement on minimalist values protected and promoted by more than one narrative that will permit us to function together in the midst of our diversity.

The novel *Watership Down* (Adams, 1972) reveals the importance of narrative in the reconstruction of life together after a group of rabbits loses its warren to a housing development. This analysis comes from Stanley Hauerwas (1981) in his illustration of narrative ethics that employs this novel. The rabbits establish a community, which they name "Watership Down," defined by goods that they agree upon at a corporate level. Guiding their development of this community is a larger story of the legendary rabbit El-ahrairah. El-ahrairah is a mythological prototype or character illustrating the challenges of life as a rabbit in a delightful and dangerous world. His wise, cunning, and careful action emerges in tales told by the rabbits in their journey to find a place to establish their new community. These stories reflect a larger narrative that provided guidelines for the rabbits as they established their dwelling place. The story of a given community makes manifest goods that the community protects and promotes. Such is the reason that stories like *Lord of the Rings* (Tolkien, 2004) capture the attention of both young and old. What makes these works interesting is the power of narrative that guides the characters. We find characters within the novels who attend to stories that propel their action. Hauerwas (1981), in *A Community of Character*, takes the important insights of MacIntyre on narrative and brings them to life in exemplification. This work of Hauerwas and the work of Bellah on the limits of individualism (Arnett, Fritz, & Holba, 2007) suggest that the communicative insights of Walter Fisher are extraordinary—stories matter; as Fisher (1987) states, we are "homo narrans" (p. xiii). We live in a story-laden world. For the study of communication ethics in a world of difference and for an understanding of dialogue that attends to the reality of differing ground upon which communicators stand, the work of Walter Fisher was paradigmatically ground breaking. His insights provided a way to understand multiplicity that did not begin with the person, but with the narrative ground upon which a communicator stands (Arnett, 2005).

Dialogic Communication Ethics

Dialogue, understood as the communicative exchange of agents embedded in a particular historical moment, a particular sociocultural standpoint, and a particular set of experiences, requires us to stand on our own ground while being open to the Other's standpoint. A dialogic approach to communication ethics recognizes the importance of meaning that emerges in discourse between persons. A dialogic communication ethic acknowledges multiple goods that give rise to and emerge in ongoing conversations, protecting and promoting the good of learning. A dialogic approach to communication ethics, or a dialogic ethic, recognizes that human beings live within an ongoing conversation that began well before a specific interpersonal interaction begins and continues without conclusion (Arnett et al., 2006). Such an ethic protects and promotes the unexpected revelation that emerges between and among persons, a revelation owned by no one and meaningfully important to many. Paula S. Tompkins (2015) reminds us that a current generation assumes the charge to teach ethics. This charge embraces a conviction about the importance of the Other, even to the extent of acknowledging interruptions that call us into account.

We are born into a world already formed, already in conversation. This understanding of dialogue assumes the importance of narrative; narrative gives birth to a particular set of social practices, virtues, and understandings of the good carried forth in dialogue. A dialogic ethic does not assure the "right" answer; it works to assist in meeting whatever diversity is before us, whether we like it or not. The key to dialogue is what Buber called the "between," that which emerges, which no one can force to appear or make happen. A dialogic ethic is the protector and the promoter of the emergent, the unexpected, and the unforeseen—it is the communicative home of hope for an idea, a viewpoint, or an action that has not yet been apparent. A dialogic ethic is the dwelling of communicative hope beyond our control but which, when recognized, brings the unsuspected, the unknown, and the unplanned together. We cannot demand dialogue and its gift of the unexpected, but, when it happens, we engage in communicative practices of gratitude, for the emergent answer comes as a gift outside the demands of the communicative partners. The work of Charles Brown and Paul Keller (1973) began the movement to connect dialogue and ethics. Later, this connection continued with the work of Johannesen and colleagues (2008), John Stewart (2011), Baxter and Montgomery (1996), and Anderson and Cissna (Anderson, Baxter, & Cissna, 2004; Anderson, Cissna, & Arnett, 1994), reminding us implicitly and explicitly of the ongoing connection of dialogue and ethics. Arnett (2017b) outlines the coordinates of the everyday and awesome task of ethics in the meeting of others in *Levinas's Rhetorical Demand: The Unending Obligation of Communication Ethics.*

Standpoint Communication Ethics

Standpoint theory originated with the work of Sandra Harding (2009), working from a feminist epistemology. Harding frames standpoint theory as an illustration of gender-driven perspectives. Standpoints of gender, race, ethnicity, class, and so on shape our conception and understanding of goods worthy of protecting and promoting. Some feminist scholars raise the question of whether or not the notion of standpoint theory risks deluding a gender perspective, with an emphasis on the reality of multiple standpoint projects (Crasnow, 2009, p. 190). There is recognition that standpoint is collective, not individual, and that it requires interrogation of the "perceived naturalness of the dominant groups' power" (Harding, 2009, p. 195). Standpoint theory examines the taken-for-granted. One cannot confuse standpoint theory with the given; it explores and questions normative assumptions.

Arguments between and among standpoint feminists and empirical feminists shape nearly 25 years of scholarship. Kristen Intemann (2010) argues that within standpoint theory there is an empiricist commitment to experience. What guides the two perspectives, according to Intemann, is that everyday experience influences the interpretive interplay between persons. Standpoint is not abstract, but the very experience within which one dwells and recognizes the world.

The work of Rita Felski (1989) and Nancy Fraser (1990) united standpoint theory with Habermas's explication of the public domain. Standpoint not only constitutes what one values and how one interprets, it ultimately gives birth to counter publics. Standpoint has a constitutive implication for understanding multiplicity and diversity in the public domain, composed of diverse publics (Jackson & Banaszczyk, 2016, p. 393).

© Rawpixel.com/Shutterstock.com

Standpoint recognizes that power shapes identity, difference, and the space we inhabit and that which distances us from others. Standpoint points to a basic recognition: Human beings understood collectively are "embodied knowers" (Rouse, 2009, p. 207). Standpoint acknowledges the situated nature of knowing. Since Harding's view of standpoint, the debates are numerous and the emphasis consistent: experience, power, and the collective embodiment of persons matters. It shapes our understanding and alignment with others. For example, families from different cultures or social classes may have different expectations about what is appropriate to serve as a meal when guests are visiting. Some cultures might expect a three-course meal, whereas other cultures might consider serving leftovers equally hospitable. Even within a culture, some individuals may have moral objections to specific foods such as meat that others would consider commonplace. Navigating differing social contexts requires an awareness of the variety of standpoints that guests bring to the table.

The following section illustrates the application of each of the approaches to communication ethics, addressing the issue of drinking alcohol on a college campus. In the United States, the practice of alcohol overconsumption has been a source of contention and conflict in many arenas, particularly on college and university campuses. The Prohibition era will forever mark the ongoing ambivalence of this country about alcohol consumption.

The College Campus: Communication Ethics Perspectives

Drinking alcohol has been a contested good in many cultures and contexts. Some cultures understand alcohol as a legitimate good of human life that promotes sociability and relaxation. Some cultures understand alcohol as a significant part of a tradition, important to sacred rituals. Other cultures or groups forbid the consumption of alcohol. Each of the approaches to communication ethics offers a way to think about the consumption of alcohol as a good (or not as a good) or as connected to a good (or to that which is not a good). We review each approach below as it applies to the case of five friends enrolled at an educational institution faced with issues related to alcohol consumption.

A **democratic approach to communication ethics** finds the good in a public process for collaborating on ideas, customs, and rights, protecting and promoting the good of public decision making. Imagine five close friends who attend the same college and understand that drinking is an issue requiring responsible decision making. The five friends make a pact to discuss and deliberate about the rules they will follow when attending parties with alcohol. After discussing many options during a number of meetings, they develop a set of guidelines for the group. The practice of discussion and deliberation illustrates a democratic communication ethic. Some of the democratically generated guidelines that emerge from their deliberations include decisions about electing a designated driver who will refrain from drinking when the friends attend parties requiring transportation and decisions about which parties to attend and which ones to avoid based on the likelihood of intensity of alcohol consumption at the event.

A **universal-humanitarian approach to communication ethics** assumes a built-in guiding ethical principle that is part of human nature, protecting and promoting the good of duty and responsibility to human beings. From this perspective, if Ivan is the designated driver on a given evening, he will abstain from drinking as a duty to his friends based on a promise he made and as a duty to the larger society in order to fulfill his obligation not to drink and drive as required by law. He fulfills the rational obligation of understanding that if everyone were to break promises, the notion of promising itself would have no meaning for human society; if everyone broke the law, contracts among persons would have no meaning. His fulfillment of this obligation also shows respect for his friends as valuable human beings; he should not put them in danger by drinking and driving. The practice of keeping a promise to his friends, keeping the law, and fulfilling the duty to protect human life illustrates a universal-humanitarian ethic.

© Chris Byrne/Shutterstock.com

A **codes, procedures, and standards approach to communication ethics** requires defining guidelines for evaluating appropriate ethical conduct and then protecting and promoting the good of this corporately agreed upon set of regulations. From this perspective, the group of five friends understands that their college has an ethical code of conduct regulating drinking on campus. For example, the students must know the university rules for student drinking, identifying the codes, procedures, and standards for this campus.

A contextual approach to communication ethics recognizes variations in culture, persons, and settings when applying communication ethics principles, protecting and promoting the good of the particular. In certain contexts, the good of alcohol consumption may clash with other goods. For example, in a party where most people are under the drinking age, the consumption of alcohol by someone who has attained legal drinking age may not represent the most salient or important good. Additionally, consider the case of someone who is having difficulty with alcohol abuse and is trying to stop drinking. A close friend of that person may choose not to order a drink at a restaurant when they are dining together, stating, "I think I'll have a soda with my meal. I don't want a beer right now." Ethical communicative choices about drinking or refraining from drinking in different situations illustrate a contextual communication ethic.

A **narrative approach to communication ethics** assumes that persons' lives find direction through stories about the way the world is or should be, protecting and promoting the good of particular narratives or stories. Narratives themselves are host to goods that underlie, constitute, and shape them. For some, a life story recognizes the good of alcohol consumption in moderation for contexts of celebration and relaxation; for others, alcohol has played such a strong role in a story of abuse and neglect that it cannot fill the role of a good in that life. A family with a history of alcohol abuse may have an elaborate story about the dangers of alcohol and compelling reasons for abstinence. A colleague had a mother who watched her father die of alcoholism after she had seen the same fate befall two uncles. The mother, as an adult, never permitted alcohol in the house for any occasion. Her husband honored her request, as did the rest of the family. As the children became professionals and functioned in much different environments with much different narrative limits on drinking, there was one constant story—no drinking in Mom's home. Stories matter; they shape our lives, defining virtuous communicative practices consistent with the goods of a given narrative.

A **dialogic communication ethic** acknowledges multiple goods that give rise to and emerge in ongoing conversations, protecting and promoting the good of learning. After a night of heavy drinking resulting in regrettable behavior, unwise choices, and physical illness, the five friends discuss their experiences. Through their conversation, they realize how lucky they are to be alive and, more importantly, recognize that the actions that occurred should never occur again. Of course, there is no guarantee that dialogue will open the unexpected. However, it is amazing what the emergent unknown can bring to us when it appears unexpectedly as an idea or a road less traveled. The emergent unknown can change a life—for dialogue is the home of a hope we cannot own, but can only invite.

A **standpoint communication ethic** suggests that the ground upon which one stands and meets the Other shapes one's understanding of the good, protecting and promoting differences in gender, race, ethnicity, affectivity, and culture. As the five friends continue to learn about healthy alcohol consumption, they embark on a travel abroad experience that shows them how other cultures view alcohol and its consumption. They learn that in some cultures, alcohol is seen as a social activity regulated by community norms, and local restaurants frown upon visible intoxication in public places.

These seven approaches to communication ethics point to theoretical differences that lend themselves to differing views of the good. Diversity lives in many forms; differing understandings of communication ethics reflect such ongoing diversity. As Chesebro (1997) reminds us, different communication systems bring forth different values shaped by the society of which they are a part.

[N]ot all people share the same values. Multiple systems of human communication exist, in part, because different sets of values govern symbol-using (see, e.g., Chesebro 1973). But, far more important in this essay, the values regulating any particular human communication system are influenced by societal systems. (p. 126)

Engagement with communication ethics diversity begins with understanding differing basic approaches to communication ethics: democratic; universal-humanitarian; codes, procedures, and standards; contextual; narrative; dialogic; and standpoint approaches. Each approach offers insight into the complexity of communication ethics in theory and action, with each protecting and promoting a given sense of the good.

COMMUNICATION ETHICS: REFLECTION AND ACTION

1. Locate a student handbook for your college or university and list several goods the institution identifies as worthy of protection and promotion. How are these goods discussed in the handbook?
2. Consider a situation that required you to make a difficult choice. Assess the situation using three of the following approaches in your communicative analysis: democratic; universal-humanitarian; codes, procedures, and standards; contextual; narrative; dialogic; standpoint.
3. Which of the approaches to communication ethics seems most helpful to you in this situation and why?
4. Locate the web sites for the National Communication Association (NCA), the Public Relations Society of America (PRSSA), and the American Advertising Federation (AAF) to find their codes of professional ethics. Do these professional communication organizations share any guiding principles?

ENGAGING COMMUNICATION ETHICS THROUGH LITERATURE: *LES MISÉRABLES*

Les Misérables illustrates elements of each approach to communication ethics. A democratic communication ethic emerges in the hopes of the revolutionaries for a more just society, with representation from peasants as well as rich nobles. Javert illustrates a prototypical universal-humanitarian communication ethic in his concern for duty without exception. His unswerving devotion to the law reflects commitment to the good of duty. Jean Valjean follows a universal-humanitarian ethic in his determination to fulfill his promise to the dying Fantine to care for her child. He carries out this duty with all his energy; likewise, he struggles between competing duties. As mayor, he brings safety and prosperity to the town; as Jean Valjean, he must save the life of an innocent man mistaken for him, risking the good he can do for the town if he is arrested and can no longer serve as mayor.

When Valjean first arrives at the village where Bishop Myriel resides, he encounters a set of codes, laws, and procedures put in place to protect citizens from harm, and these guidelines prevent him from finding a place to stay for the night. When Javert comes to find Valjean after Valjean reveals his identity to save the life of the man mistaken for him, the nun who keeps house for Valjean/Mayor Madeleine, who had never told a lie in her life, states that Valjean is not there, nor has he been there, working with a contextual ethic that honors the particular of protecting someone she believes to be honest and worthy of protection. Bishop Myriel, also known as Monseigneur Bienvenu, engages a narrative ethic when he welcomes Valjean into his home; the bishop seeks to live the Christian narrative of love for all when he identifies Valjean as worthy of the title of Monsieur, worthy of trust, and worthy of invitation into a narrative represented by the bishop's "gift" of candlesticks and silver.

A dialogic ethic arises between Javert and Valjean at the end of the book where the unexpected emergent appears after Javert arrests Valjean. Valjean asks Javert to permit him to take the wounded Marius home, and, in an unexpected acquiescence, Javert agrees, and then, just as unexpectedly, permits Valjean to go free. Though Javert cannot continue life with this contradiction between his commitment to the good of duty to the law and his own behavior in setting Valjean free, the emergent reality transforms Valjean's future. In this case, an uninvited dialogic event takes place that no one could have predicted. Javert's standpoint is grounded in a view of law enforcement. His social and institutional position frames sees the world as governed by inviolable laws, whereas Valjean's experience as a convicted and hunted criminal who has been forgiven has shaped the way he sees the world.

Communication Ethics

In the Eye(s) of the Theory of the Beholder

Common sense is seen primarily in the judgments about right and wrong, proper and improper, that it makes. Whosoever has a sound judgment is not thereby enabled to judge particulars under universal viewpoints, but he knows what is important, i.e. he sees things from right and sound points of view. (Gadamer, 1960/1986, p. 31)

This chapter examines issues of theory, diversity, and communication ethics as interrelated, framing theory as a type of lens that makes visible implicit ethical content. Different theories make visible different types of ethical content. The pragmatic importance of theory and communication ethics rests with the assumption that we need a public map of "why" and "how" we see, permitting examination of our own bias and that of others. We begin the discussion of theory with humble recognition of our limits and the need to make such positions public when doing communication ethics. After reading this chapter, you will be able to demonstrate the following learning objectives:

- Evaluate common sense assumptions as an opportunity for learning
- Explain how theories serve as a public road map in specified contexts
- Apply communication ethics theories to multiple situations

Introduction

Communication ethics theory articulates a conceptual roadmap for public decision making, pragmatically defining common sense as public admission and accountability. Today, we cannot assume that common sense emerges as a natural communicative act that we all agree upon—multiple understandings of what is good coexist in the public square. Public admission and accountability of communication ethics theory require two commitments: (1) constantly cautioning ourselves against demanding that another conform to "our" common knowledge and practices; common sense in this era requires us to recognize that there is no one standard for what we call common sense, and (2) finding ways to make a temporal "common sense" publicly known and visible.

This chapter connects the study of communication ethics to communicative practices with attention to the following three metaphors of communication ethics praxis:

1. **Common sense**—the commonly understood, taken-for-granted assumptions about the way the world works and expected communicative behaviors one will meet in navigating that world in daily life. The taken-for-granted in this historical moment is that common sense is no longer common. Theory provides a form of public common sense that drives ideas and communication ethics engagement.
2. **Learning**—without a single understanding of common sense, learning and understanding differing standpoints is a pragmatic communication ethics act.
3. **Theories**—public common sense, a public road map of a way to see, know, and understand that both broadens and narrows our insight.

Student Application: Common Sense and Contention

As one enters the first year of college and proceeds through the last day of the senior year, new phases of life call for changes in relationships, work, or living arrangements, accompanied by questions such as: "What if I do not fit in?" "What if I do not get a job?" "What if I don't like this new town?" "What if this relationship does not work out?" No longer does the experiencing of the new—in this case, new beginnings and endings of life transitions—have an answer in a **common sense** response. However, when we approach different experiences through **learning**, the unfamiliar and strange become opportunities for knowledge and new understanding.

▶

▶ **Theories** are public recordings of the learning of others, offered as a guide that helps us understand communicative events before us. Theories are public guides or maps that shape our lives, giving us insight into the way the world works.

Common Sense

"I can't believe that you don't know how to throw a baseball. It is just *common sense*." "I can't believe that you're having trouble following the plot of this television show. It is just *common sense*." "I am simply amazed at your lack of knowledge of this car engine. It is just *common sense*." "How can anyone in this day and age be so clumsy with a computer? It is just *common sense*." "What do you mean you can't follow these directions? They're written in plain English—it's just *common sense*."

Contrary to our daily utterances about common sense, *common sense* is not innate, nor is it common. Common sense is a by-product of what we know and what we practice. When the knowing and the practicing of a given understanding of communication ethics becomes normative, standard, or common, then implementation of communication ethics in a community becomes a form of common sense. However, in an era of narrative and virtue contention, the doing and the practicing of communication ethics is not common, making *common sense* no longer a taken-for-granted part of communicative life.

Today, we must curtail the impulse to judge something as having or lacking common sense by what "I" know. Such a judgment imposes one's own experiences as a universal truth, forgetting the increasing texture of difference in the world around us. Alasdair MacIntyre (2016) recognizes that particularity of goods and diversity of understanding of what is good ignite conflict (pp. 214–220). Simply put, we live in a time in which one view of common sense is no more, but the importance of common sense is of no less importance in an era of differing narrative and virtue structures. We live in an era that lost common sense and simultaneously found it anew, returning to "common sense" in smaller forms.

Common sense emerges from the communities we know and the practices we do. Common sense is only common when there is familiarity with a community and its practices. Common sense dislodged from the universal rests within the local, the limited, and the provincial (Roberts & Arnett, 2008). Common sense moves from the pervasive to the petite, to a smaller, more local version. One example of this smaller form of common sense observed in groups or communities emerges around common causes or projects guided by what could be considered "public theory," positions articulated by figures who provide a central voice for that community. In popular culture, Oprah Winfrey represents the heart of such a community, enacting an implicit theory of self-improvement and service to others, as does the home schooling movement, which rests upon the theory that education that is both individualized and responsive to the values of a particular family or tradition is more useful than a general public education. Another example lies with traditions that have endured for decades, centuries, or millennia that now state explicitly and in public contexts their assumptions about the nature of reality, the world, and human life. In some cities, groups emerge that state publicly an intention to improve living conditions for that area; such temporal agreements represent a type of public theory as common sense, as well, serving as publicly agreed-upon positions that guide action. Communicative ethics danger lurks wherever a person or a group assumes that a particular local view of common sense is universally correct, dismissing too quickly the reality of difference and the bias inherent in one's view of common sense.

Common Sense: Losing the Common

To accuse another of not having the faculty of common sense misses the point on two counts. First, common sense is not an innate human faculty; common sense consists of a background of experiences from which we draw our ideas and insights for decision making. Our particular understanding of common sense emerges from what we do and what we know; the common comes from the familiar. When the common is no longer in place, communicators are no longer certain of what constitutes an appropriate ethical communicative response. Second, the term by which we refer to this age, "postmodern," is an admission that we live in an age of narrative and virtue contention, that we inhabit a world where common sense is no longer similarly accessible to all. Different persons with contrasting backgrounds and experiences make a universal background of common sense, a common pool of knowledge and practices, anachronistic—out of place and out of time. Common sense today requires us not to take commonality for granted. In a time of narrative and virtue contention, common sense rests in the eye of the beholder. Simply stated, the only common sense is the realization that there is no universal common sense.

The meeting of this moment of historical change is now commonplace, not just in major policy questions between governments and differing political affiliates, but in everyday communicative life. For instance, one of the authors was a little league coach for a number of years, having played organized baseball from the age of eight until his college years. Knowledge and practice of baseball over the years led to experience that generated a degree of common sense about baseball that coaches assumed; coaches understood that the entire neighborhood played baseball together as much as possible. Yet, thirty years later, as a coach, he discovered that common sense about the game was not the same. This change announced itself loudly when one young person on the team said: "Coach, can you keep my glove until the next practice? I do not want to lose my glove or forget to bring it to practice." The young player's honest question and statement announced the reality of a different era, an era with little knowledge and practice of the game of baseball

outside of formal practice sessions. The common sense about the game that came from "kids in the old neighborhood" no longer existed as a universal expectation. The common sense assumption that one played between formal practices was no longer in place. The reality of difference present in competing views of common sense takes us far from the baseball field and into questions of religion, cultural expression and practices, and social and political positions. Common sense, like a communication ethic, now rests among a multiplicity of options. Our assurance of correctness now walks hand in hand with a prudent admission of varying degrees of doubt (Arnett, 2005).

Common Sense as Communicative Practices

What generates common sense is commonality of practices. When we do the same practices over and over again, they fade into the background, moving from that which we must reflect upon before being able to employ (explicit knowing) to what Michael Polanyi (1967) called tacit knowing (implicit knowing). Imagine a first-year college student raising her hand to ask for a hall pass to use the restroom. The student's effort to ask permission might unintentionally disrupt class because she has not yet developed the tacit knowing of civility in the college classroom as opposed to high school. Third-year students, based on their experience in the college setting, have a type of tacit knowledge that leaving to use the restroom without disturbing class is a common sense practice. The question, "Should I raise my hand and ask for a hall pass?" never even enters their minds. If someone engages in the same practices that we do, common sense connects us, but when our personal and/or professional practices are different, little common sense connects us.

Thomas Paine's (1776/1984) famous treatise, *Common Sense*, rested within the everyday practices of contention against British rule, such as the Boston Tea

Party. His work revealed and contended against practices that empowered British rule over the colonies, including the practices of "owning" a country from overseas and a maintaining a military presence on foreign soil. He assumed that the reader had enough knowledge of these problematic practices and colonists' practices in opposition to them that the conclusion to resist British rule became "common sense." In short, the knowing and the doing of common practices invites common sense; without the collective knowing and doing of given practices, common sense is not a connecting link between persons.

Another example stems from public speaking and Aristotle's (1995) rhetorical device known as the "enthymeme"—a speaker who employs the enthymeme assumes enough shared common sense between speaker and audience for the audience to "fill in the blanks" or supply a missing premise in an argument without the need for the speaker to state it directly. Without common sense, enthymemes do not work at all or may backfire. For example, a student giving a speech against curricular change at her school may assume that her audience is opposed to a requirement of an additional course in language study. Her statement, "Every student would now have to take more language courses," uttered as though such a requirement would be a drawback to curricular change, may not match the "common sense" of the international relations majors in her audience, who understand an additional language requirement as a beneficial and desirable change. Her assumption that all those in the audience would draw the same conclusions as she would is unwise in a moment of expected difference, impairing the rhetorical function of the enthymeme.

Additionally, as we emphasize individual distinctions over the common, we find a communication ethic having less common sense traction in a culture that lives by individualistic and "emotivistic" impulses—that is, a culture characterized by the tendency to define the "good" by "me" alone, what "feels good" or "seems right" to the self, according to "my" personal inclination or preference. A communication ethic lives wherever there is common agreement among persons about the knowing and/or the doing of practices that protect a given sense of the good. With multiple views of the good and multiple common sense understandings of the good, such a world is more akin to a patchwork quilt than to a single sewn sheet of cloth.

A Patchwork Quilt of Common Sense

When awareness of difference, differing ways of doing and knowing communicative practices, becomes the common sense touchstone of our time, agreement shifts into patches of ground or "fabric" where people have common ways of doing and knowing. From this perspective, the metaphor of a patchwork quilt unites many small understandings of common sense, many "petite localities" or places of agreed-upon goods. What holds the quilt together—indeed, what defines the quilt itself—are all the varied pieces united in their difference. Each square of the quilt in our metaphor represents a petite locality defined by a particular understanding of the good.

Common sense is not gone. Any given "common sense" rests within a localized portion of a quilt that takes shape from many particular forms of common sense; its texture includes the interplay of differing narratives, standpoints, and "ground" dynamics. Common sense ceases to have universal appeal, but it is still recognizable through the united groupings of persons constituting a larger pattern of multiplicity of goods and common sense practices. The presence of common sense as derived from some particular agreed-upon good emerges in its situatedness within a given locality or narrative ground. When differing ideas of the good become normative, common sense as a single defining pattern fades from our daily landscape.

Common sense assumes experiential agreement with communicative practices and background assumptions that guide interpretive insight. When common sense generated from common experience no longer guides us, the interpretive vision of a given person takes on increasing currency, and smaller patches of "common sense" vie for allegiance, often emerging from negotiated understandings and common practices among localized groups, communities, or relationships (see Stephen, 1994, for a discussion of symbolic exchange in marriage over different historical periods that consist of varied levels of "common sense" agreement). In short, what we see no longer gathers meaning from common practices and background assumptions, but rests in the "eyes of the beholders." When common sense at the larger societal level is lacking, common centers of common sense must sustain smaller groups of persons and institutions (Arnett, 1986).

This chapter works with celebratory thanks for the loss of a universal common sense; this reality keeps us learning from and with one another, keeping before us a sense of otherness, keeping us ever attentive to difference. Loss of the commonness of common sense leads first to learning and then to the public framing of common sense in theories that work as *Touchstones of Reality* (Friedman, 1972) that find temporal agreement. To accept the loss of the commonness of common sense requires us to embrace what we consider the central notion of communication ethics for the 21st century—learning. We engage a situated common sense that we must learn together in the doing and knowing of practices that seek to protect and promote a given sense of the good. *Common sense* rests in the knowing and the doing of those engaging similar practices.

Learning

For the study of communication ethics, the loss of agreed-upon common sense expectations is neither good nor bad, but simply a defining reality of our time. From our perspective, its loss is a major opportunity for the pragmatic importance of learning in an era of difference. This historical moment carries with it a major communication ethics assumption of this chapter: In a world of difference, one that gives rise to narrative and virtue contention, the only "common sense" is the assumption that there is no universal common sense agreement, and continual learning needs to guide us.

This assumption of the loss of agreed-upon common sense links directly with our communication ethics "first principle": *Learning is the first principle of communication ethics in an era without a universal understanding of what constitutes common sense* (Arnett, Bell, & Fritz, 2010; Arnett, 2016). If we fail to connect the loss of agreed-upon common sense with learning, we fall prey to discounting or making fun of those different from ourselves, those with dissimilar backgrounds, experiences, and practices. Ridiculing the different disregards the fact that the Other's sense of our being different is important. The strange rests with the judgment of the observer; we must fight the impulse to equate our eyes, our way of looking, with the "right" and the stranger's way of looking with the "wrong." The pragmatic response for communication ethics to the typicality of difference characteristic of a postmodern moment is to turn a problem into an opportunity. The recognition of difference moves us from smug dismissal of the alien to an opportunity for learning about understandings of common sense different from our own. The loss of common sense is the learning opportunity for this moment; we live in an era when implementation and imitation are simply insufficient.

The commitment to learning moves an understanding of this moment from a sense of loss to a communicative conviction that this is a wonderful moment of communication ethics opportunity; the loss of normative standards makes pragmatic the unceasing impetus for learning in this century. This loss of common sense is the key for generating what Emmanuel Levinas (1998) called joy in this moment! For Levinas, joy comes from meeting the historical moment before us and embracing the responsibility that such a moment calls forth. The joy of our responsibility is to take up the action of learning with the mantra that the loss of common sense is actually a good. One may not applaud this loss of common sense in private life, but public acceptance is a pragmatic necessity if working with difference that defines our time is to energize rather than enflame conflict, anger, and resentment. Learning mandates that we encounter the textured differences of human life, giving up the demand that others conform to our expectations. As we learn about and from unlike communicative backgrounds that house dissimilar and, at times, competing understandings of common sense, we encounter *a second assumption of this chapter—differing pools of common sense lead to different understandings of the "good."*

Learning from differences requires attentiveness to contrary and contrasting narratives and standpoints, each of which gives rise to what we call, in academic terms, a theory that attempts to offer public guidance, a public recording of learning. Just as a roadmap provides direction to a particular location, a theory offers guidance in different life circumstances. Graduating seniors might look to different theories in their particular industries to give informed answers to interview questions. We gather guidance from narrative practices that point us in a given direction. A narrative emerges from three communicative acts, as understood from the vantage point of communication ethics. Ronald C. Arnett and Pat Arneson (1999) draw upon the work of Walter Fisher (1987) and Barnett Pearce

(1989) to provide a vocabulary that assists understanding the value of narrative to the study of communication, First, the notion of "speech act" articulates a good that requires our protection and promotion. Second, when a given speech act that carries a given view of the good takes on characteristics that involve main characters and a sense of plot, it becomes a "story." Third, when a story takes on corporate agreement among at least some number of persons, their belief in a story that protects and promotes a given sense of the good takes on the power of guidance, moving the story to narrative status. We understand a theory as a public admission of a given petite public narrative about a particular communication ethic, offering us both clarity and limitations.

Communication ethics theory as the carrier of a given sense of the good is the interplay of narrative and standpoint. Such theory is a public admission of learning that invites a form of scholarly common sense open to question from other "common sense" positions. Such difference commences with standpoint and narrative that skew the seeing and the construction of a given communication ethics theory. For this project, we define theory as dependent upon narrative and standpoint. The loss of confidence in a vision of universal truth requires us to take ever so seriously the importance of peripheral vision, the ability to see things outside of our direct line of sight, out of the corners of our eyes. In our peripheral vision, we sense the reality of multiplicity, the reality of difference all around us in daily communicative life—the existence of multiple theories of the good.

Theories

The subtitle of this chapter, "In the Eye(s) of the Theory of the Beholder," provides deliberate ambiguity about the singular or plural emphasis on eye(s). At this juncture, the ambiguity of singular or plural becomes salient. When connected to a theory, the notion of eye moves to the plural—by the stress on the plural of "eyes," we suggest one eye wide open and the other with a patch covering its vision and multiple people engaged in the looking. A communication ethics theory, like any theory, both opens the world, permitting us to see with clarity, and simultaneously occludes our vision. A theory both illuminates and obscures. Lisbeth Lipari (2017) differentiates atomistic and holistic theories, with the former attentive to singularity and particularity and the latter emphasizing interrelationships. Texture and complexity fuel human engagement with others, making holistic interdisciplinary theories appropriate for such analysis. However, she acknowledges that the pinpoint focus of an atomistic theory can at times shed light upon a given action that would go unnoticed from a grander holistic perspective. A theory guides, which permits us to discern the unnoticed while augmenting additional discoveries. The knowing adoption of theory keeps one's eyes on the given that we meet through the interplay of narrative and standpoint, ever watchful about the limits of our own vision; unlike the Cyclops, we have another eye on what we do not know and on the limits of what we see. *A third common sense communication ethics assumption of this chapter is that each theory offers us vision while limiting our ability to see other possibilities.* Theory guidance meets the limits of our unique standpoint, a place that both enhances and colors our vision. Theory takes on the function of situating our eyes in the doing of and knowing about a given sense of the good. Theory is a public academic guidance system that gives us a form of common sense with one another as we agree upon the seeing and doing of a given communication ethic.

In the Eye(s) of the Theory

This section examines the way theory works as a guide to direct our attention or vision, moving the metaphor of "eye" from person to the theoretical perspective itself. When we take on or subscribe to a given theoretical perspective, we rest in the eye of a theory that began with an initial observation textured by a standpoint that became accepted as explanatory lens for human understanding of an experience or phenomenon. Before turning to the discussion of theory, we return briefly to notion of "common sense"; we contend that a communication ethics theory is a public statement of learning that works as common sense for those that concur with its guidance.

The clichés that we so commonly use carry common insight and simultaneously function as cul-de-sacs if taken too seriously or retained when their time is past. For instance, "in the eye of the beholder" assumes a modern common agreement that the autonomous person guides decision making. This bit of common sense rests better with a time prior to awareness of diversity of race, ethnicity, and gender that situates what Sandra Harding (1991, 2004, 2009) called "standpoint." For example, someone working two jobs to make ends meet may not value spending hard-earned money at an expensive restaurant on a meal that costs as much as a day's work. Yet, from the standpoint of another, such expenditure is not a waste of resources, but a chance to enjoy fine cuisine as one of the important pleasures of life. Diversity of perspective has always existed, but now has moved to the forefront of our awareness, gaining renewed attention and theorizing. Commonality of perspective and a shared sense of the good existed prior to postmodern recognition of diversity, a byproduct of the hegemony of particular powerful groups who gave voice to and supported the public visibility of that commonality.

When standpoints move from unreflective socio-cultural backgrounds to reflective positions, they begin to take on theoretical currency. Communication ethics theories are the public manifestations of implicit or explicit assumptions about what is worthy of our focus of attention; in short, what is the good that a given ethic should protect and promote? Communication ethics theories become public confessions (Arnett, 2005) of communicative assumptions worthy of protecting. It is the good of a given theory that offers direction and competes against one or more rival views of the good. In a time of competing views of the good, communication ethics theory assumes a confessional role of public disclosure of the good that rests "in the eye of the beholder of the theory." Competing views of ethics emerge not only from competing theories but from competing communicative practices—what we know and what we do together shapes our understanding of common sense.

If one is to engage human life from the standpoint of scholarship on communication ethics, the phrase "in the eyes of the beholder" becomes "in the eyes of the theory of the beholder." Theory establishes a perceptual field that provides a temporal place for common practices and agreement. In the study of communication ethics, theory becomes a petite place, a "touchstone" from which one can gather common sense. Competing theories result in competing views of common sense—hence, "in the eyes of the theory of the beholder" rests a temporal public accounting of common sense. The patchwork quilt metaphor mentioned earlier provides difference and texture that shape a public memory. Intellectually, theories shape our public communities of memory, constituting an ongoing texture of complexity rich with multiple views of communication ethics.

Theories as Public Memory

Situated public memory, as articulated by Greg Dickinson, Carole Blair, and Brian L. Ott (2010), houses our common interests and commitments. Memory activates keeping issues in the forefront of consideration. Memory narrates finding communal connections. Memory animates with emotion and affect. Memory is partisan and invites contested terrain. Memory depends upon the symbolic and codes. Memory is historical. Each of these characteristics of memory suggests that its public presence is both powerful and contestable (pp. 6–11).

A theory is not a narrative, nor is it a standpoint in the sociocultural sense; it is a conceptual and metaphorical space that locates the interplay of narrative and standpoint. A theory is an offspring of a larger narrative and reflective of a given standpoint. For instance, social exchange theory assumes that people make rational judgments about what each partner in a relationship has to offer. Relational partners exchange relational goods and try to achieve an outcome where the rewards are greater than the costs (worth = rewards − costs) (Homans, 1958). Social exchange theory connects us to yet another level of theoretical engagement, another standpoint in the larger narrative of human cooperation—the standpoint of a capitalistic culture. Social exchange theory is the interplay of a larger narrative of human cooperation and competition and the sociocultural standpoint of a capitalistic society; it is an explanation of the common sense of a narrative of cooperation within the standpoint of a capitalistic society (e.g. Blau, 1993; Roloff, 1981).

When offered as *the* way of engaging human interaction, social exchange theory can become a form of communication ethics propaganda. When a communication ethics theory is but one of many ways of engaging another, it takes on a petite or particular form of common sense. Theories are common sense collections of knowing and doing practices that advance a given sense of the good. They carry implicit and explicit communication ethics, advancing a given sense of the good.

The theories that shape our vision—our understanding—of communication ethics, may be quite explicit, highly developed, and well known. Yet, on the other hand, the theory may be implicit, housed in a simple phrase such as, "When the going gets tough, the tough get going." The ethic of tenacity under duress is not one held by all. Such an ethic is a compressed "rough-edged" practical theory for engaging the difficulties of everyday life. However, someone who does not hold such a view simply sees a fool continuing to work when all seems lost.

An unreflective theory of convention rests in statements throughout the history of the United States such as "never give up, never give up." One then wonders who could live a life like that: never give up, never give up. Franklin Delano Roosevelt's (1946) statement, "We have nothing to fear but fear itself"; Rosa Parks's nonverbal statement uttered loudly with her refusal to give up a seat

© Gino Santa Maria

on a bus; Abraham Lincoln's utterance delivered eloquently on the eve of war (Carr, 1906), framing the future for a divided nation—in each case, the implicit or explicit theory that guides a person mattered; such is the storehouse from which families, communities, organizations, cultures, and nations find the reason, the sense of "why," for doing what others see as simply impossible. It is not the person who provides the energy to keep going in the midst of defeat that matters, but a view of the world within which the person lives and walks: "Never give up." Theory functions as a form of public memory, both in its primitive and reflective forms, with ethical consequences.

Theory as Story-Laden Communication Ethics

One can discount the power of a public memory that rests in aphorisms and quotations. However, it was the genius of Walter Benjamin, the literary critic and philosopher, that urged him to collect quotations (Caygill, 1998). In a time of darkness and lack of clarity, Benjamin reminded us of hope, not in elaborate theories, but in petite theories caught in small reminders of community worth remembering. He offered us traces of memory in the amazing number of quotations he compiled and protected. The good within the quotations was a reminder, a communicative call to public memory about a given aspect of human life that offers light in the midst of darkness, the unknown, and the less than clear.

Communication ethics theory understood as public memory is qualitatively different from unreflective standpoints, quotations, and aphorisms; yet, in some ways, it is very much the same. The importance of direction guides each. A public memory registers the good of never giving up; it is composed of thousands of petite theories, many of which are fragments of grander or larger theoretical assumptions. The study of communication ethics may not give one the tenacity never to give up—there are ingredients to a life other than stories or theories—but such a story or theory gives one a better chance than no insight at all. Additionally, in a world of diversity, one must ask: "What is the petite theory or story that guides a person?" It is the story that guides the person—it is the theory before the eye that shapes the beholder. Theories and stories matter—from them we find our vision, our way, our understanding of the "good." A theory about a communicative good is a story about the engagement and doing of communication ethics (Arnett, 2002).

Imagine that Travis has done poorly on his first two exams in a research methods course required for his major. His friends urge him to drop the class, arguing that next semester he could take the course from an easier professor. Travis refuses to give up, determined to seek tutoring and to invest extra time and energy to learn what is difficult for him. He learned this tenacity through a father who, despite repeated layoffs, continued to seek and find employment to provide for his son's education. Travis understands the importance of hard work from a father who constantly worked hard for him and the rest of the family.

A communication ethics theory as public memory is a guide for a given sense of the good. A scholarly theory is a public proclamation that one can follow, test, and consider. A theory of convention or scholarly insight gives one immediate access to a public memory that moves one from decision making without guidance to decision making within a community of persons, many of whom no longer walk this earth, but whose lives still give a meaningful sense of credence to a given theory or public memory.

A theory promotes and protects a given sense of the good. A theory gives us eyes to see a given sense of the good—it both opens and limits a view of communication ethics, becoming a form of theoretical vision with pragmatic import for the study and practice of communication ethics. The theory works to keep a given sense of the good in our public memory. Our shared knowledge and practices constitute a communicative background, which shapes public memory and what we deem as common sense.

The emphasis on eye(s) as theoretical perspective connects to the notion of story. Communication ethics considered from different stories engages the Other differently. For instance, Paulo Freire's (1972) learning model offers a story of education and literacy to and for the oppressed (Arnett, 2002). Freire's theoretical perspective on literacy tells a story of liberation for the disenfranchised; his communication ethic tells the story of the good of public participation. Levinas (1998) reminds us of the good of "I am my brother's keeper" (Cohen, 1998, p. xii), a story reflected in the face of the Other that points away from the color of the Other's eyes to an ethical imperative not to kill the Other. In daily life, we find opportunities to live this ethic. For example, perhaps you are angry with a friend who failed to show up last night after promising to meet you for dinner. When you see her the next day, you are ready to express your anger in no uncertain terms, but when you come to face to face with her and look into her eyes, you see not the hurt she has caused you, but a reminder that this specific person matters, that this friend is irreplaceable, that you have responsibility to this person and to the relationship, and you ask gently, instead, "What happened last night? Are you okay? I missed you." Julia Wood (1992) reminds us of the "web of relationships" that shapes our communicative action and our identities, a theoretical story of interconnection. Theories protect and promote a given good; theories direct communicative action that instantiate that good. In the field of communication ethics, we leave the world of the routine when theory becomes primary; we enter a public recording of a public memory.

Theory connections to communication ethics continue with the work of many, with persons like Clifford Christians offering salient insight. The following quotation points to ongoing theoretical questions that guide his work. These questions link theory and communication ethics as story.

> Agnes Heller points us to a new model of communication ethics. Rather than searching for neutral principles to which all parties can appeal, or accepting moral relativism uncritically, the feminist social ethics that she represents is rooted in a complex view of moral judgments as integrating facts, principles, and

feelings in terms of human wholeness. She escapes the reductionistic and static view of humans as rational beings, while bringing our humanness decisively into the public arena. Heller's model of good persons, everyday life, and dynamic justice advocates an integrated view of the human as whole beings—body, mind and spirit. Her philosophical anthropology reorients accountability and autonomy to contemporary conditions rather than discrediting them. The normative ideal of her ethics is the subjection of all institutions and structures of power to communal-collective deliberation. (Christians, 2002, p. 64)

Christians points to a public form of common sense—not total agreement, but the importance of communal-collective deliberation, which other theories would just as quickly dismiss. The key to theory is the public articulation of a given worldview, the telling of a public story. Communication ethics theory as story is a public recording of a given understanding of a good that calls for protection and promotion. The good is in the eye of the theory.

COMMUNICATION ETHICS: REFLECTION AND ACTION

1. Consider the last major life transition you experienced. Perhaps it was entering a university or college setting, changing a major or job, relocating, or developing a new and meaningful relationship. In this change of direction, what "common sense" did you look to for guidance and understanding of this event?
2. What opportunities for learning about others' cultures, religious/faith traditions or narratives, and life commitments exist on your campus? How might you engage these opportunities to learn from others who are different from you in some way?
3. Choose a theory that addresses human behavior, interaction, and/or communication from any of the classes you are taking or have taken thus far in your program of study. What are the theory's implicit and/or explicit communication ethics assumptions? What good or goods does this theory protect and promote? What are the implications of this theory for the study of communication ethics?

ENGAGING COMMUNICATION ETHICS THROUGH LITERATURE: *LES MISÉRABLES*

In the beginning of *Les Misérables*, we see competing versions of "common sense." The common sense of the villagers emerged from their unreflective understanding of "social correctness." For them, it was just common sense to reject a convict released from prison; it was common sense that such a man had no potential for constructive contribution and was a social outcast, unfit for society. The bishop, Monseigneur Bienvenu, worked from a different background theory, a different common sense drawn from a commitment to caring for others. Jean Valjean's experience with the world before he met the bishop formed a background theory of social injustice toward those who have nothing, with no hope anywhere for the poor; their only option: self-protection at any cost. His rejection by the townspeople reinforced that theory, making it just common sense for him to steal from the man who had welcomed him. The bishop's forgiveness permitted Jean Valjean to learn an alternative background theory different from the one he carried with him. His future communication practices became a new common sense, situating him within a narrative that protected a different good and, in the end, the only memory worth passing to his "daughter" and the life before her. Within that memory lives a view of a good carried forth by human faces of Jean Valjean, the bishop, and even Javert. It is a memory carried forth by human faces whispering ever so softly and with tenacious consistency— there is a good of human care beyond the convention of social rules. This good calls us into communicative action to protect and promote a good of care, a public memory beyond conventional common sense.

Dialogic Ethics

Meeting Differing Grounds of the "Good"

> Dialogue is the encounter between men, mediated by the world, in order to name the world. Hence, dialogue cannot occur between those who want to name the world and those who do not wish this naming—between those who deny others the right to speak their word and those whose right to speak had been denied them. Those who have been denied their primordial right to speak their word must first reclaim this right and prevent the continuation of this dehumanizing aggression. (Freire, 1972, p. 88)

This chapter presents dialogic ethics as pragmatically necessary in a time in which multiple communication ethics identify this historical moment. Our time lives with differing narrative and virtue structures, placing any communication ethics theory within the realm of limits and temporality, unable to offer guidance for decision making in all places and for all time. A communication ethics theory offers grounded reasons for particular actions in a given moment. Specifically, dialogic ethics is a historically responsive answer to differing ethical backgrounds that situate contrary and contrasting senses of the "good." Living with the routine of change and difference, we must remember that we are not the first people or historical era to live within the ongoing presence of difference, but we may be the first to live in an era when the acknowledgment of difference defines public discourse and scholarship. We can see this shift in narrative perspectives in the difference between reactions to World War II and the Vietnam War only a few decades later. The conflict of World War II secured enough common agreement about "goods" such as democracy and human rights to propel unified action against the Nazis. The Vietnam era, in contrast, brought conflict within the culture of the United States regarding the most ethical course of action. Since that time, narrative fragmentation and diversity has only increased, bringing the reality of multiple perspectives into the foreground. This book engages the mantra of difference with a pragmatic spirit, privileging learning. Our discussion of dialogic ethics emphasizes a pragmatic need for "learning more" from the Other, alterity, and difference. Our view of dialogic ethics assumes a minimalist and modest agenda, to learn from difference—such learning is our entrance into communication ethics in action in this historical moment. After reading this chapter, you will be able to demonstrate the following learning objectives:

- Explain the importance of dialogic theory to communication ethics
- Assess various dialogic coordinates
- Describe a dialogic learning model of communication ethics

Introduction

This chapter connects the study of communication ethics to communicative practices with attention to the following four metaphors of communication ethics praxis:

1. **Dialogue and difference**—begin with the ground under our feet, the narrative that gives shape to what we consider good, and learning from the ground of the Other, calling us to attend to the meaning emergent in the meeting of a given historical moment. Difference is the key to learning and living well in a postmodern culture. Difference is the energy that makes dialogue possible.

2. **Dialogic theory**—situates background assumptions about dialogue in three major elements of human meeting: the different grounds/narratives from which self and Other begin the conversation and the emergent temporal answer given life by the meeting of such difference.

3. **Dialogic coordinates**—suggest communicative elements needed to invite dialogue; these five coordinates are learning from listening, refraining from the demand that dialogue take place, acknowledging bias, recognizing that not all communication is or should be in the form of dialogue, and keeping content and learning foremost. Invitation guides the basic assumption of dialogic ethics.

4. **Dialogic ethics**—assumes the importance of the meeting of communicative ground that gives rise to a particular sense of good and is simultaneously open

▶

▶ to learning and emergent insight that belongs to an ontological reality between persons, not to any one person in a conversation. Dialogic ethics begins with meeting what is before us—the good, the bad, and the ugly. Such an ethic rejects demand and the occasionally heard comment, "We need more dialogue." This statement only assures the impossibility of dialogic ethics, which hides from the ongoing demand made by oneself or another.

Student Application: Negotiating Difference

Throughout one's educational experience, one encounters diversity—economic, racial, social, religious, and national, to name but a few domains of difference. In the first few weeks of college, first-year roommates often experience the interpersonal tension that arises from differing expectations about sleep schedules, study habits, cleanliness, and visitors. Encountering someone different permits **dialogue**; one begins with understanding the narrative ground and commitments that anchor one's own life and learning those of another. **Difference** is one key to learning, inside and outside of the classroom. In situations involving encounters with difference, **dialogic coordinates** emerge that invite one and another into dialogue. These moments occur as one walks with someone to the next class or finds a friend in a crowded lunch area, or as one grapples with ideas in the classroom. **Dialogic ethics** makes us aware of differences that occur in our day-to-day lives with others, fostering a continuing conversation with respect for other people and ideas, living out a commitment to learn from difference in daily conversation.

Dialogue and Difference

A dialogic communication ethic begins with an understanding of dialogue responsive to content arising from narrative ground that anchors persons in conversation. Viktor Frankl (1963), whose entire project addressed human meaning, was fond of quoting Nietzsche's statement—"[A person] who has a *why* to live for can bear with almost any *how*" (p. 121). Dialogic ethics embraces the why and the how of engaging difference, framing learning as the foundation of the 21st century. Dialogic ethics is the meeting place for learning in an age of difference.

This era, which some call the crumbling of foundations and others, a time of foundations in contention, provides, ironically, one major foundation for this work—learning. Learning is the anchor in an era that rebels against universalistic foundations. Difference opens the door to learning. Dialogue opens the door to other persons and ideas.

In their edited volume on dialogue, Rob Anderson, Leslie Baxter, and Ken Cissna (2004) thoughtfully outline differing schools of dialogue encountered with regularity in the communication field. Our work situates dialogue within two

(Buber and Gadamer) of the four traditions (Martin Buber, Hans-Georg Gadamer, Jürgen Habermas, and Mikhail Bakhtin) outlined by these scholars. Additionally, this work brings two other contributors to the forefront of conversation about dialogic ethics: Paulo Freire and Hannah Arendt.

The Content of Dialogue

Buber (1955) defines the differences among monologue, technical dialogue, and dialogue as points along a continuum, with each defining relational distance and intimacy differently. All three are relational, but only dialogue responds to emergent insight between persons. Monologue looks to the self for answers, and technical dialogue looks to public feedback. Gadamer (1976) frames dialogue as a meeting of respectful difference—one's own bias meets that of another text or person, encountering Otherness, not similarity. Gadamer points to a "meeting of horizons" in which the bias of the interpreter and the text meet, requiring the attentive respect of each.

Freire (1972) reminds us of the liberating importance of dialogue for learning, employing face saving in order to keep the focus upon the learning, not upon fear and embarrassment (Arnett, 2002). Freire (1972) warns against the "banking concept" of learning and unreflective response to psychological demand in the service of making someone "feel better."

Arendt (1978) is not ordinarily considered a dialogic scholar; however, her contribution warns us against a "popular culture" view of dialogue that embraces first and foremost the importance of belonging to a social group; she writes about the person who wants acceptance so badly that reflection on whether or not the group is worth joining goes forgotten. Dialogic ethics rejects belonging as a communication ethics first principle. The question that guides a dialogic ethic is, "To what do I want to belong?" Arendt gives us a term to understand the danger of wanting to belong too badly; the *parvenu* is the person willing to give up all in order to belong to a given social group. Recently having acquired social status or wealth, for example, this person wants to fit in, but remains an "upstart" or "pretender" in the eyes of members of the group to which this person wants to belong. Arendt reminds us that the struggles and dangers of middle school or junior high do not subside with adulthood. We often seek to belong for the wrong reasons. Dialogic ethics keeps the focus on content questions, such as, "What do I want to belong to and why?" The persons, groups, and institutions with which we associate shape us and the narrative ground on which we stand. Our reflective consideration of the goods protected and promoted by those we seek to join opens our awareness of the implications of belonging to a given set of friends, a particular group, or an admired institution.

The insights of Buber, Gadamer, Freire, and Arendt provide our understanding of dialogue that extends to the Other and the historical moment, foregoing a focus upon the self alone, attending, instead, to the demands for learning that surround us in a time of narrative and virtue contention. Dialogic ethics assumes that learning transforms us, catching us by surprise; such learning emerges out of the meeting of differing positions. Learning through engagement with the Other, with that which or whom we do not know, reshapes us. As we learn from difference, we are transformed and changed. Think of how learning has transformed those you know—the absent-minded child who becomes a world-renowned musician, the awkward youngster who becomes a professional athlete, the "geek" who becomes a CEO. What these persons have in common is that learning transformed and reshaped their possibilities.

Dialogic Theory

This section outlines the interplay of multiple authors who shape our understanding of dialogue. We present core ideas for our engagement of Buber, Gadamer, Freire, and Arendt as an initial orientation connected to our dialogic ethics theme that privileges learning over unreflective belonging, beginning with the work of Buber.

Martin Buber

Buber suggests that dialogue lives outside of demand and is not "normative" in day-to-day interaction. Dialogue is not "the" way to communicate or a common mode of communication. Dialogue is only one way to communicate with another. Buber reminds us about the relational importance of monologue that seeks to tell with primary focus on what one already knows; of technical dialogue that seeks to encourage the exchange of information; and genuine dialogue, where insight emerges between persons, insight that belongs to neither one nor the other. Dialogic ethics assumes the importance of technical dialogue *and* genuine dialogue, considering the former what we can engage regularly and the latter a human gift that brings insight and meaning beyond expectation. Dialogue is both the learning of technical dialogue and the gift giving dialogue that emerges as a byproduct, not planned or engineered, but ever so responsive to the unexpected moments of communicative encounter.

Deborah Eicher-Catt (2017) emphasizes the importance of Maggie Jackson's book, *Distracted: The Erosion of Attention and the Coming Dark Age* (2008). Her point is that the world, understood as a tool, or something simply to be used, moves our attention quickly from one issue to another. Our engagement with distinctiveness and uniqueness falls to the wayside as we construct an increasingly disenchanted world. Such a place is void of the revelatory and the unexpected, the "ah ha" of everyday meeting of others. She points to enchantment as the byproduct of human dialogue, ever attentive to difference between persons and the revelatory that propels surprise, appreciation, and wonder.

Contrary to its common denouncement, monologue has an important place in communicative life. There are times when the Other should "tell" us information; we simply take notes and listen. One of our colleagues uses lecture as the primary way of engaging learning in his classroom. We are supportive of him as he reminds students and us that monologue is a healthy and needed part of life.

Ironically, to refuse ever to be part of a monologic environment makes dialogue impossible, turning dialogue into a demand. If one takes music lessons, a skilled teacher may go on and on about music theory as if there were no one else in the room. Yet, much learning emerges—notes, memory, and listening take the telling and turn it into learning. To demand that each exchange be dialogic is to overvalue one's own significance. Yet, when this same teacher works with young people, there is a reaching out that encourages their playing and practice. He begins not with theory, but with asking about their week and looking over the practice schedule that he asks them to record. He then asks them to evaluate how well they can play a given piece of music, connecting their evaluation to practice time. He works with them gently, with the music connected to practice. He works each week to link quality of performance with time spent on a given piece of music. Watching him work with a younger performer illustrates technical dialogue at work, and there is joy in watching the smile on the teacher's face in the "telling" to his older student, bringing monologue into the conversation as a teacher and musician. If one wants to learn, then valuing monologue is a beginning. If we do not value another's telling, we move to dialogue upon demand, and dialogue, by definition, resists the demand that communicative life meet "my" standards. For a more complete understanding of dialogue, see the recent work of Ronald C. Arnett (2012b, 2014, 2015).

© Africa Studio/Shutterstock.com

Buber moves the conversation to discuss the interplay of images in a relational exchange, involving six tacit communicative exchanges, including (1) my image of myself, (2) my image of the Other, (3) my image of the Other's image of me, (4) the Other's image of the Other, (5) the Other's image of me, and (6) the Others image of my image of the Other, illustrating different perspectives on self and other. When image no longer dominates, dialogue is possible. Yet, the very effort to "try to be in dialogue" makes it impossible, keeping one's image of oneself as a "dialogic person" more important than the dialogue itself. Much of life is more akin to technical dialogue than to "true" dialogue, attending to complexity of images of self and other in informative exchange. Theories that seek to bring these images together thrive. For instance, John Stewart (2011) discusses a transactional model of communication that integrates these differing images. The insight of Pearce and Cronen (1980) in their depiction of the coordinated management of meaning reminds us of the ongoing complexity of bringing diverse perspectives together. The still ground-breaking work of George Herbert Mead (1962) in symbolic inter-action theory details differing images of "I" and "me" (p. 173–178), with the latter more attentive to image construction. Mead's work is particularly important; he considers communicative interaction the primary shaper of the self-conceptf.

In essence, the six dimensions of image summarized by Buber point to a reality sustained by one theory after another. Images matter. One must negotiate images without confusing the notion of image with the engagement of human dialogue. A dialogic ethic begins with the assumption that one cannot take on the image of a "dialogic person," a "dialogue maker," or a "dialogue broker." To do so is to move dialogue into a disguise, the image of being dialogic. Much of life requires negotiating of images more akin to monologue or, at best, technical dialogue.

Suppose that Madison's and Terrell's instructor has just assigned them to the same group for a class project related to service learning. They do not know each other at all; their initial encounters consist of small talk and opinions about the project, which involves interviewing children in after-school programs to determine learning needs. Each student works with images of self and others, negotiating images that present themselves as concerned, collaborative group members. Terrell, however, does not want to appear overly eager to excel; he presents a different image.

Over the course of the term, Madison and Terrell engage in a great deal of technical dialogue focused on information relevant to the project. Sometimes, however, one of them will reveal something that generates a response in the other. For example, Terrell once remarked, "I am glad we are doing this project. I wish I had had this type of support in an after-school program when I was growing up." Madison then asks questions about Terrell's life; the two are surprised to discover that an entire hour has passed, and in the process, several new insights about each other and the project emerged. Looking back on their experience, Madison states, "It is funny, but we never intended to get into such a deep discussion. I learned more about Terrell than I thought I would just working on this project. At first, I thought he just wanted to get the project done to fulfill the course requirement, but now I see that it means a lot to him. I also understand this project differently than I did at first, and that would not have happened without our discussions."

Images begin the conversation, and information emerging between persons offers an unexpected ending. The process of dialogue often begins in monologue and technical dialogue, only to surprise us with its emergence when least expected. If we move the conversation about images and dialogue to dialogue and difference, we open the discussion to the dialogic work of Gadamer, who reminds us of the importance of bias to human communication and learning. Dialogue begins with difference.

Hans-Georg Gadamer

Gadamer (1976) begins dialogic engagement with the assumption that bias is central to human understanding. Biases guide our unique insights and contributions to everyday life. Gadamer rejects the assumption that we can or even should eliminate bias. Monica Vilhauer (2009) engages Gadamer's notion of bias with an emphasis on play. What we bring to an activity—our own unique skill set and our own limitations—establishes particularity of engagement. Indeed, the admission of bias and its importance is the most controversial element of Gadamer's work, but, in a time of difference, his comments take on immense pragmatic currency and are central to any commitment to learning. Differences between and among images permit us to engage textured readings of complex issues. For Gadamer, the first step toward dialogue is admission of bias. The second step is to respect the bias of the Other. The third step is a willingness to permit the "fusion of horizons," the interplay of two differing images, to shape a given direction. The final step is a reminder similar to that offered by Buber—meeting the Other can affect one's worldview, for good or ill. The ultimate dialogic outcome is not some pristine end state that brings contrasting perspectives together. The final answer is yet another emergent bias shared between persons. In short, dialogue begins, ends, and begins again with bias in Gadamer's world.

Tanisha, a second-year student, and her Spanish professor are having a discussion about grades. Tanisha has a B average and is striving for an A. Her professor insists that grades are less important than learning the language. Tanisha explains that keeping her scholarship rests on her grades. Her professor argues that the lifelong benefit of studying the language should be a primary concern and that many businesses seek to hire persons who speak more than one language. Through their discussion, each begins to see the issue in new ways. The professor decides to permit all students to elect to complete additional assignments to augment their grades. Tanisha understands that this additional involvement will increase her own commitment to learning the language, which will benefit her in the marketplace. What all finally agree is that language learning is important in an age of diversity. The student and the professor begin with different biases and, in this case, find a bias agreeable to both. Such is not always the case; dialogue of biases does not always result in agreement. The link between bias and difference finds even more emphasis in the dialogic commitments of Paulo Freire and his commitment to literacy and the oppressed. Freire connects face saving and learning as vital elements of dialogue.

Paulo Freire

Freire (1972) contends that the invitation to dialogue is impossible between persons of unequal power. He assumes that a major common set of interests and power equity must be in place before dialogue can take place. He works at saving face for the oppressed and the disadvantaged, not for those in power who are inattentive to the needs of those without power. His position on dialogue is quite different from that of Mahatma Gandhi (Duncan, 1972), another 20th-century activist and dialogic thinker working to remove oppression from groups with little power. Gandhi engaged "enemies" through "satyagraha," or loving resistance. Freire, on the other hand, reserved dialogue for those wanting to learn, those with similar commitments. Whoever assumes the position of telling and refuses to listen to the Other is an unlikely candidate for dialogue. Awareness of the bias of inequities opens the door to change and beginning conversation.

Learning presupposes that we have something to learn that is different from our current knowledge base. Dialogue is a mechanism for such learning. Freire spent his entire professional life working with learning and difference tied to dialogue. He assumed that the oppressed, the disadvantaged, and the dismissed of society could and would learn through dialogue, meeting difference responsively. Freire understood that those on the outside of power must engage difference, learning to read the practices and norms of a dominant culture. Such learning from difference is not new; those without power have met such a challenge in one society after another. What is new is that both those with and without power often feel like outsiders; such a reality sets our common table. In an era of difference, from a communication perspective, there is a need for a dialogic mantra—learn from difference or miss the point of the 21st century.

A dialogic communication ethics assists the Other, saving face in order to protect and promote an environment of learning. Saving face, however, is secondary to keeping the environment open to learning; sometimes monologic clarity must open the way for others to learn. For example, during an intensive language learning experience, a group of young men from a country with historic norms of male privilege and power worked to keep women from that country who were also enrolled in the program from learning the language, using social ridicule as their weapon, only to have another man from that same culture step forward and name their acts of bullying. Each day another male participant stepped forward out of silence to rebuke those who had run over many. Each day the hope of dialogue found protection from those who refused to accept the denial of opportunity to these women and employed monologue to clear the way for learning—permitting those of us on the outside to see a dialogic ethic protected by monologue at the right time and in the right proportion. The celebration of monologue is one of the ways in which we can, ironically, at times, make the invitation of dialogue possible and decrease the danger of what Arendt (1958/1998) called the "social," the blurring of public and private life.

Hannah Arendt

The effort to impose dialogue on settings that do not authentically call dialogue forth forces a false sense of openness and attentiveness to another, trying to make communicative structures intimate and friendly. Genuine life in the public sphere requires communicative distance. The contrast to this constructive view of distance manifests itself in a company that calls employees a family, and then lays people off and unleashes disenfranchised employees. Communicative health begins with an honest recognition that public places require distance and that private life or vocabulary is not for sale or misuse in the workplace.

Arendt (1958/1998) sought to preserve the natural dialectic of public and private life, with each sphere offering a differently textured response to human life. To blend the two realms forfeits the natural dialectic between public and private. In short, feigning good will and closeness is just that—feigning. Such communicative action is the reason for cynicism, defined as a response to unmet high expectations (Arnett & Arneson, 1999) and propelled by those interested in a "managed smile" (Arnett, 1992) rather than what Hyde (2005) refers to as genuine "acknowledgement."

© file404/Shutterstock.com

The impulse to move the private into the public accompanies the person of convention, as Arendt (1978) detailed the plight of the parvenu, as discussed earlier in this chapter—the person on the outside who works to accommodate, doing everything asked without ever securing acceptance. The sadness of this effort, which stems from social pressures to belong, is that not all persons find affirmation or a sense of public worth from those in power. Sometimes, it seems that no matter the accomplishment, a given group of people will not accept the outsider. Arendt's work calls us to avoid equating dialogue with belonging. If the goal is always to belong, dialogue, ironically, becomes impossible; we return to a focus upon image that upholds social space and blurs differences between public and private communicative life.

Consider Frederic, who moves to a private college in a rural town. His nationality is different and his mannerisms do not reflect the standards of other students. He is an outsider. Unknowingly, he begins to take on parvenu status, trying to fit into a community that finds him odd. He begins to say "yes" to each request made of him; he becomes the most helpful person he can be. Yet when there is a party, he receives no invitation. No matter how much he seems to assist others, the "outsider" status seems to follow him. Frederic becomes depressed; his only goal is a genuine welcome into the group, which goes unfulfilled. He returns home at night thinking of other ways to assist in hopes of eventual acceptance. Arendt's advice to Frederic would be simple but unconventional—belonging cannot be the primary goal of an outsider. You cannot make others welcome you, Arendt would suggest. The only hope is to do work and projects that one considers important with or without recognition. Belonging is wonderful, but the parvenu takes belonging to an unachievable status, failing to ask two questions: Is this group even worth joining? Am I doing tasks that are worth doing with or without their approval? Parvenus begin to give away their souls for an approval that will forever lie beyond their reach. Arendt reminds us to beware of the need to belong that takes us too far too quickly into the hands of those who are best kept at arm's length.

This chapter on dialogic ethics begins with a basic assumption. Whatever is most important in engaging another begins and ends without demand. We can demand that another do a full day's work. However, we cannot demand that another love a given job. We can demand that a person show up on time, but we cannot demand that the person's heart be in the task. Dialogue is no different. We can demand the recognition of differences, which is a monologic communicative gesture and, at times, necessary. We cannot, however, demand dialogue. We can be attentive to dialogic moments only by protecting the validity and, indeed, the sanctity of monologue and technical dialogue. Monologue and technical dialogue make dialogue possible, and, when they go unclaimed as important communicative actions and the demand for dialogue becomes primary, the opposite happens—monologue takes center stage and dialogue walks alone behind a closed curtain. A pragmatic respect for monologue and technical dialogue makes dialogue possible and calls for dialogic coordinates wary of demand.

Dialogic Coordinates: Without Demand

What makes dialogue and dialogic ethics possible? What are the coordinates for engagement? The authors mentioned previously all point in a given direction: respect communication that is not dialogic. This respect is, paradoxically, the beginning of dialogic ethics. Otherwise, dialogue remains banished from communicative possibility due to our demands. The coordinates are five in number. First, be a learner and a listener—attend to content or ground that shapes your own discourse and that of another. When monologue and technical dialogue come your way, seek to learn. One must place respect for content over style and delivery system. Sometimes great ideas come in packages we do not wish to encounter. Second, demand for dialogue moves us from dialogue into monologue and concern for our own image of how communication "should" be. Third, acknowledge bias; it is inevitable. To admit where one is actually permits the possibility of change from new insight. Fourth, acknowledge that not all communicative arrangements offer the possibility for dialogue. Fifth, keep dialogue connected to content and learning, remaining ever attentive to new possibilities that emerge "between" persons. To do so keeps Arendt's fear (1978) at arm's length—the impulse to use a feigned dialogue to belong to groups that might be at odds with the good or goods one holds dear. Contrary to the assumption of a parvenu, belonging is not the first principle of dialogic life; being attentive to what emerges between persons is foundational. In the words of Buber, it is the emergent common center that bonds persons and brings a sense of belonging; belonging is simply a by-product that emerges outside our control. Finally, find ways to nourish the natural dialectic of public and private communicative life, foregoing the temptation to blur them by trying to create "nice" or friendly spaces from places that require some professional distance, avoiding what Buber called the overrunning of reality (Glatzer, 1966). The reality is that not every organization is a community, and few businesses honestly fit the vocabulary of family. Even a family-owned business must navigate the complex interplay of public and private relationships in the various roles that each family member serves in the organization. Dialogic ethics finds nourishment from foregoing the ongoing communicative temptation of demand, even the demand that all communication take on dialogic characteristics.

© rusty426/Shutterstock.com

Dialogic ethics eschews demand, whether for communicative style or content. It is about a call to attend to the historical moment before us, not a demand for an era or a moment only to our liking. Dialogic ethics rejects "a bad-faith form of paradigmatic confidence" (Arnett, 2017a, p. 97). Shifts in the historical moment shake our confidence appropriately when we must protect and promote what we formerly took for granted or begin the search for another good. Change begins with meeting what is present without constant lament. Can you imagine a batter in baseball demanding that a pitcher throw a particular type of pitch? Can you imagine a weather forecaster demanding that the day be sunny? These demands fall clearly into the realm of the ridiculous. However, it is possible to imagine a person who speaks no language other than English going to a country with another tongue only to demand that all speak English. It is possible to imagine your coworker, Shavon, demanding that another think just like she does. These latter two events are certainly imaginable, but, from the perspective of dialogic ethics, fall into the domain of inappropriate demand.

Dialogic ethics begins with one basic prescription—respect whatever is before you and take it seriously. The reality before us is all there is; we must learn from what presents itself, whether wanted or not. Jujitsu is a martial art that uses the weight of another's body as leverage in self-defense. Dialogic ethics works as a form of moral jujitsu, using the weight of the historical moment against it by refusing to resist and, instead, leaning into its demands. While another is lamenting a situation, a communicator who is working from a position of dialogic ethics asks, "How can I meet this situation, not with demand, but with an intense desire to learn?" Such a position does not suggest agreement, just recognition of what is before us as the door to learning. From this pragmatic meeting emerge listening and learning unencumbered by demand. Demand keeps the focus of attention on what was or should be, not on what is. In dialogic ethics, the move to intense attentiveness to the historical moment before us permits new possibilities to emerge. Dialogic ethics is not about "getting my own way," but about meeting what is before us—like it or not.

One effort at a form of dialogic ethics emerged with the term dialogic civility (Arnett & Arneson, 1999). A book, *Dialogic Civility in a Cynical Age*, and an essay titled "Dialogic Civility as Pragmatic Ethical Praxis: An Interpersonal Metaphor for the Public Domain" (Arnett, 2001) moved ethics and dialogue into public domain discussion attentive to Adam Ferguson's (1767/2004) work on the Scottish Enlightenment that introduced civility as a pragmatic counter to warring feudal clans, offering the possibility of cooperation beyond the basis of bloodline alone.

Arnett (2001) did not suggest that all communication should be dialogic or civil, but sought a safe place for engaging difference when such a place is not present. It is legitimate to question calls for civility that may mask hegemonic power structures; the work of Arendt points in this direction with her consistent warning against parvenu status. In some settings, civility offers minimal common ground that permits diverse groups who share the goal of continuing the public conversation and maintaining civil society to engage life together. Additionally, it is possible to engage in conflict and keep civility at the forefront. Gandhi did so with his "satyagraha" campaigns based on dialogic foundations that brought Indian independence from the British. He resisted the use of "duragraha," stubborn persistence. Gandhi received criticism for making friends with his enemies. Martin Luther King, Jr. received similar complaints about his own method of conflict engagement. In short, the concerns about civility are both real and hardly new. One has to decide on which side of this argument one intends generally to land; in this book about communication ethics literacy, we selected the company of Gandhi and Martin Luther King, Jr., with the tempered reality brought to us through the insight of Arendt. Such a considered and tempered view of civility resonates with that of Harlan Cleveland (2006), who argues for respect for differences around a common center.

As Lisbeth Lipari (2014) indicates, dialogic ethics welcomes us into a communicative house not owned by me or the Other, but occupied by both (pp. 197–198). Dialogic civility engages a form of communication architecture that attempts to design a place of communicative safety, not for all time, but for a moment, a temporal moment in which difference can meet with the project of learning, temporarily bracketing a triad of domination that seeks to defame, discount, and dissect the Other. Such a project seems unduly ideal, requiring of us more than we are commonly able to supply. Yet, we do supply such places—safe houses for victims of domestic abuse, halfway houses for those working their way back to everyday employment, shelters of hospitality offering meals, without question, for transients—any organization, any school, any home that offers sanctuary for another is such a place.

Dialogic civility was an effort to frame a public "communication ethics architecture" for a communicative sanctuary. Those with great confidence in their own insights are unlikely to want or need a place of safety, but those on the outside, those without, those who cannot make or break a communicative moment, need places of sanctuary, places to think and places to work with ideas and to exchange them with others. Dialogic civility is, in musical terms, a form of "rubato," in which one takes the notes out of their normal rhythmical flow. "Rubato" gives one a sense of pause or elongated time. Dialogic civility was an effort to offer a sense of rubato in daily life. A sanctuary is, indeed, a place of musical prolongation for those seeking reprieve from situations and persons that seek to defame, discount, and dissect. For a moment, we step out of a time signature of social competition into a place that is different, a form of sanctuary, a place where persons of difference can meet without threat to their dignity as persons.

The limits of the term "dialogic civility" begin with the term "civility," which comes with a conventional expectation of conformity to a social structure. The task of this work is to reveal how dialogic ethics works in both civil and uncivil environments, with the first ethical mandate to meet what is before us, whether we approve or not, and with the second to respect the necessity of monologue and technical dialogue. Dialogue begins with meeting difference, and difference often meets us with a jarring that generates a typical expression of discontent—"If only this situation were something other than it is." In dialogic ethics, the response is pragmatic and curt: if we want to change it, we must first meet this radical form of otherness of which we may not approve and which we may not want. Change in contentious moments can happen, sometimes with a minimal dialogic gesture—I cannot make you like me, but I will remain in this seat. Rosa Parks's voice was powerful not just because it signaled a new future; she transformed a nation. As she remained seated, the world began to shake with vibrations from an ethical echo that united the past, the present, and a future to be (Arnett, 2006b). From a perspective of dialogic ethics, such change begins with recognition and learning of that which is before us, both the desired and the unwanted.

A Dialogic Learning Model of Communication Ethics

A dialogic model of communication ethics begins with four questions. First, what does it mean to "show up"? Dialogic ethics assumes the necessity of countering unreflective concern fueled by absence and lack of interest. Reflection is the first step in attentiveness, which serves as a rhetorical interruption announcing repeatedly that "our" or "my" narrative ground does not have equal support from many others. We live with a constant reminder that we do not all share the same narrative ground. Second, what is the communication ethics position from which I work, and how does it inform my interaction? This question highlights the call to reconnect word and deed, saying and doing consistent with my ground or narrative that offers ethical guidance. Third, how can I offer the Other opportunity to articulate the position or ground that shapes a communication ethic? Learning hinges upon this pragmatic gesture toward the Other. Fourth, how can communication ethics work as a learning model based upon self-reflective accountability? Communication ethics requires recognition of the importance of attending to the Other. The Other, I, the content, and the historical moment matter, each pointing to the importance of learning.

Dialogic ethics stresses the situatedness of ethical communicative interaction between persons. In ethical communication, we recognize that persons, narrative ground, and the historical situation shape, guide, and restrain our actions. We seek insight into the potential effects of our communication and how those effects themselves find meaning, judged by standpoint, situated in and on narrative ground, informed by the moment before us, and responsive to the Other's position.

Taking communication ethics into a dialogic perspective requires meeting and understanding various communication contexts and applications. We offer the following guidelines as the first step to communication ethics literacy. Dialogic ethics demands learning that makes ongoing efforts at communication ethics literacy possible.

1. Listening—without demand: What is happening in a given moment? Whether we like or dislike that moment, we must engage the question (s) of a given moment.
2. Attentiveness: What are the coordinating grounds upon which stand the self, the Other, and the historical moment?
   a. The ground of self: the ethical/narrative commitments that guide us.
   b. The ground of Other: the ethical/narrative commitments that guide the Other.
   c. The ground of the historical moment: the question announced by a given moment. For instance, World War II announced the question, "How do we protect democracy?" Today, the question is, "How do we meet and defend against terrorism?" There is much disagreement on the answer to the question, but there is agreement that this moment has a common question with recognition that not one answer, but multiple answers, emerge as the response. We should expect no less in a moment of contending narrative and virtue structures.
3. Dialogic negotiation: What temporal communicative ethics answer emerges "between" persons, pointing to communicative options for action, belief, and understanding?
4. Temporal dialogic ethical competence: What worked, and what changes might now assist?
   a. Evaluation/self-reflection: reflection upon one's own ethical or narrative commitments.
   b. From knowledge to learning: the key is not to "tell," but to learn from the Other, the historical moment, and reflective understanding of communicative action.

Dialogic ethics *listens* to what is before one, *attends* to the historical moment, and seeks to *negotiate* new possibilities. Dialogic ethics is a conceptual form of marketplace engagement, ever attentive to conversational partners and their "ground," the historical moment, and the emerging "possible" that takes place in the "between" of human meeting.

Dialogic ethics embraces learning and considers the impulse to "tell" without understanding the Other a counter action to the kind of ethical engagement needed in a world of acknowledged difference. In the edited volume *Moral Engagement in Public Life: Theorists for Contemporary Ethics* (Bracci & Christians, 2002), Arnett (2002) cites Freire, who reminds us of such a commitment:

> To criticize arrogance, the authoritarianism of intellectuals of Left or Right, who are both basically reactionary in an identical way—who judge themselves the proprietors of knowledge, the behavior of university people who claim to be able to "conscientize" rural and urban workers without having to be "conscientized" by them as well; to criticize an undisguisable air of messianism, at bottom naïve,

on the part of intellectuals who, in the name of the liberation of the working classes, impose or seek to impose the "superiority" of the academic knowledge on the "rude masses"—this I have always done. (p. 165)

A dialogic ethic begins with understanding our own ground and our own understanding of the good. It accompanies the desire to learn from the Other through engagement of difference. Next, one attends to what emerges in the meeting within a given historical moment. The emergent responds to dialogue as an invitation, not as a demand, and is open to learning. The works of Buber, Gadamer, Freire, and Arendt urge us to meet what is before us, to learn from difference, to be attentive to difference, and to eschew the impulse for demand, even the demand for dialogue itself. As in much of what we do, increased literacy depends upon our commitment to learning what we do not know—dialogic ethics lives within this postmodern "common sense" of learning that must supersede the impulse to tell in this historical moment.

COMMUNICATION ETHICS: REFLECTION AND ACTION

1. Consider the model of dialogic ethics presented in this chapter. Write a story focused on conversational engagement between two persons that describes this model in action, identifying the elements of the model and each stage of the model throughout the conversation between the two persons.
2. Identify a person who holds a position different from yours on an issue to which you are strongly committed. In class or in another location, plan a meeting in which the goal of each person is to learn about and then articulate the other person's position. After this conversation, assess the interaction using the elements of the model of dialogic ethics.

ENGAGING COMMUNICATION ETHICS THROUGH LITERATURE: *LES MISÉRABLES*

At the beginning of *Les Misérables*, Monseigneur Bienvenu, the bishop, visits a dying revolutionary. The bishop was a staunch opponent of the French revolution. The dying man explains his own position on the revolution, providing evidence and arguments for the bishop to consider. The bishop, in turn, presents his position. At the end of the conversation, the bishop reconsiders his original views and asks the man for his blessing. The bishop was open to learning from a man who represented a position the bishop opposed. Through the presentation of alternative viewpoints, new insight and learning emerged. Without abandoning his commitment to the faith, the bishop found a new understanding for some of the goals of the French revolution.

When the bishop first encounters Jean Valjean, he is aware of the different background narrative that Valjean embraced, fully aware of the possibility of personal harm and loss. Nevertheless, the bishop invites dialogue, a meeting with the Other, without demand, permitting events to emerge without an attempt to control what happened by protecting his property or his person. When the police apprehend and return Valjean, a dialogic possibility emerges once again through invitation by the gift of the candlesticks, which the bishop insists that he had given to Valjean, who had inadvertently left without them. The bishop invites learning with a hope that the gift of candlesticks might carry a life-changing sense of light. In the demands of that time, we witness the learning of a bishop and a convict and the triumph of an emerging communication ethic attentive to the Other, both of which would otherwise falter by a telling inattentive to difference.

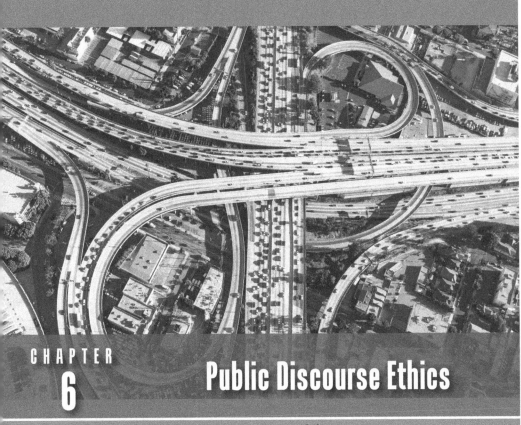

Public Discourse Ethics

Public and Private Accountability

> The public realm, as the common world, gathers us together and yet prevents our falling over each other, so to speak. What makes mass society so difficult to bear is not the number of people involved, or at least not primarily, but the fact that the world between them has lost its power to gather them together, to relate and to separate them. (Arendt, 1998, p. 52)

This chapter begins with the assumption that public communicative space needs reclamation. Two initial presuppositions about the importance of public space guide this chapter. First, Hannah Arendt (1958/1998) was correct in announcing the danger of the loss of public and private life; these differing communicative arenas provide a natural dialectic in which each calls the other into accountability. Second, in this historical moment, it is essential to recover the importance and clarity of the public arena in order to assure the communicative vibrancy of both public and private life. Public discourse ethics seeks to protect and promote the "good" of the public arena. After reading this chapter, you will be able to demonstrate the following learning objectives:

- Assess the quality of our public engagement with one another
- Recognize a public standard that is not based on your own opinion
- Differentiate your own public and private ethical positions

Introduction

Public discourse ethics protects and promotes a place of conversation for diversity of ideas and persons. Public discourse ethics nourishes the public arena as a conversational space that provides a pragmatic welcome for difference. Private life, unlike public life, eschews difference, finding definition in commonality of interests and commitments. The public arena takes us into a world of difference, into the "marketplace of ideas" (Fraleigh & Tuman, 1996), where multiple ideas and communicative behaviors contend for status in the public world before us.

This chapter connects the study of public discourse ethics to communicative practices with attention to the following three metaphors of communication ethics praxis:

1. **Public discourse**—conversation about ideas in civic/community contexts marked by diversity of perspectives requiring thoughtful public engagement. It is not the notion of one to many that makes discourse public, but confidence that one has a public audience who will listen, agree, and/or contend with ideas delivered in the public arena. Public discourse examines differing insights that shape our public engagement with one another.

2. **Public decision making**—involves discerning a course of action with full recognition that other alternatives exist. The standard for public decision making is not one's opinion, but an idea, theory, story, or action known by a group of persons and offered as a public decision-making map. For instance, calling someone to account for plagiarizing requires that there be a public standard that roots the decision making/judgment in a public evaluative base.

3. **Differentiation of public and private space**—identifies two spheres of life that shape and inform each other by maintaining their separate identities. The key to this differentiation is the reclaiming of a natural dialectic of accountability where one can call one dimension of communicative life into question by the other, texturing a clear understanding of one's public and private positions.

Student Application: What is Public and Private Space?

Public discourse allows for the articulation of many different ideas, providing a forum for idea testing from multiple perspectives. For example, the internet has become a place where multiple ideas enter a technological public space. Social ▶

▶   media platforms such as Facebook and Instagram have become contexts within which ideas and personal descriptions enter the technological public realm. Much of our **public decision making** involves engaging different voices and, as a public, deciding what is appropriate and inappropriate as we engage the public space of the internet. **Differentiation of public and private space** asks us to reflect on the private information we want to share with the world. In an information age, we find others willing to share all sorts of information with the public, making the private seem almost nonexistent. Consider the extent to which private conversations become public through cell phone conversations, often losing differentiation between public and private space.

Public Discourse: The Public "Good"

Public discourse works to protect and promote the public good. Multiple approaches to public discourse offer insights, such as the work of Karl Wallace (1955) on principles governing public decision making, Franklin Haiman's (1982, 2002) writings on free speech, and Ronald C. Arnett's and Pat Arneson's public framing of dialogic civility (Arnett & Arneson, 1999) as a metaphor for the public domain (Arnett, 2001), which addresses public decision making in civic society and everyday interaction in professional organizational settings. In each case, the governing concern is the public good. In the case of public decision making, multiple voices contribute to information directed toward action in the public realm, encouraging a "habit of search" (Wallace, 1955, pp. 6–9) that seeks publicly defendable information and evidence, working under the assumption that openness to multiple perspectives governs public debate over issues. Freedom of speech suggests the value of multiple perspectives in the public domain, even those with which we may disagree.

Through presentation of diverse ideas, standpoints gain adherence within a public sphere of multiplicity. Professional civility in the public domain suggests that within organizational settings, the public standard of an organization's mission guides behavior of employees and other organizational representatives (Arnett, 2006a; Arnett & Fritz, 2003). Janie Harden Fritz (2013) supports professional civility through communicative virtue, which frames public practices that direct organizational action. Professional civility protects employees' private lives from intrusion in public settings, and the public sphere protects us from individualistic cliques and relational connections that exclude on the basis of personal liking or disliking. Attention to the public mission protects the good of a healthy private life.

Public discourse ethics is a home for diversity of persons and ideas; it is the habitat for public decision making. This space is not an aesthetic warehouse for ideas of difference, but the living quarters for communicative ethics action—decision making about the temporal "right" answer in a given situation and in a given moment. Public discourse ethics is the welcoming home of *difference* and *temporal public decisions*, requiring us to provide a public map of accountability.

Public discourse ethics is a form of "idea gardening" that protects and promotes the public arena. Small plot gardening seeks to feed a family by attentiveness to a first principle, the soil. When gardening, one must protect and promote healthy soil by seeking a diversity of crops and practicing crop rotation. Additionally, one must decide what a weed is and what harvestable crops are, with knowledge that what we consider edible plants and what we consider a weed change over time. For instance, one of the authors recalls how, each spring, his grandmother had his family pick the dandelions, not as weeds, but for salad. She loved the soil and gardened with the hope of protecting and promoting the soil, making careful decisions about what one should use for food, wasting as little as possible. The author's grandmother might understand public discourse ethics as "idea gardening"—protecting and promoting diversity of crops (ideas) and wasting little, keeping the garden—in this case, the public arena—safe for another year of supplying the family, always with one final reminder: "Be careful what you call a weed."

© Kaleb Kroetsch/Shutterstock.com

Public Decision Making: The Good of Public Accountability

Public discourse ethics requires public accountability, providing a map, a trail, a set of clear steps in the decision making that makes possible our following of public reasoning that gives shape to a given idea or behavior. Public accountability involves three communicative commitments: (1) to diversity of ideas, (2) to engagement of public decision making, and (3) to a public account for continuing a communicative practice or changing that practice. A given communication ethics decision in the public arena protects and promotes a place where one can decide. It protects and promotes the importance of making decisions in the public arena while remaining open to change, offering clarity of rationale for maintaining or changing a given position.

The public arena is not a place of ideology where there is one idea; it is a robust place of multiple perspectives and ideas. Public discourse ethics lives with the unity of conviction and self-questioning. Protecting and promoting public discourse ethics is akin to the work of a public library that protects and promotes books without dictating what to read and what to think; it is akin to the responsibility of an adult to encourage a young person to play an instrument or a sport without dictating which one to choose. Public discourse ethics protects and promotes the "particular" by an act of irony. The public arena promotes a safe space for contesting ideas, making it possible for us to figure out the particulars from a wealth of possibilities. Public discourse ethics is the art of discernment, protecting a general sense of home for ideas in order to preserve differing particular ideas and positions, promoting learning of difference in the public sphere.

Eclipsing the Ethical: Undue Confidence and Unsubstantiated Opinion

The public arena is the place that protects and promotes discernment among diverse ideas. The public arena lives and prospers when public space for conversation, not one's own opinion, is the ultimate good. This chapter assumes two unethical acts in public discourse ethics: (1) refusing to permit ideas contrary to one's own to enter the public domain, and (2) refusing to make a decision after grappling with contending ideas. Public discourse ethics rejects both sides of an unethical public arena coin: lack of access and lack of accountability for decisions. The goal of a vibrant public arena is to avoid communicative action based on ideological certainty that seeks no new knowledge, just the opportunity to tell, *and* an unwillingness or inability to make temporal decisions.

The public arena does not offer the final answer; it is the place where one takes a grounded stance, engages the grounded stances of others, and makes

© Allexxandar/Shutterstock.com

a decision. It is the ground of decision making with short- and long-term consequences for people and societies—for both good and ill. We need to hold each decision within a sense of suspension or doubt, ever open to change and ever wary of change without clarity of conviction for the "why" of a given amendment. The pragmatic reason for the caveat of doubt is twofold: change beckons when previous decisions that were once valid no longer work and when poor quality ideas surface and take us in problematic directions. One example of such decision making and subsequent change in the United States is the Prohibition era. From 1920 to 1933, the manufacture, sales, and transportation of alcohol was illegal. The cessation of National Prohibition illustrates change in response to new circumstances; prohibition did not bring about the hoped-for results, and the country moved in a different public direction with a decision to repeal the 18th Amendment to the Constitution.

Public discourse ethics lives in the everyday life of a college or university. Working with first-year students, we often hear, "I do not know what to major in; I am simply lost." From the vantage point of public discourse ethics, the conversation needs to be reframed as, "What an opportunity!" Confusion is not novel; it is part of our lives today. One begins to manage the confusion by simply picking a major without carving the choice in stone. One takes the general education electives, buying some time; one works with professors to figure out strengths; one decides, keeping open a window of doubt responsive to the possibility of change. About one-third of students change their majors before graduation (Stanek, 2005). Public discourse ethics requires us to discern, decide with some self-questioning, and change our minds when necessary. Our task, then, as graduates, is to send back money, keeping the doors of opportunity open for many who will follow and will come confused, hoping to find a direction in a public space of contending ideas.

Much of life meets us without our knowing the appropriate or necessary action or response; we are often clueless because the circumstances are new and an excess of choices makes us, all too often, feel overwhelmed, a theme central to Erich Fromm's work, *Escape from Freedom* (1994). Fromm penned his contribution shortly after World War II, yet his concern remains. Imagine a small child whose enormous collection of toys makes it impossible to play creatively. Fromm's metaphor of escape from freedom refers not to escape from choice but to escape from a multiplicity that overwhelms us in the decision making. Just like the child with a surfeit of toys, we encounter multiple choices; to live in this moment of flux requires a discernment that unites decision, doubt, change, and gratitude for the general that gives space to the particular. We turn the tables and upset the unethical impulse for unsubstantiated opinion, pivoting toward a public rendering of ideas, choice, decision, and change—or continuing with a current position. We struggle against efforts to vanquish this public home of ideas, decision, and change; we protect the public space of idea engagement.

Differentiation of Public and Private Space

The first move to protect public space as the home of diversity of perspectives is to understand that diversity thrives upon differentiation of public and private space. This chapter works from a basic assumption—communication ethics in private life depends upon the strength of communication ethics in public life. Public and private communication ethics support and enhance one another. Public discourse ethics resists the infusion of private life into the public in order to protect the sanctity of both realms, providing safety and shelter for texture and difference in communicative life (Arnett, 2006a). For example, it is important for students to be able to attend class as a public event. Perhaps two roommates share a class. Conversation with the roommate in the context of the class deals with public ideas. When the roommates return to their dorm room or apartment, they enter the private sphere of personal conversations and private friendship, constituted simply by discussing with one another information not shared in public.

The need to protect public space does not rest in theory alone, but within lived experience in school, beginning in elementary school and junior high, then continuing on into high school, college, and professional life. We find that some minimize others' productivity by moving into conversation about who likes whom and comments about how "I" would run all this differently. Private discourse in the public arena is akin to "junior high" discourse that rejects anyone different from oneself or any idea different from one's own. This form of discourse continues throughout life wherever there is a rejection of difference, demanding that others or activities be as "I" so proclaim. Such private discourse that invades the public arena seeks not to change public policy, but to enhance the self relationally.

Granted, we cannot draw a precise definitional line in the sand between the terms "private discourse" and "public discourse" (Arnett, 2006a). Yet, on the other hand, to assume that one can equate the two is equally unhelpful. Public discourse ethics depends upon the natural dialectic of counter-questioning from public and private realms of human life. Such communicative action can, at times, offer wisdom beyond that which conventional opinion claims as "right."

The life of Dietrich Bonhoeffer is a good example of public and private spheres of life and discourse. Bonhoeffer, a theologian and pastor, engaged in resisting the Nazi party in Germany, protesting the Third Reich and the atrocities of Hitler during World War II. Through letters, speeches, papers, and personal actions grounded in a counter-narrative to Nazism, he confronted the public assumptions of the society at that time, offering a contending position to Nazi control. It was the private world of his family and his church that permitted Bonhoeffer to counter the norm of public life in Nazi Germany. Bonhoeffer's *Letters and Papers from Prison* (1997) offers an insight into the courage granted by a private life to contend with a public arena no longer deemed conscionable. With others, Bonhoeffer was able to bring another perspective to public life. The example of Bonhoeffer is important in that he needed the private to counter the public; his private position offered opposition to the public position at that time. His story provides clarity about the difference between private and public and the fact that one dialectally informs the other.

Identity emerges with clarity through differentiation. The study of another language, one alien to one's home tongue, takes one into a public arena of language beyond one's private expectation that all speak the same language. One may learn to understand one's home language better in comparison with another. Identity of the first language finds clarification in the meeting of difference in the form of another language. Learning within a public realm assists knowledge of one's own private position. The intimate, tied to the private, and the more distant, tied to the public, reinforce the unique identities of each. However, what some contend is a fundamental mistake of our time is a banality of insistence on blurring public and private discourse, foregoing a natural dialectic that Hannah Arendt consistently called forth in her writing.

Resisting an Invasion of Banality—Protecting Difference

Public discourse ethics protects and promotes the public arena, a place where difference lives. When we attempt to make the public arena a private place of agreement, we move private commonplaces to a public form of banality, a form of extreme commonness, taking away their uniqueness and special nature. For instance, the distinctiveness of friendship rests with the private information shared with a limited number of people. If everyone knows the private information, then the friendship is no longer defined by unique knowledge of one another. To be distinctive and special, close friendships need the value of private information.

It is possible for the public to invade the private, and it is possible for the private to invade the public. Communication technology provides us with greater access to others than at any time in human history. If one is not careful, public commitments erode private time with family and friends as cell phones and text messages make contact with the office not only more possible, but more expected. The infusion of the public into the private comes from an invasion of banality, a banality of access. It is not uncommon to be at a theater and hear a phone go off or hear another talking quietly (or not so quietly) on the phone. At a football game, it is interesting to see the number of people responding to email while watching the game. The focus of attention moves from friends and family (private) to the workplace (public) very quickly. The infusion of the public into the private occurs as we blur the differences between the realms. Likewise, a student intern who spends time texting friends while on the job is permitting private friendships to invade the public internship site. Both forms of communicative exchange—public and private—enrich our lives; however, when the wrong communicative space (public or private) invades the other, a fundamental communication ethics violation occurs.

A basic assumption of this chapter is that public life forced upon the private and private life forced upon the public are both fundamental communication ethics violations. This violation gives life to Martin Buber's statement about the danger of "overrunning reality" (Glatzer, 1966, p. 65). To assume that everyone can be a personal friend overruns the reality of personal differences that propel us to varied associations with others. To assume that everyone should share our personal commitments overruns the reality of individual choice. One cannot force the public area to be excessively private, and one cannot force the private to be disproportionately public.

If one watches a television show based on interview and discussion midday during a typical week, one finds a conversation involving topics that many of us would consider private discussed openly on (public) television. It does not take long to recognize that the basic assumption of such an entertainment genre involves two basic ingredients: (1) participants who do not know or care about the difference between public and private information regarding their own lives, and (2) an audience who does not know the difference, or, if they do know, find themselves entranced by the amusement of watching another violate public space with what many would term inappropriate private disclosure. Such shows count on an audience finding entertainment in voyeurism, watching others make fools of themselves through the violation of public and private communicative lives.

The temptation of such "voyeuristic television" is one that meets us each day. Granted, making fun of another is not new; this behavior is as old as the social construction of the first human communities. However, television and the internet make possible what was at one time limited to a local community. Many left small towns to enter urban environments in order to find more distance—to protect the difference between private and public communicative life.

The last fifty years have been an experiment with the collapsing of public and private communicative life. Phrases like "this company is a family" and "we are all friends here" and the need to know information about another that is unnecessary for the job or the task are simply commonplace. As one employee stated, "I go out and party with those at work; I must to keep my place in the company. If I do not go, then the conversation is more likely to be about me; to protect my job, the talk needs to center on another."

Richard Sennett (1974) refers to the notion of the "tyranny of intimacy" (p. 340) as imposed private life in the public domain. This tyranny begins when the private moves into the public. When persons become too close, there is no space for privacy or freedom of movement. In close relationships, we nurture private intimacy for that very purpose; however, when all of one's relationships become unduly close, the feeling of closeness becomes oppressive. Public discourse ethics questions any attempt to decrease the difference between public and private space. The reasons are threefold. First, democratic debate requires an active and a protected public space. Second, when we knowingly find public amusement in the private life of another, voyeurism propels our entertainment. Third, if we are to protect and promote the private communicative lives of persons in a community, such differentiation is necessary. Private life is that which one would not share in public. Not everyone is a friend, and to offer the same information through self-disclosure to each person lessens the chance that genuine friendships that have a private domain will emerge. Protecting and promoting the public domain assures a private communicative life.

We can act as communicative voyeurs by taking the focus of attention off our own responsibility and work. Janie Harden Fritz and Becky L. Omdahl's collaboration regarding *Problematic Relationships in the Workplace* (Fritz & Omdahl, 2006; Omdahl & Fritz, 2012) includes perspectives that encourage a focus on productivity and mission that provides professional connection, avoiding the invasion of the deeply private into the public and keeping attention away from gossip about others (Arnett, 2006a) while still engaging in friendly, constructive interactions with others (Omdahl, 2006). The modern impulse in a company to talk about another is no different than living in a small town and gossiping about the "different" one. Yet, it is for this very reason that we must reclaim a clear sense of public life. Furthermore, what is different changes, leaving behind old assumptions.

© f11photo/Shutterstock.com

The Public as Sacred Space

Public discourse ethics assumes that the public arena is a "sacred space"—a space protected, honored, and valued. To nourish this space is to keep before us diversity of ideas and persons while keeping the private arena differentiated and clear. In a world of difference, the sacred becomes a general public place, a large home for differing particulars. In a changing world, public discourse is the communicative ethics protector of difference among persons and ideas; our task is to keep the public domain safe for difference. Naturally, there is debate about what procedures should be central in the protection of the public domain—such approaches vary from the insight of Karl Wallace (1955) and his commitment to public space as a place for democratic deliberation to the Frankfurt School work of Jürgen Habermas (1984), which seeks a form of communicative ideal in procedural inclusion. However, consensus rests in the conviction that the public domain makes deliberation among differences possible.

Scott Stroud (2016, 2017), in his emphasis on the "democratic riddle," argues that democracy is far more than the cliché, "One person, one vote" (2017, p. 29). Democracy is a habit of social association in which partisan argument makes space for views counter to one's own. Stroud's concept of democracy, derived from Dewey, gathers together with "moral and spiritual association" (Dewey, 1888/1969, p. 240; Stroud, 2017, p. 29). Put differently, democracy nourishes social magic in which the committed attend to the commitments of others.

These theories seek to protect and promote the public domain through two basic assumptions. First, it is unlikely that we can exhaust every option related to the public domain; there are multiple authors and multiple theories calling for its renewal in differing ways. Second, the theories have one common agreement— protect and promote the communicative vitality of the public domain. Whatever challenges the legitimacy or the vitality of public space is at odds with the communicative ambition of communication ethics in the public domain. We protect diversity in the public domain as we intentionally differentiate the banality of idle chatter, which functions like the lure of fast food, from public discourse. We, like others, find much comfort in familiar fast food when traveling; even when it does not taste particularly good, at least it may remind us of home. However, the public arena is not our home. We should never feel totally comfortable in such a place; if we do, there is a good chance that we have excluded others. When we begin to feel too comfortable, we have most likely turned the public domain into a place where one can legitimize refusing to learn another language or to listen to what one does not already believe. We attempt to control our public lives to the extent of overrunning reality (Glatzer, 1966), inviting only what we can control.

We live in a culture in which instant gratification manifests itself in immediate recognition. It is not uncommon to receive a phone call from someone seeking to sell us something, during which the unknown person on the other end of the line uses our first name, overrunning reality with manufactured familiarity. There is much right with the hope of the familiar, but there is something amiss with a familiarity that bypasses stages of natural relationship development.

As a culture, we have been convinced, incorrectly, that imagined familiarity increases the quality of our communicative lives. This chapter assumes otherwise. Whenever there is an effort to overrun reality with undue familiarity in the public domain, we should be wary. If an ad suggests that we can get a loan without any future financial worry, we should wonder about the veracity of the claim. If one hears that a college degree can be "had" in one year without ever going to class, one should be suspicious. If a weight loss program argues that one can lose weight without effort, one must question the claim. We live in a time of immediate gratification that works on an old Barnum and Bailey adage: "There is a sucker born every minute." When we overrun the time that it takes to know another, we run an immediate major private risk and a long-term major public risk. The first is the risk of confusing the presentation of personality with character. Style lives in the question of personality, not in the character of communication ethics. Second, we put at risk a public domain that makes our private lives even richer.

One begins to understand the significance and importance of the public domain as one uses the adjective "public" in front of everyday nouns. For instance, what does it mean to have a public friendship? What does it mean to have a public commitment to an institution? What does it mean to have a public identity? In our discipline and for this chapter, we ask: What do the terms "public speaking" or "public discourse" suggest? Put differently, how are friendship, commitment, identity, and speech different when the term "public" works as an adjective, shifting the texture of the word that follows?

One of the writers remembers his mother issuing the following admonition whenever the family went out to eat or attended a public function: "Remember to use your indoor voices." There is interesting irony in the reminder to use indoor voices in a public place. The suggestion reminds us that a public place calls for lower individual volume in order to permit many voices to have an audible chance in the public domain. In the public domain there is seldom only one issue that drives conversation. Lowering one's voice not only permits another to have communicative space, but also permits distance in the public arena, making a place for others. In communication ethics, we must not forget to attend to multiple voices and work to welcome those not yet at the table of public decision making.

Protecting the Voices of the Unseen and the Unheard

This chapter connects public discourse ethics with discourse justice that seeks to defend the neighbor, the unprotected, the person or persons without bloodline or money to protect themselves. Discourse justice attends to Kenneth Andersen's (2003) communicative ethics of the unknown "third party." Andersen was insightful in connecting public discourse responsibility to a world larger than persons present in a given conversation. Public communicative ethics begins with a concern for communicative justice that attends to the unknown, the unheard, and the unseen party in a conversation.

The civic engagement of Spoma Jovanovic (Jovanovic, 2012; Jovanovic, Steger, Symonds, & Nelson, 2007; Poulos, Hamilton, Jovanovic, & Moretto, 2015) begins with social history and follows with pragmatic action, nudging and, at times, demanding social change. She cites H. L. Goodall's (2016) reminder that democracy is an experiment that requires active participation and, at times, public challenge of those who flaunt their power and their privilege (Jovanovic, 2012, p. 7).

We begin with a basic assumption—do not falsely yell "fire" in a public place, an opinion stated by Chief Justice Oliver Wendell Holmes in 1919. Such a communicative act opens the possibility of danger to many who are unknown, unheard, and unseen. Public discourse ethics protects and promotes a communicative public space where the unknown, the unheard, and the unseen have a voice. The theme song from the old but enduring Walt Disney television show, *Zorro* (Foster, 1957), points to the importance of justice when one cannot see the other, finding justice "out of the night": "Out of the night comes the strangest sight—a horseman known as Zorro." The song calls for a hero living within a story of justice for the forgotten, who works for change to protect and promote the welfare of the unknown, the unheard, and the unseen, those not in the center of our vision. Andersen was correct in reminding us to protect a place where the voice of the unknown and the unseen, those not in the center of our vision, calls forth our commitment to public discourse ethics.

Hannah Arendt (1958/1998) gives us insight into the "why" of the public domain, the importance of differentiating public and private arenas, and, finally, what actually constitutes the public domain. This chapter presents public discourse ethics as protection and promotion of the good of the public domain. Arendt warns of gross ethical misconduct that misshapes the public domain—thinking only of oneself, being inattentive to those unknown, unseen, and not in the center of our vision. Arnett, in "Biopolitics: An Arendtian Communication Ethic in the Public Domain" (2012a), states that democracy must counter the dominator and those framing public policy on arguments of biopolitical exclusion. Such action prohibits "the biosubject from exercising sovereign power" (p. 230). Democracy assumes that each one of us matters. Biopolitics assumes that human beings often go ignored and displaced when their biological characteristics are different from those exercising influence and power. The biosubject is a political actor. He or she is you and I. Such concerns caused Arendt to cite Kant's emphasis on an "enlarged mentality"; our concern must be greater than ourselves alone (Arendt, 1982). An enlarged mentality takes into account those not at the table.

Arendt, a Jewish woman, was one of the major figures to speak on the events surrounding the Eichmann trial. Adolph Eichmann was on trial in the 1960s for his role in World War II as the primary architect of the Nazi "final experiment," the killing of millions of Jews and the orchestrating of the concentration camps. She coined the term "banality of evil" to outline her position on Eichmann (Arendt, 1963, p. 278). She contended that he was a common man following orders and constructing a bureaucracy to implement the "final solution" for those unknown, those unseen, those not in the center of our vision. During Eichmann's trial, Arendt was constantly amazed at his use of clichés to defend his own actions. The use of clichés seemed consistent with the evil seemingly so shallow that only rules, orders, and bureaucratic application could guide the action.

Arendt (1996) took issue with Kant, who once stated that stupidity originates from wickedness. She suggested that all too often it is the opposite—evil stems from "thoughtlessness." It is the battle against thoughtlessness that nourishes, for Arendt, our primary hope against a banality of evil that lives within an environment where the light slowly dims over time, leaving us unaware of the darkness before us. Carol Brightman (1995), in her preface to a collection of letters between Arendt and Mary McCarthy, highlights this point:

> Tocqueville was right: "Since the past has ceased to throw its light onto the future, the mind of man wanders in obscurity"... [I]n Arendt's view, [the obscurity] holds promise—not unlike the darkness Dante enters in the middle of the dark wood. Deliverance comes if first the traveler dares to tell the fearful things that he has seen. (p. xvii)

Brightman reminds us of the necessity of putting our standpoint into words, offering an account for our actions. Countering "thoughtlessness" requires us to engage a public arena that demands an accounting, an offering of a public mapping of the decision making that generated the telling. In the context of a college or university, changes in curricular requirements call for public articulation of reasons for such decisions. Students, accrediting bodies, and other constituents of the educational institution look for thoughtful reasons for actions that will affect many.

Reclaiming the Public Arena

The public arena works best when one does not attempt to dominate such space. Ideas in the public arena change, but the sanctity of the public arena remains. We somehow seem to think that speaking louder and taking up more space is what we should do when entering the public domain. The communication ethics

© Marco Rubino/Shutterstock.com

commitment to protect and promote a given sense of the good makes it necessary to temper one's individual voice, making room for an entire chorus of possibilities. Communication ethics, in this case, states: "Protect and promote the public domain." Public discourse ethics begin with an assumption that there needs to be a space, a ground upon which one can stand, that permits many to have a voice. The public arena is such a place, a place where light makes itself available to all.

Of course, the public arena is not an ideal open place for all. Such a reality does not stop an ethical obligation to make it better. We protect the public domain when we keep our own interests as secondary and public space as primary. We protect the public domain when we embrace a world of difference. We protect the public domain when we fight tendencies to want our commonplaces to be those of all persons. We protect the public domain when we fight our desire for banality. We protect the public domain when we understand the importance of a robust private and public life. We protect the public domain when we remind ourselves and others that feeling a lack of comfort in the public domain is good—it is good because the public domain is a place that welcomes difference, not taken for granted commonality.

We promote the public domain with a public discourse ethic that keeps this space sacred, at the heart of the human drama. The public domain is the place of contention and difference, change, struggle, traditions, and beliefs that are often at odds with one another. Yet, the moment we permit our desire for complete agreement to overcome this sacred space, we defame human life, and communicative action moves toward words like imperialism, totalitarianism, and "me"—"my kind of ideas and people." Public discourse ethics protects and promotes a space bigger than "me," bigger than the horizon of my vision, a place that makes me a bit uncomfortable, that requires me to learn, to join, and to try to make a difference without ever dominating this sacred space with my ideas alone. Through protecting public space, we protect private space, as well. In public discourse ethics, the responsible public communicator follows the insight of David Zarefsky (1995):

> The goal of communication study is understanding what it means to be an articulate person, one who is able to participate effectively in relationships with messages and people, whether in the intimacy of private dialogue or in the deliberations of the public forum. (p. 103)

The quality of our lives rests in the interplay of difference that begins with the natural dialectic of public and private communicative domains.

Pointing to a Dialogic Ethic in Public Discourse

Public discourse ethics points to a dialogic ethic in the manner of listening, attentiveness, and negotiation in the demand for a communicative return of the public and a viable and differentiated communicative space. The following model summarizes a dialogic ethic applied to public discourse, highlighting major points in this chapter.

1. *Listening—without demand: What is happening in a given moment? Whether we like or dislike that moment, we must engage the question(s) of a given moment.* Public discourse ethics assumes a dual understanding of the notion of demand. First, there is the demand for public space; second, there is the knowledge that no one can demand that another listen to one in that public space. The demand is for the platform; however, the demand to listen is beyond the pale of our communicative reach. Communicators must take responsibility to engage the public arena rhetorically, recognizing that every standpoint, every narrative, carries persuasive impact.

2. *Attentiveness: What are the coordinating grounds upon which stand the self, the Other, and the historical moment?* Attentiveness to how one engages difference in this historical moment drives public discourse ethics, protecting and promoting the public arena as a communicative space for engaging alterity, or radical otherness. In the public arena, we meet the not yet known, that which often makes us uncomfortable.

   a. *The ground of self (the ethical/narrative commitments that guide us) and*

   b. *The ground of Other (the ethical/narrative commitments that guide the Other).* The ethical ground shapes public discourse ethics of self and Other, providing a place for public decision making. A conceptual public map permits self and Other to understand public decision making, taking the power from unsubstantiated opinion.

   c. *The ground of the historical moment (elements of the time in which we live, including "relational time" of the persons in conversation).* Decision making in the public arena is not static and changes with the demands of the historical moment. The public arena is a rhetorical home, seeking temporal answers to emerging new questions.

3. *Dialogic negotiation: What temporal communicative ethics answers emerge "between" persons, pointing to communicative options for action, belief, and understanding?* Public discourse ethics requires repeated negotiation; public space gives no answers, only opportunity to keep the conversation going.

4. *Listening, attentiveness, and dialogic negotiation constitute temporal dialogic ethical competence. What worked, and what changes might now assist?*

   a. *Evaluation/self-reflection (reflection upon one's own ethical/narrative commitments).* Attending to the question of what is a good public discourse ethic leads to a pragmatic answer: without participation in the public space and accompanying challenge and change, continuing traditions have no forum or testing ground. Public discourse ethics makes a space for conversation, taking us not to truth, but to conversation, discovery of temporal answers, and constant change, as well as a reinvigorated understanding of tradition, as persons and the historical moment call forth alternatives.

b. *From knowledge to learning (the key is not to "tell," but to learn from the Other, the historical moment, and reflective understanding of communicative action).* Public discourse ethics, with a stress on temporality, suggests that knowledge gives way to learning, which gives way to more knowledge, which gives way to more learning, rejecting the temptation to cast knowledge in stone, placing our first responsibility on the commitment to learn in the public arena.

5. *Dialogic ethics listens to what is before public communicators, attends to the historical moment, and seeks to negotiate new possibilities. Dialogic ethics is a conceptual form of marketplace engagement, ever attentive to conversational partners and their "ground," the historical moment, and the emerging "possible" that takes place in the "between" of human meeting.* Public discourse ethics listens to contrasting ideas, is suspicious of demands for a single viewpoint, and is attentive to persons and the historical moment, connecting the public sphere to temporal answers and the inevitability of change and reexamined traditions. Public discourse ethics protects and promotes a space where temporal answers, inevitability of change, and human voices with an obligation to provide a conceptual map of decision making meet and shape tomorrow with the limits of insight from today.

COMMUNICATION ETHICS: REFLECTION AND ACTION

1. The distinction between public and private discourse emerges in the difference between a relationship that is formal and distant and one that is close and intimate. Think about a relationship that began as a "public" relationship and moved to the "private" level. What changes in communication can you point to that marked that shift?

2. Sandra Petronio (2003) discusses boundary management and self-disclosure, a topic with great relevance for thinking about public and private discourse. Consider a situation in which you have been in conversation with someone and were aware that you wanted to keep the conversation on a public level—and the person kept moving the discourse to private topics. What conversational choices did you make in order to maintain boundaries that you believed were appropriate?

3. Identify a public context in which persons with different private positions on an issue need to work together to accomplish a task (not necessarily related to that issue). What conversational choices can those persons make in order to get the work done? What sense of purpose or "why" might guide the project?

ENGAGING COMMUNICATION ETHICS THROUGH LITERATURE: *LES MISÉRABLES*

In *Les Misérables*, we observe how private and public domains interact with one another. When Jean Valjean takes on the identity of Madeleine, his private life remains hidden. His public identity engages the people of the town, his workers, and, when he becomes mayor, the personnel connected with the operation of the town's government. Mayor Madeleine works to stay within the realm of the public, protecting his private life and space. He recognizes the importance of differentiating public and private domains. His labor in the political realm of the town assists the good of the town; he operates not for private gain, but for public improvement.

In one fateful instance, Valjean saves the life of Fauchelevant, a man trapped underneath a cart that has fallen upon him in muddy terrain. No one is willing to attempt to lift the impossibly heavy conveyance, which sinks deeper and deeper into the mire, beginning to crush the chest of the pinned man. At the risk of revealing his own identity, Valjean/Mayor Madeleine takes on the task of rescue. He exerts his remarkable strength to lift the cart just enough to give others the courage to join the rescue effort. He knows his publicly responsive action drew Javert's attention. Valjean's heroic action witnessed to a basic fact: Only one man had the strength to lift such a load: Jean Valjean, the convict.

Valjean's life testifies to protecting and promoting the good of public space. Even when Jean Valjean (as Mayor Madeleine) turns himself in, revealing himself as the true Jean Valjean to save an innocent man's life, his communication ethic in the public domain is a public decision that protects and promotes the public good of those under his watch as Mayor Madeleine. Time and time again with an enlarged mentality in operation, he protects the public domain at his own expense.

CHAPTER 7 Interpersonal Communication Ethics

The Relationship Matters

In the light of the ideal of authenticity, it would seem that having merely instrumental relationships is to act in a self-stultifying way. The notion that one can pursue one's fulfilment in this way seems illusory, in somewhat the same way as the idea that one can choose oneself without recognizing a horizon of significance beyond choice. (Taylor, 1991, p. 53)

Interpersonal communication ethics differentiates itself from other forms of communication ethics by attentive concern for the relationship between persons. The transition from high school to college creates opportunities to develop new interpersonal relationships as well as strains on existing relationships at an increased distance. Interpersonal communication finds its identity in the ethical mandate to protect and promote the "good" of the relationship (Fritz, 2016). When the interaction no longer nourishes the relationship, "interpersonal communication" moves into another form of communicative interaction. This particular understanding of interpersonal communication attends to the good of relationship as the carrier of identity of the communicative exchange, situating the exchange within an ethical framework. After reading this chapter, you will be able to demonstrate the following learning objectives:

- Define interpersonal communication ethics
- Demonstrate distance in various relationships
- Analyze the particular elements or attributes that shape a given relationship

Introduction

This chapter suggests that the implicit interpersonal communication mandate to protect and promote the good of relationship shifts to an explicit defining feature of interpersonal communication, simultaneously defining interpersonal communication ethics. Protecting and promoting the good of relationship, however, does not presume interpersonal agreement. One can abide by an interpersonal communication ethic that protects and promotes a given good underlying a given understanding of a relationship and not garner the approval of one's communicative partner. This chapter moves interpersonal communication ethics outside the realm of subject and object or the one enacting relational care and the recipient of relational care to a gestalt understanding of relational attentiveness and care. Interpersonal communication ethics rejects both the realm of self-approval, what Alasdair MacIntyre (1984) called "emotivism" (p. 11), decision making by personal preference, and an exaggerated need for relational approval from the Other that can lead to interpersonal colonization. Interpersonal communication ethics calls forth a responsibility toward the notion of relationship that resists ownership by the self and the Other. In short, interpersonal communication ethics is not about "me" or "you"; it is about a co-constituted communicative benchmark or standard that calls both parties to accountability for something that defines interpersonal communication—the relationship.

There are multiple forms of communication, with one form, interpersonal communication, privileging the relationship as the interpretive guide to information. Not all communication is or should be interpersonal in nature, but when interpersonal discourse centers the conversation, relationship takes center stage. When interpersonal discourse is the communicative task, the relationship becomes the heart of the exchange, tempering the gathering and use of information.

This chapter connects the study of interpersonal ethics to communicative practices with attention to the following three metaphors of communication ethics praxis:

1. **Interpersonal communication**—works with the good of the relationship between and among a small number of people (two to four).
2. **Distance**—provides necessary space for each communicative partner to contribute to the relationship.

▶

▶ 3. **Interpersonal responsibility**—begins with each person's commitment to active care for the interpersonal relationship, owned by neither and nurtured with or without the support of the Other. Interpersonal responsibility adheres to the insight of Emmanuel Levinas: abandoning the expectation of reciprocity for attentiveness to a call to responsibility with or without the approval of the Other.

Student Application: Relational Responsibility

Interpersonal communication pervades our lives. Each relationship calls for unique levels of distance and different responsibilities. Each college student enters a time in life when **distance** with family members and close high school friends begins to emerge. Distance ultimately changes these relationships, permitting a form of engagement appropriate to a new stage of life. Some close high school friends disappear from our lives until there is a break in the semester, and other friendships become stronger and last throughout our college years and beyond. In each case, **interpersonal responsibility** involves caring for an interpersonal relationship. As one seeks a path in life, interpersonal relationship responsibility invites a balance between distance and closeness in each relationship, which defines the quality of our interpersonal lives via relational dialectics (Baxter & Montgomery, 1996; Stewart, 2011).

Interpersonal Communication

The study of interpersonal communication encompasses a variety of theories, approaches, and topics. Definitions of interpersonal communication range from the close and intimate (e.g., Miller & Steinberg, 1975) to the public (Arnett, 2001). Theoretical approaches as diverse as dialogic (e.g., Anderson et al., 1994; Anderson et al., 2004), social exchange (Roloff, 1981), uncertainty reduction (Berger & Calabrese, 1975; Berger & Gudykunst, 1991), social (Leeds-Hurwitz, 1995), communibiological (Beatty, McCroskey, & Valencic, 2001), and intercultural (Oetzel & Ting-Toomey, 2011) populate the scholarly landscape of interpersonal communication. The most recent *SAGE Handbook of Interpersonal Communication*, now in its fourth edition (Knapp & Daly, 2011), identifies the current state of research in interpersonal communication, representing scholarship primarily from a quantitative perspective. Reviews generated over the last decades (e.g., Ayres, 1984; Roloff & Anastasiou, 2001) offer a number of organizing frameworks through which to understand the rich and diverse area of interpersonal communication study. Additionally, Leslie Baxter and Barbara Montgomery (1996) offer a thoughtful discussion and critique of approaches to interpersonal communication.

This chapter works with a minimal set of coordinates in the discussion of interpersonal communication: a small number of communicators, interest in maintaining a relationship among the communicators, and attentiveness to historical situation (topic and contextual constraints). Theorists discuss differences in

© marekuliasz/Shutterstock.com

interaction and communication dynamics when the number of communicators in a context moves beyond two (see, for instance, Miller & Steinberg, 1975). Traditional approaches to interpersonal communication include the situational and the developmental (Miller, 1978), assessed by the number of persons in the relationship (the situational view) or the closeness of the relationship as it progresses toward greater intimacy (the developmental view). Our position is closest to the developmental view, although our understanding of development does not revolve around psychological intimacy, but on increasing recognition of the nature of relational responsibility emerging between and/or among communicative partners.

Our view of interpersonal communication begins with three basic assumptions. The first is that interpersonal communication is but one form of communication. We do not connect all dyad exchanges with the term interpersonal communication. When the relationship is primary, interpersonal communication guides the encounter, but when some other communicative good, such as discourse directed toward accomplishing an organizational goal, is primary, and relationship care assumes the form of client attentiveness, a vehicle used for maximizing profit, the communicative exchange comes closer to business and professional communication. We do recognize, however, that relationship care occurs in both private and public contexts. We do not limit interpersonal communication to private discourse alone (see Bridge & Baxter, 1992); interpersonal attentiveness to relationships often defies neat categorizations.

The second assumption is that interpersonal communication nourishes the relationship in order to bond responsibility between persons, not to further careers or advance political agendas. This view of interpersonal communication is deliberately narrow, permitting us to differentiate it from other useful and different communicative forms that may involve dyadic communication.

The third assumption is the recognition that there are multiple ways to study interpersonal communication within the discipline of communication. This chapter acknowledges the foundational work on interpersonal communication developed by authors such as Charles Brown and Paul Keller, Gerald Miller, John Stewart, Charles Berger, Michael Roloff, Julia Wood, Barnett Pearce, and Leslie Baxter, to name but a few. Their work represents multiple methodological and epistemological approaches to interpersonal communication, including social scientific (both quantitative and qualitative), rhetorical, and philosophical perspectives. Celeste Grayson Seymour (2011) thoughtfully explicates a modern, postmodern, and premodern framing of interpersonal relationships. Her task is to highlight a view of interpersonal communication that does not reify subjectivity and individualism but takes ongoing participation in everyday life as the formative principle of communication. Even though the investigative strategies are different and, at times, in contention, there is a common heart within these approaches—the relationship matters in interpersonal communication.

The authors of this work understand interpersonal communication as relational nurture, with the assumption that relationships need to grow and change and negotiate a variety of complex dialectical tensions (Baxter & Montgomery, 1996). Information, the demands of context—even the speakers themselves—take a subordinate position to a privileged good: the relationship. One does not engage interpersonal communication ethics when the good of relationship does not guide the exchange; at such moments, another form of communication dominates. Clearly, interpersonal communication does not happen in all places where one might assume it finds its home, such as in families or communities of worship. Interpersonal communication ethics has a pristine view of relationship—less driven by social exchange than by desire to assist the relationship without expected utility or reward. Levinas is correct; it is burden that provides meaning and insight for a life well-lived.

Interpersonal communication takes place wherever privileged concern for the relationship guides family members, business partners, friends, musicians, or athletes to attend to the good of relationship. The privileging of relationship begins, ironically, with the necessity of interpersonal distance (Buber, 1966). Relationships need space for growth and change, an assumption that runs counter to popular assumptions of the need for "closeness" in relationships (Arnett, 2002). Perhaps the difference between relationship care and interpersonal domination rests in a willingness to cultivate space for relationship growth and change.

Distance

The particular nature of a relationship and its constitution matters, as does the type and form of communication. One major metacommunication ethics assumption is that one cannot impose a singular form of communication on all interactions—not all communication episodes and contexts are the same. We often unknowingly make an unethical communicative move in demanding a particular form of communication in a setting that does not naturally, appropriately, or even pragmatically call forth such a form of communication. Note that the unethical lies with the demand, not with a mistake. One can mistakenly engage the wrong communication without ethical infraction; the ethical question arises only in the demand of the communication to fit "my" approval.

One of the practical ways to lessen the impulse for demand is to recognize the interpersonal importance of distance. As one holds an object too close to one's eyes, the details fade and blur together. It is only with distance in place that one is able to see more clearly. The old adage that absence makes the heart grow fonder has much to do with our losing sight of the importance of a person or an institution due to too much proximity.

Distance permits us to see the details more clearly. The particular matters so much that one must honor distance, permitting one to see with clarity. As Martin Buber (1966) warned, beware of the person who overruns reality. "Overrunning reality" means attempting to be closer than time, interaction, and interests have yet made possible. When we overrun reality, we lose the sense of distance necessary for careful relational growth. Distance is necessary if we are to honor what we meet; otherwise, we attempt to turn the Other into ourselves. All of us know people who are consistently "ahead of themselves"; such persons are difficult to teach, befriend, or advise. This point is important, for in our culture we too often misuse "interpersonal skills" to decrease distance between persons. Buber would suggest that such a move dishonors the Other, missing the uniqueness of contribution that the Other can bring to the table of conversation. When you get too far out in front of yourself, you lose perspective on what you do not know.

Generally, we conceptualize distance as nothing more than empty space. More accurately, it is the ontological home of the communicative relationship between persons. In the case of interpersonal communication, distance is the ontological home that nurtures and permits a particular relationship to change naturally. Laurie Moroco (2005) addresses the importance of phenomenological distance in interpersonal relationships, permitting appropriate space to texture relational development. Lisbeth Lipari (2014) points to the danger of routine and unreflective engagement with others (pp. 183–185). Undue closeness can both smother the Other and take the Other for granted. Relationships require a distance that yields care and attentiveness to difference.

When one of the authors was small, his father would take him fishing. The boat had to go very slowly in a lake full of logs and stumps, obstructions that made navigation difficult and, simultaneously, created excellent conditions for fishing. Frequently, the distance between where the boat started and the perfect fishing spot seemed to take forever to traverse. Slowly, they covered a distance that never seemed to decrease, and as soon as they had fished in one spot for a while, the father moved to another. Years later that young boy, now a grown man, can only remember catching a few fish, yet there were literally hundreds. What now remains in memory is what was always in the distance, that which occupied the "space" between here and there, which became the here leading to another there. Logs floating, birds perched upon them, turtles sitting on the logs, an occasional water snake, moss, waves, the shore line, grass, the changing colors of the water, the sun, and two companions, a father and a son. It is in the distance between the here and the there that memories live. It is what happens in the distance between the here and the there that shapes the texture and richness of a life—and a relationship.

© AjiaK/Shutterstock.com

Bob Hope, an American comedian and actor, sang for decades a song of gratitude, "Thanks for the Memories." Philosophically, distance makes memories possible. Saying, "Thanks for the memories" is akin to giving thanks for what happened between a here and a there. Relationship, as understood in this chapter, requires a responsibility for memories that change both through shifts in perspective and through additive adjustments of novel experiences that enter and alter one's memory—in this case, an interpersonal communication memory called "relationship" that lives in an ontological home of distance.

Distance is interpersonal space that nourishes the very thing that keeps persons together interpersonally—relationship. The distance between us is an ethical responsibility, not a flaw or a limitation. Distance is the home of our responsibility—in this case, responsibility for an interpersonal relationship. Now, consider again the father who took his son fishing—he nurtured a relationship as a dad that called him to love the outdoors, hard work, and dependability. Today, what lingers so many years later is his interpersonal responsibility that never let him forget what he should do as a dad, or, in the words of this chapter, the importance and the power of distance—the holder of a relational call. He nurtured a relationship that lives beyond death.

The importance of distance keeps us from equating interpersonal communication with ever more closeness. It is possible to be concerned about a relationship with another and use multiple ways of attending to the heart of the interpersonal life of those persons together. The assumption of interpersonal communication ethics is that no matter how close the relationship, one must nourish a space for distance, a space for distinctiveness of persons, and a home of relational responsibility between persons. For instance, when the son of one of the authors was young, he asked the following question: "Dad, are you my friend?" The answer given quickly was, of course, "Yes." Then, as the conversation continued, the dad remembered his relational responsibility and offered a correction. "Son, I love you. You can count on me as your friend unless I must choose between friendship and being your dad. If I must lose your friendship to help you as your dad, I will do so without a blink." The relationship mandated by being a dad and a son takes precedence over friendship in this interpersonal exchange between father and son; responsibility for a particular type of relationship keeps the heart of this interpersonal communication nourished. Distance calls us to nourish a relationship that is historically appropriate, not necessarily the definition of relationship that we demand of the Other or want for ourselves. The interpersonal relationship calls us to do what we consider necessary—in this case, as a parent, not as a high school companion. Interpersonally, the relationship we have with another matters—it is the defining ethic in our interpersonal communication, and it is our ethical responsibility to nurture that relationship.

Interpersonal Responsibility

Ernest Boyer, when working as the Director of the Carnegie Institute for Teaching, was asked to define the conditions for student success: "What makes a great student?" The answer was not what a crowd of educators expected. Arnett (1992) reports his response: "He replied, 'A parent, friend, teacher, or someone significant offering a sense of hope that the young person is worthwhile and can and will succeed'" (p. 102)—a mom, dad, brother, sister, cousin, teacher, coach, religious leader—anyone who says, "Come hell or high water, I am with you and will help you succeed." Such a mentor becomes a champion, facilitating a relationship that assists the Other. Interpersonal communication from an ethical standpoint is not about saying the "right" thing or looking as if one has all the ideas worked out; it is simply about not losing sight of a key ingredient—my relational responsibility to the Other.

The ethical dimension of interpersonal communication moves the focus from relationship alone to responsibility for the relationship, a relationship that is about something—for instance, in the previous example, the "something" is success against all odds. This chapter attends to the "habits of the interpersonal heart," a relation that calls forth our responsibility. We often hear someone complaining that another person does not have good interpersonal skills. This chapter defines the interpersonal good as attending to responsibility appropriate for a given relationship. An interpersonal ethic is not the same as an interpersonal aesthetic/ style that seeks to "win friends." This chapter privileges responsibility for a relationship that one seeks to nourish over the Other's "feeling good" and one's own "feeling good." Aesthetically appealing and "feel good" discourse have a place, but they are not the same as relationally responsible interpersonal communication in which attentive concern for the relationship is more important than how one appears as a communicator.

The ethics of interpersonal communication moves interpersonal communication to the realm of responsibility for the relationship. Paula S. Tompkins (2009) aligns ethical practices with relational embeddedness in narratives of consequence and meaning. As one seeks to know another, it is important to listen to the narratives of consequence that shape the conversation. Placed in ethical language, the move from interpersonal style to interpersonal responsibility for the relationship highlights the difference between personality and character. Good personality, or interpersonal style, linked with interpersonal responsibility, or character, leads to long-term relational health; good personality without character foregoes the long-term obligation to attend to relational responsibility, forging a form of interpersonal sophistry marked by style alone and absence of interpersonal ethics—for the relationship is the content that guides character in an interpersonal ethic.

The good that interpersonal communication ethics carries is that of the relationship. The notion of responsibility engages a communicator with an ethical charge to attend to practices that bind a given relationship together. The conceptual irony of this manner of understanding interpersonal communication is that something other than the Other's perception must guide the interaction. This view of interpersonal communication does not place liking as primary, but, instead, responsible engagement of a given relationship. What does it mean to be a teacher, a mom, a friend, a colleague? In each case, one asks what the necessary relationship is and how one can work interpersonally to nourish the relationship that one seeks to support. In each case, it is the relationship that takes on a sense of particularity, the defining characteristic of the notion "relationship of"—the particular characteristics of an emergent "relationship between" with a defining preposition.

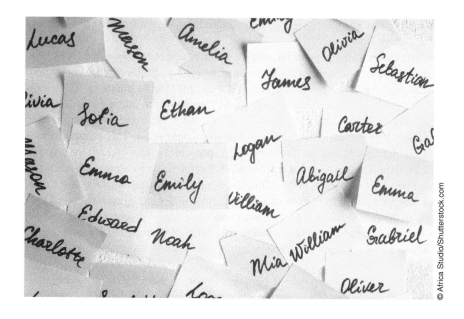

© Africa Studio/Shutterstock.com

The Particular Matters

The focus of attention in this view of interpersonal communication is both simple and demanding—how does one support, enhance, and nourish a relationship that exists between two persons? The first assumption in interpersonal communication from the standpoint of interpersonal communication ethics is that the nature of the relationship matters. As an earlier example stated, a dad is not necessarily a friend, and a student is not necessarily one's colleague, and on and on; the particular relationship matters. Levinas (2000) addresses this concern in his work *Proper Names*. The naming matters. Naming announces the relationship of dad, teacher, student, or friend. The proper name begins with a general reminder of a relationship played out in the particular between persons. When I say the terms "son" and "daughter," they unite the general immediately with the reality of particular faces. The works of George Herbert Mead (1962) and Seyla Benhabib (1992) give additional insight into the difference between a "generalized other" and a "particular other," with an interpersonal ethic gathering strength, meaning, and direction from the particular relationship. The particular matters in the shaping of the relationship. As persons and historical circumstances change, the relationship shifts, as well.

The particular shaping of a given relationship results in a call to a particular communicative responsibility. As a relationship changes, so does one's responsibility, redirecting and reshaping the interpersonal communication taking place within it. Emmanuel Levinas states that ethics begins with action that displays

"I am my brother's keeper" (Cohen, 1998, p. xii; Levinas, 1998). How one lives out that relational calling is dependent upon the particular demands before the communicative partners. Interpersonal relationship lives not in the abstract, but in the particular; the exact nature of what is ethical in interpersonal communication lives within a unique particular that changes with persons, with time, and with the historical demands before us.

Hesed and the Shadows of Demand

Interpersonal communication ethics presupposes that one cannot impose a particular type of relationship on another, nor can one demand a relationship from another. To impose or to demand a particular type of relationship violates the spirit of interpersonal communication. Relationship development in interpersonal communication requires attentive care without the specter of demand. Relationship development in interpersonal communication lives by "hesed," a Hebrew term that suggests an obligation for the good of the community (in this case, the relationship), but not a demand. Communities find the importance of bonding relationships through differing worldviews. Contractualism gathers people with a legal agreement. Committalism requires a collective obligation to the task. Covenantalism permits people to work with one another when liking is no more (Strom, 2013). To permit demand to govern all interpersonal interaction moves such discourse into technique and image-centered communication, forgetting one's responsibility to the relationship. In interpersonal communication, the only long-term protection for the communicative partners is a commitment to a relationship nourished by "hesed"—relationship responsibility enacted without response to the demand of the Other, attentive, instead, to the demand of the proper name of a given relational connection.

Interpersonal communication lives within a space of multiple "hesed" commitments. First, the relationship cannot be demanded, and, secondly, there is an irony in that one cannot demand that no demand ever be uttered. Interpersonal communication ethics is the place of occasional demands.

One cannot make the demand that there *never* be a relational demand in interpersonal communication. Upon occasion, in interpersonal communication ethics, one can demand that another attend to a relationship that has seemingly gone unattended. This demand works as a rhetorical interruption, calling for a change in one or both parties' focus of attention. A demand, however, cannot sustain an interpersonal relationship long term; eventually, and sooner rather than later, the concern for relationship development must return once again to "hesed" status. To make repeated demands for a given communicative action is to move the communicative gesture into something quite different from interpersonal communication. Both demand and the notion of "hesed" have unique characteristics that guide communicative life in interpersonal communication ethics.

Undue demand lives in the rush to turn a new acquaintance into a friendship without letting the relationship develop on its own. "You will be my friend now!" destroys the fragile structure of an emerging relationship. The narrow ridge upon which interpersonal relationship engagement finds its balance defines the "unity of contraries," such as the necessity of relationship and impossibility of its long-term demand (Buber, 1948). The question of how to engage another interpersonally finds an answer within the terms of the relationship and a caution to beware of "overrunning [the] reality" (Buber, as cited in Glatzer, 1966, p. 65) of relationship limits at a given time in a given moment. Relationships change, but most often on their own without our forcing or making a particular relationship materialize. We can invite. We can demand on occasion, never forgetting that we cannot own the relationship or our image of what we demand that relationship to be.

Persistent demand without attentive change from the Other moves interpersonal communication from relational attentiveness to relational obsession and control, terminating an interpersonal communication relationship that gives way to a darker, more insistent form of interpersonal interaction that this chapter deems interpersonal colonization and that Cupach and Spitzberg (2004) term "the dark side" of interpersonal relationships and attraction. In short, it is not demand that is problematic, but the movement of the occasional act of demand that offers a needed rhetorical interruption to demand as the normative foundation of an interpersonal relationship, moving us from interpersonal communication to interpersonal colonization. Just as we cannot demand dialogue at all moments, neither can we demand interpersonal relational attention as we would prefer it, on our own terms, at all times.

It is the shadow side of interpersonal communication, propelled by persistent demand, which reconfigures interpersonal communication ethics into something else temporarily masquerading as relational concern. Yet, it is the shadows, the possibility of demand not enacted, that give power and meaning to the light of relationship sustained by "hesed." For example, you may not appreciate your friend's constant "nagging" to spend more time together. Yet, the awareness that your friend desires your company points to the value of the relationship.

Without demand, relationships suffer, and with constant demand, relationships cease to have the character of what this chapter calls interpersonal communication ethics. Demand emerges from the propelling force of desire for the relationship with a particular Other. If one is unconcerned about the Other or the relationship with the Other, one simply does not care. On the other hand, constant demand does not permit a space for response to a particular Other to emerge. Demand creates a focus of attention on the relationship that becomes too intense for "hesed" to emerge and stifles a sense of voluntary engagement from reciprocal desire. Constant demand creates a different sort of bond than relational concern. Our misuse of demand plays itself out in our undue confidence in learning interpersonal skills more as an effort to "win friends and influence people" (Carnegie, 1936/1981) than as a call to responsibility to nurture a relationship.

The Limits of Interpersonal Skills

Consistency of demand takes the relationship into one's own hands, moving from interpersonal communication that requires co-constituting communicative life together to a unilateral focus—"my" image of what should be. Such is the danger of too much emphasis on interpersonal communication skills. No skill is the sole answer to all problems and demands before us. Interpersonal skills are not exempt from the reality of limits. The line between working with another and manipulating another vanishes when one takes on too much responsibility for the Other's communication and response. The key to interpersonal communication is invitation to relationship building, not smooth discourse at all costs. Baxter and Montgomery (1996) recognize the complicated nature of interpersonal relationships in their work on relational dialectics, highlighting the messiness and unpredictability of relational dynamics. They remind us of the difficulty of a goal of undue control of the communicative process with another.

Janie Harden Fritz (2016), examining interpersonal communication ethics, explores the reality of increasing options related to social communication technologies. She reminds readers of a basic reminder from Jacques Ellul to ask not, "Can it be done?" but rather, "Should it be done?" (Ellul, 1954/1964, p. 436). Creative engagement of social communication technologies linked to reflection about the wisdom of their use is more likely to facilitate relational engagement between and among persons (Fritz, 2016, p. 11).

Additionally, interpersonal communication ethics recognizes responsibility to the relationship, not demands that one makes on the Other. Interpersonal communication ethics does not live long on the ground of demand to meet "my" standards and my understanding of a relational reality owned by neither partner in the communicative action. This chapter recommends that an advertisement for a position in the business world refrain from asking for "outstanding interpersonal communication skills" and request, instead, "good business and professional communication skills," which do have a demand component. The notion of business and professional communication requires adherence to a public standard of discourse and interaction.

The key to interpersonal communication ethics is not "Who has the best communication skills?" or "Who communicates in the way I think best?" The key to interpersonal communication ethics lies in the answer to this question: "Do given persons work to honor a relationship, whatever the consequences?" If the relationship changes, one's responsibility has to change. The guiding key is the relationship, which works as a beacon calling forth our responsibility to the Other. Interpersonal communication ethics rests not in our hopes or wishes or those of another, but in something that we invite and can never create alone, a relationship that calls us to responsibility.

Wanda and her good friend Stacy are about to leave a party. Wanda notices that Stacy is too impaired by alcohol to drive safely. Wanda says to herself, "I know my responsibility to this relationship. I will not let my friend drive home in this condition." In that moment of interpersonal communication ethics, one does not know whether the Other will approve or even be willing to keep the friendship; however, at that moment, it is not the delight of the Other that drives one's action, but a standard much more powerful and demanding—the heartbeat of responsibility for the Other calling us forth in a phenomenon properly named "relationship." In interpersonal communication ethics, relationships matter, as Brown and Keller (1973) highlight in *Monologue to Dialogue: An Exploration of Interpersonal Communication:*

> We rest our lives on our values, the vaporous wings of a prayer. These values must be confirmed by others or they die and we die. Research has demonstrated time and again that each of us is unique in our perceptions, there being no more alikeness among friends than among strangers or enemies. Friends are united and confirmed in their common ideals. (p. 206)

In interpersonal communication ethics, the common ideal begins with a relationship that both consider worthy of responsibility, a responsibility that keeps the difference between character and personality ever present in interpersonal life together.

Pointing to a Dialogic Ethic in Interpersonal Communication

Interpersonal communication ethics points to a dialogic ethic in the manner of listening, attentiveness, and negotiation. The following model summarizes a dialogic ethic applied to interpersonal communication in relationships, highlighting major points in this chapter.

1. *Listening—without demand: What is happening in a given moment? Whether we like or dislike that moment, we must engage the question(s) of a given moment.* Interpersonal communication ethics is wary of demand, even of the demand to do away with all demands. The importance of *hesed* frames an interpersonal communication ethic attentive to a particular relationship. The form of the relationship is not subject to our demand or our interpersonal communication preference. We engage the relationship in its particularity.

2. *Attentiveness: What are the coordinating grounds upon which stand the self, the Other, and the historical moment?* Attentiveness to relationship and the kind of relationship, "relationship of," is the defining feature that centers the good of an interpersonal communication ethic.

   a. *The ground of self (the ethical/narrative commitments that guide us) and*

   b. *The ground of Other (the ethical/narrative commitments that guide the Other).* The ethical ground that shapes interpersonal communication ethics for self and Other is a commitment to something beyond the communicative partners, to a relationship that defines communicative life together.

   c. *The ground of the historical moment (elements of the time in which we live, including "relational time" of the persons in conversation).* A relationship is not static and must change with the demands of the historical moment. In fact, this view of relationship makes it akin to a phantom; it is there and ever changing, denying our impulse to reify it into a given, demanded, solidified state.

3. *Dialogic negotiation: What temporal communication ethics answers emerge "between" persons, pointing to communicative options for action, belief, and understanding?* The interpersonal understanding of a relationship requires fresh negotiation in friendships, in relationships with significant others, and with parents. Negotiation reminds us of the consistency of change that "I" can never control, but that "we" must negotiate together.

4. *Listening, attentiveness, and dialogic negotiation constitute temporal dialogic ethical competence. What worked, and what changes might now assist?*

   a. *Evaluation/self-reflection (reflection upon one's own ethical/narrative commitments).* Attending to the question of what we do in interpersonal communication ethics is a deliberate self-reflection. It is akin to the self-writing that Foucault (1997) challenged us to do habitually. In this case, the evaluation is up to "me," not "us," or otherwise we fall into the temptation of demand once again under the guise of "just doing evaluation."

   b. *From knowledge to learning (the key is not to "tell," but to learn from the Other, the historical moment, and reflective understanding of communicative action).* There is no interpersonal communication ethic that is set in stone; as the relationship changes, so do our responsibilities. The key is to link the relationship with the responsibilities.

5. *Dialogic ethics listens to what is before the relational partners, attends to the historical moment, and seeks to negotiate new possibilities. Dialogic ethics is a conceptual form of marketplace engagement, ever attentive to conversational partners and their "ground," the historical moment, and the emerging "possible" that takes place in the "between" of human meeting.* Interpersonal communication ethics listens to relationship needs, limits demands, connects responsibility to the relationship, and attends to the inevitability of change. In interpersonal communication ethics, the responsible "I" follows what Michael Hyde (2001) called a call of conscience—in this case, connecting one's interpersonal responsibility to a particular understanding of a given relationship, ever attentive to the inevitability of change.

COMMUNICATION ETHICS: REFLECTION AND ACTION

1. Assess three of your interpersonal relationships in terms of each person's relational responsibility to the self, the Other, and the relationship.
2. Consider these three relationships again. How has each relationship been "negotiated" at different points in its "relational time"?
3. What "hesed" commitments are engaged in these three relationships? Recall that "hesed" refers to things that must be done for the good of the relationship, but cannot be demanded.
4. Consider a favorite motion picture, or one that you have recently viewed, that features an interpersonal relationship. Assess this relationship according to the model of dialogic ethics presented at the end of this chapter.
5. Working with one or two other students, identify a scenario that you believe is a common interpersonal communication ethics challenge encountered in everyday life. Identify elements of the model of dialogic ethics at the end of this chapter that are relevant to the scenario you identified. Take turns enacting responses that represent elements of interpersonal communication ethics discussed in this chapter.

ENGAGING COMMUNICATION ETHICS THROUGH LITERATURE: *LES MISÉRABLES*

Understanding *Les Misérables* as a novel about interpersonal communication ethics opens a creative window into interpersonal relationship responsibility. As one's relationship changes, the responsibility that one has for the Other also changes. When Jean Valjean, galley slave of nineteen years recently released from prison, finds a place to stay at the bishop's home—a bishop known as Monseigneur Bienvenu (whose name translates to English as "Welcome")—he steals silverware, runs away in the night, and is captured with the property in his possession. After the capture, Jean Valjean finds himself with the authorities back at the bishop's front door. The bishop is ever so happy to see him, stating to the police that the silverware was a gift to Jean Valjean, but that he "forgot" to take with him two silver candlesticks, which he was now glad to give to Valjean. It is the relationship of a Bishop of Welcome to a man with an embittered soul that begins the novel. Jean Valjean eventually shifts his life, working to assist others at his own expense.

When the Bishop of Welcome meets Jean Valjean, both distance and responsibility mark their engagement. The formal title of "Monsieur"—"sir"—by which the bishop addresses this newly released convict offers the space of dignity to a wounded soul. Without prying into the details of Valjean's life and intentions, the bishop offers a public welcome of distance. Upon the gendarmes' return of Valjean after apprehending him with the stolen silverware, the bishop protects and promotes the good of the relationship. He enacts the relational responsibility he took on the previous evening by permitting distance again, this time distance from Valjean's intention of theft. The bishop grants distance from even the individual intention of Jean Valjean, offering the possibility of a renewed relationship "between" the two. As Valjean leaves, the good of the relationship endures through time as the bishop tells Valjean to use the resources to become an honest man.

In *Les Misérables*, interpersonal communication ethics directed toward the good of relationship emerges over and over. Marius and his grandfather, when we first encounter them, have essentially destroyed their relationship. Their political disagreements result in conflict that drives them apart. Near the end of the novel, Marius's grandfather, overjoyed to find that Marius is alive, communicates with him in a very different way. Together, Marius and his grandfather reconstruct their interpersonal relationship, and the discourse of each honors the good of the relationship.

In reading the novel, one walks into an interpersonal world of responsibility for relationship. The bishop nourished a relationship of welcome without the certainty that the wounded spirit before him would change, but with knowledge that his responsibility to this man called him to compassionate action. Throughout the novel, Valjean continues to nourish a relationship based upon gratitude, responsive to a Bishop of Welcome. The echo of the bishop's interpersonal responsibility takes Jean Valjean into a world of burden taken up for others with a reason to help, and even suffer, all in the quiet name of a relationship that shaped his action from a distance—somehow, the gift of the candlesticks brings a flicker of light, becoming an eternal flame that illuminates places where only shadows would otherwise rest. The bishop's act of passing the candlesticks offers light that brings a new sense of sight, permitting attention to others, no longer masking the good of interpersonal responsibility "for."

Organizational
Communication Ethics

Community of Memory and Dwelling

> The home, as a building, belongs to a world of objects. But this belongingness
> does not nullify the bearing of the fact that every consideration of objects, and of
> buildings too, is produced out of a dwelling. (Levinas, 1969, pp.152–153)

A large part of communicative life finds meaning in concerted action with other persons within organizations. Organizational communication ethics represents the dwelling place (Levinas, 1969, p. 152) of communicative practices that form our life together (Bonhoeffer, 1978). Organizational communication ethics is about the kind of dwelling place we construct in our life together. Studies indicate that we now spend up to 70 hours a week in some form of organizational action (Hewlett & Luce, 2006). Technologies such as email and smartphones put employees within organizational reach to an ever-increasing degree, prompting responses to messages received at hours beyond those of the traditional workday. In all these commitments, our organizational life takes on the characteristics of a particular type of dwelling, a particular home for communicative practices. The good of organizational communication ethics rests within the very dwelling place we construct. The guiding question for organizational communication ethics is, "What type of dwelling does a given organization want to be, claim to be, and function as?" After reading this chapter, you will be able to demonstrate the following learning objectives:

- Define organizational communication
- Explain the importance of a dwelling place that gives an organization a sense of uniqueness
- Differentiate between organizations and institutions

Introduction

There are as many different goods as there are different organizations; the uniting theme is the implicit or explicit commitment to a type of dwelling place. Organizations host a variety of persons with different understandings of the good; organizational communication ethics recognizes the need for a minimal common understanding of a given good in each organizational setting, requiring one to take responsibility for the dwelling that the communicative practices construct.

Differing approaches to organizational communication work to support, alter, or displace a particular sense of the good, a given understanding of the communicative life of a specific organizational dwelling place. In short, one advocates a given view of organizational communication because of its perceived status as "better," which carries an ethical assumption that some good, a given vision of a dwelling place, requires protection and promotion in a given organizational arrangement.

This chapter connects the study of organizational ethics to communicative practices with attention to the following four metaphors of communication ethics praxis:

1. **Organizational communication**—the orchestrating of communicative practices through formal and informal structures of events and persons in a given organization to accomplish a given purpose or purposes.
2. **Dwelling place**—the type of communicative home a given organization invites by its communicative practices. The notion of home does not suggest all warmth and care; indeed, there are homes that are far from this reality. A dwelling place is a gathering of communicative practices and stories that gives an organization a sense of uniqueness, separating a specified organization from others within the same industry.
3. **Organizations and institutions**—formations working together to establish a gestalt identity, with the latter providing a background identity that guides and shapes the horizon of possibilities played out in a particular fashion within a particular organization.

▶

▶   4. **Community of memory within organizations**—the pragmatic equivalent of an organizational conscience, providing a reminder of what has and has not worked and what particular actions did and continue to do for communicative life together, shaping a given dwelling place in a particular fashion.

Student Application: Finding a Dwelling Place

As one engages a diverse number of campus organizations, such as Lambda Pi Eta, the official communication studies honor society of the National Communication Association, the Public Relations Student Society of America (PRSSA), an American Advertising Federation (AAF) student chapter, other student groups, fraternities and sororities, religiously affiliated associations, and places of employment, one must negotiate, through communication, the coordination of tasks with others. **Organizational communication** focuses on the form of communication needed to get a particular task done. Each of these organizations is an element in a larger set of institutions. For example, a college or university is one organization that makes up the larger sphere of institutions of higher education. As we enter different organizations, differing **dwelling places** invite us to use our time in quite contrasting ways. When one decides to pursue higher education, one must figure out which particular organization out of all the institutions of higher education provides the best fit or right dwelling place to shape one's future. Upon graduation, one must identify an employing organization that will provide such a sense of fit and potential dwelling place, as well. A **community of memory within organizations** reminds us of the ongoing story of a particular organization, permitting us to examine our communication within a given organization to discern what type of communication protects and promotes a given good for that organization.

Organizational Communication

Organizational communication is the orchestrating of communicative practices that announce how formal and informal structures of events and persons in a given organization interrelate to accomplish a purpose or purposes. Organizational communication has been a focus of study for many decades, from the foundational work of Redding (Tompkins & Wanca-Thibaut, 2001) to today's contributions from a growing number of scholars. *The SAGE Handbook of Organizational Communication* (Putnam & Mumby, 2014), now in its third edition, traces its history and development, providing an overview of topics addressed in this multifaceted area.

Organizational communication addresses communicative practices and discourse processes among and between peers and between employees and leaders/managers. Questions of how organizational culture and meanings emerge through communicative exchanges, how communication mediates perceptions of

organizational life, and the work of language in relation to power in organizational settings are representative topics within the scope of organizational communication. Perspectives in the field of organizational communication are varied, including critical, postmodern, feminist, queer, and social constructionist approaches (e.g., Allen, 2005; Ashcraft & Mumby, 2004; Buzzanell, 2002; Deetz, 1992, 1994; Deetz & Mumby, 1990; May & Mumby, 2005; McDonald, 2015; Mumby, 2015) and a variety of topic areas ranging from work relationships (Fritz & Omdahl, 2006; Omdahl & Fritz, 2012; Sias, Krone, & Jablin, 2002) and leadership (e.g., Fairhurst, 2001, 2011) to communication processes such as organizational socialization (e.g., Jablin, 2001; Kramer, 2010) and uncertainty reduction (Kramer, 2003). Methodological perspectives on organizational communication vary, as well (Corman & Poole, 2000), including postpositivist (Corman, 2005; Miller, 2000) and interpretive (Putnam, 1983; Cheney, 2000) approaches.

Organizational communication ethics addresses the practices and functions of communication in organizations that protect and promote a particular good that defines a dwelling place. Specific approaches to organizational communication ethics include those identified by Conrad (1993) and Seeger (1997), and explorations of ethical implications of organizational actions from particular standpoints on the good hail from a number of approaches, including feminist, dialogic, and critical perspectives (e.g., Ashcraft, 2005; Buzzanell, 2002; Deetz, 1994; Deetz, 2001; Deetz & Mumby, 1990; Mumby, 2000). Critical perspectives, for instance, offer explicit frameworks that seek justice and participation of all organizational members (e.g., Deetz & Mumby, 1990). Feminist theorists (e.g., Ashcraft, 2005;

Buzzanell, 2002) challenge patriarchal conceptions of the good for organizational life, offering alternative perspectives of goods for organizational experience, highlighting the clash of competing goods in organizational practices. For example, Ashcraft (2000) highlights feminist concerns for power equality through a quest to reunite public and private spheres of life and ethical communication practices in her study of an organization guided by a feminist philosophy of organizing.

Implicit within approaches to organizational theory and communication is a view of the good for human engagement in organizational life. For example, each of various approaches to organizational communication structure and function, including classical, human relations, and human resources approaches (e.g., Miller, 2015), offers a different understanding of the good in the nature of assumptions about human beings, about work, and about communication that holds implications for the type of dwelling place that defines a particular organization.

Dwelling Place

Our view of the good in organizations begins with the notion of dwelling place: organizational communication ethics centers on a particular good that defines a dwelling place, which then shapes communicative practices and our interpretive engagement with a community of memory. No organization is ethically neutral; communicative practices announce daily a given understanding of what is good and what is not good within a given organizational structure. Each organization constructs a particular sense of dwelling that welcomes some and dismisses others. No dwelling place can please all, and no dwelling place can remain alive and well without change. Both the true believer in a given dwelling place and the critic engage a dialectical dance, keeping a given dwelling place from declining from the irony of too much appreciation, on the one hand, and constant and relentless criticism on the other.

Stanley Hauerwas (1981) calls the lament about organizational politics void of knowledge about how organizations work to protect and promote a given sense of the good. Within any organization are competing goods that require negotiation in order for the organization to carry out its work. If this negotiation does not occur, the dwelling place loses its vitality and declines due to a smugness of mission or utter disrespect for the organization, with both actions taking the future of the place for granted. Disaster rests with the inarticulate, a failure to take account of the organizational mission and purpose explicit in day-to-day life. Both the "settler," someone who has been with an organization for a significant period and takes for granted the long-term reality of a given organization, and the uninformed, who makes demands unattainable by a given organization, court this danger. The settler fails to acknowledge the importance of public articulation of organizational goods. The uninformed member simply does not know enough about the organization's missions and purpose to articulate them to self or others;

this member makes demands because of lack of knowledge of what is possible in the organization. Just as people do not have every talent or possibility, neither do organizations.

Janie Harden Fritz (2013) articulates the importance of protecting and promoting the good of place. She outlines the pragmatic necessity of mission attentiveness. She suggests that without understanding the identity of an institution and its associated horizon, excellence goes without ongoing creative nourishment. Attentiveness to organizations and their community of memory, for Fritz, is one of the key expectations of professional civility (pp. 154–172).

This discussion of organizational communication ethics does not seek to define the "right" sense of the good for a given organization; such a task rests with the organization itself (Nicotera & Cushman, 1992). Identity comes from the ongoing workings between the "saying" and the "said" of organizational life that seek to protect and promote a given sense of the good. Explication of the "saying" into the "said" permits organizations to have public commitments to a given set of ethics as first principle. This approach moves the importance of Levinas's (1998) "said" (p. 233) to the forefront, giving a given dwelling a public ethical address.

The "saying" refers to the current living practices that manifest a given good; the "said" refers to memories of past and current, "living" practices that form a substrate for future communicative action. For example, if Sandra is struggling in a college class, the "saying" takes shape in her proactive efforts to seek assistance from her professor by raising her hand in class or visiting during office hours. As students follow Sandra's example, they cultivate a specific organizational culture that begins to define the quality of scholarship at that institution. Eventually, those practices become the "said" that guides future interaction in such a place of learning. This requirement for action on the part of the student protects and promotes the good of responsibility for one's life and actions. The "said" rests within the public story or policies of the organization. As new "sayings" encounter testing in everyday life, they shift to the "said," serving as public guiding positions. When the "said" no longer assists a given organization, hope rests in the ongoing creativity present in "sayings" that emerge and later become another set of public "saids" of an organization.

Marshall Scott Poole and Robert McPhee (2005) consider a structurational framework for organizational communication theorizing that resonates with this understanding of the "said" as a set of resources to guide the "saying" of current communicative action. As the demands of a given historical moment shift, an organization must find within itself the resources with which to respond to historical changes and demands, beginning with reflection upon the past and present values of an organization (the "said"). A reflective sense of the organization works to promote a given sense of the good in the public "said" of tradition that lives in mission statements and the organizational saga (Clark, 1972). The "saying" of its response to new challenges guides the communicative action of change and prompts the recollection of what once was that might again assist the organization. The dialectic of the ability to articulate the publicly stated (the "said") with attentive response to a changing historical moment (the "saying") increases the chances of protecting and promoting a given good in different communicative environments and shifting demands.

An example of the relationship of the "said" to the "saying" rests in the current historical moment that addresses new member orientation to student-run college clubs (Kase, Rivera, & Hunt, 2016; Salo, 2010). Associations such as sororities and fraternities seek to protect and promote their traditions and values. In previous generations, hazing practices afforded camaraderie and community-building in the formation of a particular group identity—a "saying" that contributed to a "said." This new historical moment calls for change. Current hazing practices can require degrading, humiliating, and dangerous activities to demonstrate a new member's commitment to the group, an unacceptable approach to new member orientation. To respond to this new historical moment, reconfigured national inter-fraternity guidelines for member recruitment and education discourage or forbid hazing practices (Reisberg, 2000) in an attempt to encourage the alteration of a potentially destructive "saying." In response to these new standards, sororities and fraternities are finding constructive ways to enhance new members' engagement with the group's tradition and values, enacting a new "saying" that will contribute to the continuing "said" of group traditions. The "saying" evokes change, and the "said" works to preserve and make public the expectation for retaining a given group's charter.

The power of change in the "saying" manifests even at the level of entire countries ceasing to exist due to revolution, invasion, or gradual shift and erosion. Given the fragility of entire nations, one cannot assume that an organization will continue in perpetuity. Historically, the story of Rome reminds us of this possibility. Organizational communication ethics attends to the ongoing interplay of the "saying" and the "said," or what Burke (1954) so aptly called *Permanence and Change*. Organizational communication ethics, learning from the ongoing relationship of "saying" and "said," begins with the connection between institutions and organizations, which begins the first step of keeping an organization grounded, decreasing, to a small degree, the likelihood of its losing its way through inattentiveness to the grounded practices that give it a particular identity. The following section examines the interplay of organizations and institutions; each functions as a "saying" and a "said" for the other, a context of change and stability.

Organizations and Institutions

This chapter brings together two terms that are not synonymous, but closely aligned—organization and institution. The terms texture one another, calling each other into accountability. The categories of organization and institution are not identical; however, their family lineage links the identity of one with the identity of the other. Organizations find meaning within a larger understanding of the institutions that provide them with a sense of identity. Conversely, in the long run, the way in which given organizations perform shapes the identity of a given institution.

The framework of an organizational house is the institution. The institution is the legal and publicly recognized structure that permits us to understand the identity of a given organization as an entity of a given type: a bank, a university, an integrated marketing communication firm, a homeless shelter, a museum, or any other form of organization. Places of identity announce the way in which constituted life and action within the organization transpires (Cooren, Kuhn, Cornelissen, & Clark, 2011). The code of a given place calls forth "mutual forms of obligation" (p. 1162) to gain access to these organizing principles. Cooren and colleagues (2011) cite James R. Taylor's emphasis in gathering transactional glimpses of organizational communication. What takes place between and among persons in the organization reflects the manner in which organizations reflect their unique constitutive natures.

An institutional home gives identity to an organization, offering a place of connection around publicly recognized types of work. Organizations find meaning through their identification as a particular type of institution. Organizational communication ethics finds life in a community of memory invested in communicative practices that live out a sense of the good protected and promoted in a given organizational home, host to meaningful work and productivity, where public standards make clear the nature of organizational loyalty expected and given. Organizations find their identity within the shadow of an institution that provides a community of memory for the ongoing function and purpose of a given organization.

Take, for example, a financial organization—a credit union, a bank, or a savings and loan—that works within a larger institutional commitment to financial services consisting of these and other particular organizational members of an institutional community. What makes a given organization that offers financial services visible to us is an institutional reality called financial institutions; the identity of the organization depends upon the institution. From the standpoint of communication ethics, institutions and organizations work together in a gestalt fashion. Institutions provide the "background" and organizations the "foreground," with the whole of the two together creating something greater than the sum of the parts. Our ethical assumption is that identity does not happen alone or in a vacuum. We owe our identity to the background that situates our communicative life together within a given organization.

Communication ethics finds public display in an organization through four basic questions. First, what is the institution or institutions that give(s) identity, embedding and situating a given organization? Second, what particular communicative practices and particular understandings of an organization depend upon a larger institutional identity and how are they manifested? Third, how does a particular organizational communication ethic become a dwelling place of the good where communicative practices and a story-laden sense of the organization publicly disclose the particularity of a given organization within a given institutional background? Finally, how does a given story of an organization depend upon a "community of memory" that keeps alive the identity of a given place? Organizational identity emerges out of a background provided by an institution. An organizational community of memory begins with its institutional ties that offer stability and simultaneously push for change.

Community of Memory within Organizations

Organizational functions of the "what"/communicative practices and the "how"/ understanding shape an ongoing community of memory. The manner in which these communicative elements evolve in public consciousness is more often a muddling through with erratic discoveries than a clear delineation of a given direction. However, for the telling of this story about organizational communication ethics, we must begin somewhere.

This section begins with a note of thanks to Robert Bellah and his co-authors, who pointed to a major premise of this chapter—organizations are the holders of a "community of memory" (Bellah et al., 1985, pp. 152–155). The community of memory of an organization is a sense of organizational conscience, retaining what a given organization deems as good. A community of memory within an organization frames its identity and its political life. From a communication ethics perspective, organizations are carriers of a given sense of the good that offers human meaning in an organization—organizations offer places to participate, belong, play, and work; they situate our lives, giving meaning beyond our individual selves.

The good resides in the combination of "what" (practices) and "how" (understanding) that gives shape to a good for a given organization. For Bellah, the notion of community of memory is central to an understanding of life situated within something other than an individual self. Understanding the human being as an embedded agent, as opposed to an autonomous communication agent, outlines the importance of Bellah's work to the study of organizational communication ethics.

It is important to note that the memory of a given sense of the good does not assure agreement of each organizational member with a given organization's view of the good. A community of memory sets the initial argumentative parameters— guidelines that ground good reasons for a particular place—that function as a standard capable of calling into question current communicative practices, guiding change in response to the persuasive power of alternative communicative practices (emergent "sayings") that offer a contending sense of the good. Just as society in a postmodern culture lives with competing narrative and virtue structures, an organization holds more than one community of memory that offers a standard for challenge and change to other understandings of the good, other communities of memory, lived out in the daily communicative practices of an organization. Just as an individual cannot assume agreement on one view of the good, neither can an organization embrace such an assumption. The loss of universal agreement affects organizations just as it does individuals.

A community of memory works as a conscience or guide, not as a dictate; it responds to changing circumstances within an organization or risks becoming simply a dead tradition (Gadamer, 1960/1986). Bellah's use of the notion of "community of memory" is a first principle reminder that there is more to life than what he and his coworkers would consider a modern fiction, the autonomous self. Bellah and his coauthors (1985) suggest in *Habits of the Heart*:

> A primary emphasis on self-reliance has led to the notion of pure, undetermined choice, free of tradition, obligation, or commitment, as the essence of the self. . . . the radical individualist's sincere desire to 'reconnect' with others was inhibited by the emptiness of such an 'unencumbered' self. It is now time to consider what a self that is not empty would be like—one constituted rather than unencumbered . . . (p. 152).

A community of memory connects us to meaningful stories and, in addition, to others who contributed to that community of memory. What makes a community of memory possible is not "me," but those who have come before the persons who now work at the telling of a given memory at a given time and emergent new insights that become part of the communicative life recorded in a community of memory. A community of memory is alive, owned by no one person, and the product of ongoing engagement with the past through the present, engaging with a future that is not yet.

Bellah and colleagues remind us: " . . .[W]e have never been, and still are not, a collection of private individuals . . . .Our lives make sense in a thousand ways, most of which we are unaware of, because of traditions that are centuries, if not millennia, old" (Bellah et al., 1985, p. 282). For Americans, fireworks and

© rozbyshaka

barbecues are taken-for-granted communal practices associated with the annual celebration of Independence Day, even in a culture that privileges individualism. In organizational terms, Bellah suggests that we do not live within aggregates of individuals; we live in communities that are alive with memory—memory of the past that engages the present and the future. Bellah points to a communicative fact of organizational life: a community of memory points to the kind of dwelling place and the form of communication practices that shape and reshape an organizational dwelling place.

A community of memory is both a collection of the past and an engagement with the future. A community of memory is not a static worldview; it is a live engagement with the meaningfulness of a given organization, institution, or community. The stance we take on a given community of memory makes all the difference. We cannot change events, but our telling, our way of making meaning of those events, does change with time, highlighting particular understandings of the good in organizational life. It is not simply "what happened" that matters, but our public "meaning making" of that event, which can and does shift over time, that reveals our understanding of the relationship of organizational events to how we protect and promote particular goods. A community of memory lives in the exchange and interplay of "saying" and "said." When the "said" totally eclipses the "saying" of community of memory, it morphs into a rigid ideological system, losing its constructive and reconstitutive properties.

Active Engagement—Organizational Participation

A community of memory is not a place of static collection of old stories; it is the central location of active engagement for an organization. It is the place from which the new meets the challenge of history and within which the old lives on in transformation and change, shifting perspectives on itself and its relation to the present. A community of memory is the "said" of an organization that lives only when the "saying" of an organization remains vibrant. A community of memory functions like a text that informs while changing as it provides a place from which ongoing tests and challenges commence.

Ongoing communicative practices carry forth a sense of the good in everyday organizational life; these practices are active "sayings" within the organization. The ongoing challenge and reinforcement of the "saying," the daily communicative practices, keep a community of memory alive. We orchestrate ethical meaning through communicative social practices that shape and drive the structures and functions of a given organization. An organization's structured manner of inviting and discouraging certain communicative practices and functions announces what good a given organization seeks to protect and promote.

An organization's community of memory works as a holder of a given sense of the good, calling forth guidance through a public standard that provides argumentative parameters that one can use to challenge ongoing communicative practices and functions. Within a community of memory that functions as a flexible and expansive set of argumentative parameters, one finds a good that calls forth accountability, framing a given organizational communication ethic.

Accountability—Organizational Evaluation and the Good

Without the function of memory, an organization has no ethic that can provide a standard for public evaluation. In a postmodern culture, the community of memory of an organization functions as a public conscience, reminding persons of the good and its coordinates within a given organization. The connection to communication ethics lies not only in what a given organization seeks to protect and promote, but in the events and practices that it remembers. Protection and promotion of a given good guide the retention of the information or event.

A community of memory is not static; it undergoes necessary change. Just as participants in an organization are accountable to a community of memory, the community of memory itself is accountable to the demands of the historical moment. A community of memory must guide with flexibility of implementation. The daily challenge of communicative practices and changing functions tests a community of memory, offering opportunity (and sometimes demand) for addition and change. Organizational communication ethics understood from this perspective is an ongoing interplay among communicative practices and functions that test, challenge, reinforce, and, at times, change a given community of memory.

Take, for instance, a family-owned business deeply concerned about loyalty to employees, a good that guides the interaction of a given organization through a community of memory resting upon the "said" and given life through the ongoing "saying" of the practices of the family business. Each generation, each historical moment, calls forth a particular way of enacting a given good. In a previous era without social security and pensions, loyalty called for a particular form of enactment, keeping persons on the payroll long after productivity ceased. In an era of social security, pensions, and buy-outs, a differing sense of the good often seems to connect more with productivity than with a given person. Time will tell whether these changes took us to a "better" workplace or simply furthered alienation and exploitation. To affirm a given good does not assure that the decision will prove to be correct in the long run. However, when such decisions take place in public, family members, workers, and interested constituents can work for a given "said" or for the need for continuing attention to "saying" and further change. If the members of the family are honest with themselves and others, they begin to state publicly how their engagement with employees works—not through personal ties to employees, but through employee productivity. Just as in the case of the move from small towns to the city followed by the advent of the suburb, changing goods that we protect and promote do not necessarily assure a higher quality of life. Only the willingness to admit goods publicly and then to offer alternatives over time offers hope that the ongoing interplay of "saying" and "said" will find paths of correction when needed.

A community of memory finds a testing ground in daily communicative practices, the manner in which an organization shapes its functions that gather and disseminate information. The ability of given communication structures to work rests in their alliance with a community of memory or in their power to exert enough influence such that "new" communicative practices actually alter a given community of memory. Organizations risk their legacies and their vision for future action when a community of memory fades from the deliberative background central to an organization's engagement of foreground decision making. Danger lurks whenever a community of memory goes dormant, seemingly hibernating, no longer an active part of everyday decision making.

Finding, Testing, and Protecting and Promoting the Good

A community of memory does not assure that the "right" good finds protection and promotion, but it does permit a public benchmark that guides and offers a targeted place for both guidance and contention. The inability to state what an organization does and why it does what it does announces a communication ethics danger that invites pragmatic communicative consequences. The ultimate organizational communication ethics test rests within one statement: "The dwelling place is framed by the interplay of a community of memory and the communicative practices, the ongoing dialectic of 'saying' and 'said.'"

The good protected and promoted by a particular organization undergirds the organization's nature and purpose; therefore, the primary ethical principle for an organization must be its ability to articulate what it does. Public articulation provides a text from which consideration, critique, and change can emerge. The first move of being articulate rests in knowing the base location of one's identity as an

© Simone Andress/Shutterstock.com

organization. The first articulate organizational communication ethics statement is a discussion of how a given organization functions, in a derivative or embedded sense, within the shadow of a larger institutional identity.

In everyday language, we must ask, "What does this organization stand for? What is the purpose of our work together?" Without public articulation, the organizational mission and purpose cannot serve as a "common center" (Arnett, 1986) for coordinated organizational action. A well-known example today is Enron, the corporation that made headlines in the first years of the 21st century for corruption, greed, and corporate negligence. The Enron legacy has continuing currency in that the lack of reflection was simply astonishing. When asked what the company did, many had difficulty giving a clear answer. Their stammering sense of confusion should have suggested what later became apparent—they were not sure of their direction or purpose because the company was engaged in an elaborate shell game in which the moving of financial assets was more important that the actual creation of a product or provision of a service.

We witnessed this same communicative stammering a few years earlier than the Enron debacle as numerous companies that had never made a profit sought investments in the misplaced magic and unmitigated hope of emerging technology. The technology hype called us to invest in something that was not yet and never would be. As companies, one after another, collapsed, we noted the obvious—their potential never emerged. Investment in a vision is a necessary business risk. Investment in an inarticulate project, however, is simply a mistake; it is ambition propelled by greed.

Any time there is a lack of clarity about what exists, there lurks the potential for a communicative ethic devised to assist a few, with the hopes that many will not catch on to the hoax of a project that has no aim but hides behind a curtain of unreflective action. For example, Wells Fargo created millions of fraudulent savings and checking accounts without their clients' knowledge. The bank was encouraging their employees to sell multiple products to consumers for various incentives. The bankers were able to set the new account pins to 0000, allowing for bankers to enroll unknowing consumers in various banking services. Many of these new accounts incurred fees that were unknowingly paid by the consumers who were enrolled in online bill pay. Wells Fargo is paying $6.1 million to refund customers for unauthorized bank and credit card accounts (Egan, 2017).

Organizational communication ethics assumes that there is no end to ethical monitoring and that there is no pristine answer to many questions in organizational ethics. There is no way to assure ethical conduct without question. However, policies and procedures that seek to provide appropriate transparency begin to offer a conceptual map that permits us to ask, "What has been and what is the good this organization seeks to protect and promote?" and "What kind of dwelling place results and what communicative practices does it, thereby, welcome?" Communication ethics literacy suggests that the congruence between the community of memory and ongoing practices announces the good that an organization seeks to protect and promote. A community of memory can change, but while it is operative, it provides a public story-laden map for what a given organization considers the good. Given the multiplicity of understandings of the good in this historical moment, public clarity of purpose, mission, and organizational good is the common center of guidance and eventual change (Arnett & Fritz, 2003).

Pointing to a Dialogic Ethic in Organizational Communication

Organizational communication ethics points to a dialogic ethic in the manner of listening, attentiveness, and negotiation. The following model summarizes a dialogic ethic applied to organizational communication, highlighting major points in this chapter.

1. *Listening—without demand: What is happening in a given moment? Whether we like or dislike that moment, we must engage the question(s) of a given moment.* An organizational communication ethic begins with attentiveness to what constitutes a given dwelling place.
2. *Attentiveness: What are the coordinating grounds upon which stand the self, the Other, and the historical moment?* Attentiveness to the character of a given dwelling place and its manifestation of a given good that requires protection and promotion defines an organizational communication ethic that shapes self, Other, and responsiveness to the historical moment.

a. *The ground of self (the ethical/narrative commitments that guide us) and*

b. *The ground of Other (the ethical/narrative commitments that guide the Other)* point to something beyond the communicative partners, to a relationship of persons, organizations, and institutions that defines communicative life together in organizational settings.

c. *The ground of the historical moment (elements of the time in which we live, including "relational time" of the persons in conversation).* The ethical ground that shapes organizational communication ethics for self and Other is attentiveness to a community of memory and to communicative practices that remain alive and responsive to the demands of a given moment without losing the character of a given dwelling place. A dwelling place is not static, but changes with the demands of the historical moment and contributions of participants while seeking to be respectful of the ongoing character that defines it as a particular dwelling place.

3. *Dialogic negotiation: What temporal communicative ethics answers emerge "between" persons, pointing to communicative options for action, belief, and understanding?* The organizational understanding of a dwelling place requires repeated negotiation. Negotiation reminds us of the consistency of change that keeps a dwelling place vibrant and possessed of a uniqueness of character carried by a community of memory and communicative practices ever tested by changing circumstances.

4. *Listening, attentiveness, and dialogic negotiation constitute temporal dialogic ethical competence. What worked, and what changes might now assist?*

a. *Evaluation/self-reflection (reflection upon one's own ethical/narrative commitments).* Attending to the question of what we do in organizational ethics is a deliberate self-reflection driven by the question, "What is the good that this dwelling place seeks to protect and promote, and how is that protection and promotion responsive to changes in communicative practices needed in this historical moment?"

b. *From knowledge to learning (the key is not to "tell," but to learn from the Other, the historical moment, and reflective understanding of communicative action).* There is no organizational communication ethic that is set in stone. Just as there are multiple organizations associated with a given institution, there are multiple dwelling places. Our responsibility is to engage the dialogue among a community of memory, communicative practices, changes in the historical moment, and the people and demands within a given organization.

5. *Dialogic ethics listens to what is before organizational members, attends to the historical moment, and seeks to negotiate new possibilities. Dialogic ethics is a conceptual form of marketplace engagement, ever attentive to conversational partners and their "ground," the historical moment, and the*

emerging "possible" that takes place in the "between" of human meeting. Organizational communication ethics listens to the stories that frame a community of memory, connects responsibility to the dwelling place, and attends to the inevitability of change reflected in communicative practices. In organizational communication ethics, the responsible organization follows what Seeger (1997) calls a sense-making model of organizational communication ethics—in this case, connecting one's responsibility to a particular understanding of a given dwelling place, not demanding that the organization do things "my way," following a particular community of memory at a particular time, ever attentive to the inevitability of change reflected in responsive communicative practices.

COMMUNICATION ETHICS: REFLECTION AND ACTION

1. Consider any organization or campus group of which you are currently a part. How would you identify the "community of memory" in that organization or group? Are there particular people who carry or represent this community of memory particularly well? Has the community of memory changed over time? If so, how?
2. What features of an organization are most likely to make that organization a "dwelling place" for you? Are there specific communicative actions you can engage in that will help make that organization a dwelling place for others?
3. Consider, again, an organization or group of which you are a part or of which you have been a member. What good does/did this organization or group seek to protect and promote? To what extent were members and nonmembers of the organization or group aware of that good?

ENGAGING COMMUNICATION ETHICS THROUGH LITERATURE: *LES MISÉRABLES*

When Jean Valjean (as Monsieur Madeleine) builds a factory to make glass beads, he designs the enterprise to work profitably and to produce prosperity for the entire town. As an institution, the factory must generate a profitable product. As a community of memory, the organization carries within it the culture of its founder. The practices of the organization reflect the concerns of the founder, shaping worker performance. He protects women employees as they work in a historical moment of few protections for working women. When finally persuaded to accept the office of mayor of the town, he uses this governing institution to work for the good of the people in the town.

Competing goods within the mayor's realm of authority emerge when Fantine is dragged before the mayor and the police for attacking a male citizen of the town after he had thrown snow down her dress. Fantine is to be taken to prison, but Mayor Madeleine sets her free. Javert challenges the attempt to free Fantine by citing the law to the mayor; the mayor counters with other laws that state his own authority to interpret the law. We witness opposing goods represented by two communities of memory vying for adherence, each protected and promoted by a different official within the organization identified as the town government. Valjean knows that the communicative practices of decision making shape what we hold as good, framing a community of memory that offers a corporate identity for those within a given organization. Valjean's life and communicative action remind us that a community of memory requires not only an ongoing story, but also those willing to keep a given memory alive and robust. Dwelling places rely upon communicative practices and communicators unwilling to take an organization, whether a business, family, or town, for granted.

Intercultural Communication Ethics

Before the Conversation Begins

> Arendt's reflections and analyses as a social and cultural historian show . . . that such matters of "distinction" and "difference" are never merely individual but always concern the identities and social positions of collectivities. (Benhabib, 1996, p. 28)

Intercultural communication ethics protects and promotes the "good" of a particular culture, understanding culture as the shaping force behind persons and communities. An intercultural communication ethic calls us to protect and promote a given good—the culture itself. Our communication ethics responsibility is to learn about other cultures without presupposing that each culture is simply equal in ethical importance to another and to forego the assumption that the individual is primary—intercultural communication assumes that the culture is of first importance. The philosophical first principle of intercultural communication is that culture is a good that shapes individuals and communities and that this shaping has ethical consequences for persons and communities. After reading this chapter, you will be able to demonstrate the following learning objectives:

- Define intercultural communication
- Illustrate the importance of culture to communication ethics
- Construct an example of the inarticulate

Introduction

Intercultural communication ethics begins long before communication between persons commences; the communication finds nurture in cultural soil that offers either a common place for discourse or energy for difference and learning as we meet those nurtured differently than we were nurtured. Intercultural communication ethics reminds us that our communication begins with a context that predates us; it is the background scene that makes sense of foreground communicative action. Intercultural communication highlights the importance of difference in this historical moment.

This chapter connects the study of intercultural ethics to communicative practices with attention to the following four metaphors of communication ethics praxis:

1. **Intercultural communication**—the study of differences and similarities of cultural content and its influence on persons within and across different cultures.
2. **Culture**—consists of communicative practices, traditions, and stories that give identity to a group of people. Culture is a communicative background that provides meaning and stability to human life, providing an often unexamined sense of ground that makes foreground implementation of given communicative actions sensible within a given culture.
3. **Culture shock**—a feeling of disorientation experienced when encountering communicative events disruptive of one's expected routine.
4. **The inarticulate**—refers to goods that one is unable to define or pinpoint with precision, but that, nevertheless, shape and nurture a culture's communicative life and practices.

Student Application: The Unfamiliar

A number of colleges and universities offer study abroad programs, providing opportunity to travel to other countries, attend courses, and learn another culture's language and communicative practices. Even if one chooses not to participate in such a program, one still encounters contexts highlighting the importance of **intercultural communication**, meeting different cultures within a common geographical space. The **cultures** of which we are a part shape our identity, providing meaning in our lives. **Culture shock** occurs when we enter a new environment or

▶

▶ culture, one in which we encounter the unfamiliar. Culture shock can take place on the first day of school, on the first day at a new job, or as we meet cultures contrary to our own, willingly or unwillingly. Meeting the unfamiliar helps us learn about other cultures while finding out more about our own. We experience the **inarticulate** when we cannot find words to describe our experiences to others. A first-year student, for example, may experience the inarticulate when attempting to describe campus experiences to parents or grandparents who never attended a college or university. Sometimes we experience the inarticulate when we attempt to account for what we value, finding it difficult to express in concrete terms the reasons for our ethical positions.

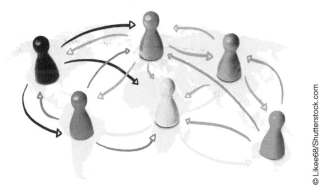

© Likee68/Shutterstock.com

Intercultural Communication

The study of intercultural communication has grown in importance with increased recognition of the changing demographic makeup of the United States and other locations, increasing awareness of a global economy, and the need to coordinate communicative activity in an ever more diverse workplace. The work of Molefi Kete Asanti (2002), William Gudykunst (2003, 2004), Bradford 'J' Hall (2005), Judith Martin and Thomas Nakayama (1998), William Starosta (Starosta & Chen, 2003), Stella Ting-Toomey (Ting-Toomey & Korzenny, 2002; Ting-Toomey, 2011; Ting-Toomey & Dorjee, 2015), and Kwame Anthony Appiah (2006, 2007, 2010), to list only a few representative scholars, have followed and expanded the work of Edward T. Hall (1973, 1976, 1990) and Clifford Geertz (1973), among others, forging important inroads in the communication discipline, establishing recognition of difference and diversity in speech communities and supporting understandings of the good in communicative practices.

In addition to recognition of intercultural difference, the work of Clifford Christians and Michael Traber (1997) offers a minimalist set of goods shared across cultures, suggesting that within great diversity lies the possibility for minimalist common ground. Their position is consonant with Sissela Bok's (2002) insights about the importance of minimalist value agreements and is a repudiation of some who attempt to turn postmodern awareness of difference into a technique that refuses to examine the possibility of temporal common ground.

Cultural differences work to provide us with insights. They also offer conflicts that tear up schools, communities, countries, and regions of the world. The power and force of difference in such places reminds us of the importance and the difficulty of difference. Yet, we can no longer assume commonality; difference is the norm. Stella Ting-Toomey (2011) discusses intercultural communication ethics as recognizing the embedded nature of ethics within a culture. Ethical practices become unreflective cultural habits. Ting-Toomey suggests that meta-ethics permits one to scrutinize and evaluate a given set of ethical practices/habits within a culture. Meta-ethics is the product of cultural knowledge beyond a limited provincial setting. The assumption that the world is smaller in that we can travel and communicate throughout the global community quickly is now commonplace. At the beginning of the 19th century, it took several days to travel by boat from New York to London. Today, at the beginning of the 21st century, it takes seven hours by plane. The travel time is quicker and the problems of the global community enhanced. We now know more about one another, and the evaluations are not always positive. Culture matters more as our connections to one another become closer. The hope of learning from one another needs to dominate intercultural communication ethics. Diversity will not cease, and the defining communicative element of this moment is that our awareness of diversity continues to increase.

Learning in intercultural communication ethics is central to a textured view of human life and perhaps to the very existence of the human community. Differences and similarities across cultures offer opportunities for learning in a postmodern moment and for negotiating temporal agreement. Intercultural communication ethics incorporates learning about different goods, the discourse that arises from and shapes the texture of those goods, and practices that enable constructive conversation in a postmodern world of difference. Kwame Anthony Appiah (2006) encourages learning from difference in a world in which we encounter inevitable Otherness. He assumes agreement on some universals across cultures, but recognizes great local variety in what cultures consider worthwhile and important. To live together we must learn from each other and from different ways of life. He argues in support of an ethic of cosmopolitanism, which refers to our obligation of concern for all humanity, for those beyond "our kind," while recognizing that particular loyalties to the local are equally important. Kathleen Glenister Roberts and Ronald C. Arnett (2008), in their edited book, *Communication Ethics: Between Cosmopolitanism and Provinciality*, explore this issue within the field of communication.

Culture

Culture at macro and micro levels is often unknown by in-dwellers, those with birthright connections to a given culture. The reason for their lack of knowledge or awareness is that one usually views the communicative actions of one's own culture as an unreflective norm, as the right way of life. One notices one's own culture when learning about another culture through meeting that culture, either by one's own initiative or when a stranger comes into our midst and begins to work in a contrasting fashion, countering our cultural assumptions. For instance, in the United States, if one makes the A-OK sign with one's hand, it is a gesture of bravo and encouragement; yet, in many places throughout the world, the same gesture carries the meaning of a significant insult.

Talking to a student whose home county is China, who knows five languages, and who has traveled to multiple countries, one of the authors asked this question: "How does one learn about culture?" The answer frames much of the material that follows. The student replied: "Do not assume you know the culture of another or even your own. Learn about each culture—watch and attend to what does not work; at such moments, the culture resists imposition from another and yourself." Culture is the often unreflective home of the communicative practices of a people. Every communicative practice carries an implicit or explicit communication ethic that protects and promotes a given good. Culture is like an invisible house that becomes visible when we bump into the limits of the walls that direct our actions and our vision without our knowledge.

A person endowed with the title of *sage* has wisdom—wisdom about the culture. However, the postmodern sage does not offer answers, just a reminder—cultures shape the onlooker and the participant. Our task is to learn about other cultures and more about our own as a byproduct. Today, the task of a sage is to suggest without dictate of accuracy, keeping before us conviction and doubt walking together in a given communicative action. The book *Dialogic Confession* (Arnett, 2005) addresses Dietrich Bonhoeffer as such a sage, bringing both conviction and doubt into the meeting of cultural crisis in Nazi Germany. There are standard-bearers of such a unity of contraries who offer insight into a model of conviction about a cultural good that falls prey to neither the excess of telling that disregards the Other nor the deficiency of a relativism that eschews all judgment. Between the realms of telling and relativism lies a view of culture that is not neutral and is not beyond dispute and change; it works as a shaping, changing guide, protecting and promoting a given view of the good.

A Shaping Guide

Culture is akin to a guide in the wilderness who is so good at the task that the follower forgets how confusing the terrain would be without the leader. Such a guide discerns differences in signs and their significance, navigating a way ever so carefully through the forest. Culture is more like a close family guide in that we are born into a given ethical framework. It takes thoughtful communicative engagement to shift from one culture to another. The novel *Zorba the Greek* (Kazantzakis, 1996) reminds us of the power of culture. The plot is straightforward at the level of culture. An Englishman who knows books meets a Greek who lives life to its fullest without spending time reading what others claim life to be. The Englishman, known as "Boss" in the story, meets one "unusual" experience after another upon encountering a culture common to Zorba. The "unusual" is that which one has not experienced. Culture shapes us to think in particular ways, and when we encounter the unexpected, or even the unimagined, we find ourselves meeting the unusual, which is simply different from our own cultural expectations.

Culture is the symbol system of a group of people that gives us interpretive clues for what something means and the significance of a given event. One of the authors met with a student from another culture and suggested that coming to class on time is a necessary good if one is to succeed. The student, however, understood the notion of success in a culturally different fashion—if someone in the community or the family needed help, he would assist, which resulted in his frequent late arrival to class. The student was asked to write a paper on engaging a different culture with a dissimilar understanding of success, which he did with cultural insight into how different cultures view the term "success" and how unlike understandings carry with them differing views of the good. The course ended with the question, "How is bilingual different from bicultural?" The same student answered: "It is culture that tells us the meaning of the words—it is a deeper form of language." The student offered important insight: culture is a deeper form of language; the student got it right and continued to come to class late, taking care of others before he thought of himself. The encounter with this student was a reminder that cultures do not treat the individual in the same fashion. Not all live in a place where the Other takes second place to schedules, requiring people to rush off in the middle of a conversation to get to an appointment on time. Not all cultures answer the door immediately.

One of the authors recalls working on an Indian reservation in New Mexico and remembers driving up to a house where he was supposed to meet a person, who saw him and walked into the house. Upon ringing the doorbell, no one answered. Later, after the author knew the person better, he asked, "Did you see me drive up that first day, and did you hear me ring the bell?" The answer was simply, "Yes." Later came the obvious question: "Why did you not come to the door?" The answer was simple: "The time was not right." The author had entered a place where time was different than he had anticipated and where the importance of one individual, namely, the author, was less than he imagined.

Individualism

From the mores of the United States, the assumption is that individuals are central, particularly when the individual is "me"; it is difficult to be part of this culture and to think otherwise than one's taken-for-granted cultural assumptions. Most members of an individualistic culture assume that each communicator engages an action or idea autonomously. The irony is that what "I" think is universal or true for all is, at best, a cultural presupposition and, at worst, cultural imperialism. The communicative supposition about the importance of the individual is derivative of a particular culture; the assumption does not originate with a single person, but resides within given cultures. The West—the United States, in particular—has a dominant cultural assumption: the individual is the point of communicative origin.

Perhaps the first detailed description of this culture began with the first suggestion of the dangers of individualism published in the participant-observation work of Alexis de Tocqueville (1830 & 1835/2000). *Democracy in America* offers a textured look at an American culture at that time, identifying issues that face us today. The importance of culture's shaping of the individual is no more evident than in the construction of the term "individualism." To take individual action and ideas as autonomous is not a reality, but a cultural construct. Tocqueville's initial detailing of individualism made clear the cultural construction of what many of us take as a human reality with universal appeal; he coined the term "individualism" as action that forgets cultural roots by acting as if it is possible to stand above all that shapes us. Tocqueville understood that individualism is derivative of or emergent from a particular culture, a product of a given culture. Perhaps it is our taken for granted love of individualism that makes culture shock a reality when we stand on soil that reminds us that life begins and ends without "me" (Arnett, in press). Intercultural communication ethics keeps before us that there is a before and an after. If "I" am the tree, there may not be noise in the forest when the "I" falls, but there is a forest that will nurture the next tree.

Culture Shock

When students travel to another country for the first time, they are likely to experience culture shock. The term "culture shock," introduced in 1954 by Kalvero Oberg and popularized in the book *Future Shock* by Alvin Toffler (1970), which built upon and expanded the concept by noting the rapid pace of change in today's society, continues to have relevance. Culture shapes us within a sense of the routine. When the routine fails, we find ourselves in shock, missing a cultural background that had previously given tacit meaning to our communicative lives. Culture shock, a natural reaction to the unexpected and unfamiliar, needs a thoughtful response; simply giving free rein to our distress is no longer a helpful response to changes in the expected. For the 21st century, a pragmatic reaction to culture shock is learning.

In daily conversation with one another, we differentiate the terms "shock" and "surprise." The difference between shock and surprise rests in the dissimilarity between something novel and unexpected and an unusual turn of events. The totally novel is what generates a "paradigmatic" difference, and the unusual turn of events is a paradigmatic addition or variation rather than a paradigmatic difference or change. For instance, movement from the horse to the automobile was a paradigmatic change. Movement from a sport utility vehicle to a truck is a variation within a given paradigm.

When we are in an environment that is akin to our own, we are more likely to experience paradigmatic variation. However, when we encounter a culture that is quite different from our own, we experience culture shock. The differences in culture within the "West" are often paradigmatic variations and the differences between "East" and "West" sometimes paradigmatic differences. The events of the first and second World Wars support the view that paradigmatic variation is no easier to engage than paradigmatic difference. Sometimes our first impulse is to find those who are like us, only to discover that variation can be as difficult, if not more so, than the notion of difference. For example, even within the United States, persons moving from rural areas to urban communities can experience culture shock from what appears to be paradigmatic variation. Paradigmatic variation tempts us to assume that we understand the Other better than we do, causing us to consider the other's actions wrong rather than different when contrary to our own. Culture shock gets our attention quickly with its disruption of the routine.

Whether the culture shock is engagement with paradigmatic change or paradigmatic variation, it introduces a disruption in how we think. When traveling abroad with others, one often hears how tired another is. The fatigue comes from the work of travel, but it also comes from disruption. We feel different when habits and conventions are not our own. Phrases emerge that announce our desire for routine: "I cannot wait to sleep in my own bed again," or "I am ready to go back to school." The pattern of everyday life is important for many of us. We find a sense of comfort in doing what we have done. Walking a well-trodden path offers a sense of comfort. Boredom does not come from engaging the same pattern; boredom comes from a sense of disappointment that what meets us is not more interesting. When we meet life in its patterned cadence, we do not find boredom; we find comfort. Sometimes we do not recognize the importance of the pattern as comfort until it is no more. As one grows older, lament often follows a phrase like this: "If I could only have one more conversation with . . ." We miss what was in the pattern of the everyday. Our fatigue emerges in moments of culture shock that require us to engage the different, the paradigmatically unfamiliar. As one student suggested, one needs to sleep well in this historical moment, because learning is demanding—we experience fatigue as we meet communicative cultural events that act as rhetorical interruptions, disrupting our normative patterns.

Difference as Rhetorical Interruption

Meeting another culture is a journey into difference. Often there is excitement in the first hours, days, or even weeks of a new place or a new culture. Eventually, however, most of us begin to miss the familiar, our own cultural home. As a friend stated, "No matter how I try to act differently, each time I travel or study abroad, I remember who I am—an American, encumbered with all that goes with our culture." Another colleague who teaches on a Protestant campus says, "I now know why I am Catholic." The same is true of Protestants on a Catholic campus. Ironically, when one has encountered great diversity as a routine experience, one may experience "commonality" as a type of difference that functions as a rhetorical interruption when one finds oneself in the presence of others similar to oneself. For instance, a white, middle-class student educated on a university campus marked by diversity of nationalities, political perspectives, and religious orientations may experience culture shock when taking a job in a small town composed primarily of white, middle-class citizens with homogeneous political and religious perspectives. We begin to grow weary of meeting rhetorical interruptions in our routine life. Lack of the routine takes us to the phrase, "I am homesick." Rhetorical interruption is the disruptive factor, calling our sense of home into question. A rhetorical interruption is simply a communicative event that disrupts our sense of the routine.

Rhetorical interruptions startle lives. Few of us would volunteer for a constant meeting of difference. Such is the reason that when students go to another country, many want to associate only with students from their school or their own country. It is difficult to have one rhetorical interruption after another intrude upon one's day. A student visited France with the hope of using French in the stores as quickly as possible. As soon as possible, the student went to purchase some local pastries. During the exchange with locals, he became confused, only to have the people in the store begin to laugh. Such rhetorical interruptions remind us that we are on the outside looking into a culture other than our own. The irony is that the rhetorical interruption is what permits us to learn; it is the reminder of difference. Charles E. Morris III, in "Context's Critic, Invisible Traditions, and Queering Rhetorical History" (2015), makes a fundamental theoretical and practical point: What is left out, what goes without stressed importance, shapes cultural history. What we bring into view, an awareness that has gone ignored and forgotten, reconstitutes our understanding of the past with insights from the present. When such moments happen, we recognize that we are not participants, but onlookers in a much larger world than we had earlier imagined.

When students travel to another culture, preparatory conversation needs to center on two issues: (1) learning from difference and (2) maintaining or acquiring one or two hobbies one can do anywhere. For example, a violinist can play anywhere and reconnect with the familiar. A serious athlete finds opportunities for exercise anywhere. Difference, rhetorical interruption, and learning require us to work from some base of the known. The routine permits us to find a place to go for comfort, offering energy for the next encounter with a person who is not sympathetic to the plight of a stranger. Our task is to discern what to keep and what to let go in our communicative engagement with the routine—when to change and when to resist.

The Local—Change and Resistance

There are times when cultural change enters one's small town, church, or place of work. What happens when a German or Japanese company purchases an American company? What happens to the people in a company who must adopt new ways of engaging work and, at times, defend old ways of doing labor? We can no longer assume a world of routine, even in our daily expected tasks.

© Arina P Habich/Shutterstock.com

On the other hand, too much routine will move us to rejection of all that is unfamiliar. A major stage production that announced change within the local was *Fiddler on the Roof*. At times, life makes us change our commitments to the routine, finding intercultural transition in our own small towns, where we must now ask ourselves, "Why do we have a '*Fiddler on the Roof*'?" The question meets the strangeness of the action and the silence of the person who lives in the village and is uncertain of the answer to a question that has the potential to disrupt local lives.

The musical production *Fiddler on the Roof* continues as a powerful announcement of disrupted routine within the local. The play announces change in many areas of ordinary life: reliance upon a matchmaker, falling in love with someone, the clash of a local ethnic culture meeting pre- and emerging revolutionary Russia. The town is no longer the same the moment the play of change begins with a glimpse of our ongoing question, "Why a '*Fiddler on the Roof*'?"

The production is about change in the local against the backdrop of the struggle for tradition. The play reveals the enduring power of tradition when accuracy is not the guide. For example, when Tevye talks, his description of his Jewish heritage is not always accurate, yet the power of his presence as a representative of that tradition is beyond dispute. It is the power of culture without complete accuracy that reminds us why tradition that offers resistance to modern fascination with efficiency and accuracy draws adherents. Culture resists by refusing to give itself up to simple accumulation of information—accuracy can actually miss the point of the power of the culture.

Tevye talks to one of his daughter's suitors, Mendel. The point of the conversation below is not simply change that disrupts tradition, but the humorous impression of Tevye's memory of the tradition:

Tevye:	As Abraham said, "I am a stranger in a strange land . . ."
Mendel:	Moses said that.
Tevye:	Ah. Well, as King David said, "I am slow of speech, and slow of tongue."
Mendel:	That was also Moses.
Tevye:	For a man who was slow of tongue, he talked a lot. (Jewison, 1971)

A culture is more than accurate data accumulated for precise recitation.

The facts Tevye recites are wrong, yet his commitment to the tradition is without question. Tradition does not rest on 100% precision, but on a general sense of direction that offers insight and meaningfulness for others. Once one gives up the demand for routine and for precision of detail, the power of culture shock begins to fade, and the manner for learning another culture begins to take on currency. A culture finds life in the precision of fuzziness and lack of articulation. Appiah's emphasis on "as if" and his stressing of "sorta" (2017, pp. 34–43) recognizes that truth dwells more often in mystery, a direction without complete closure, than in precise, pinpointed arguments. To understand another culture is not to add up a number of details about a people, but to be willing to meet the unexpected, the ambiguous, and the imprecise.

Intercultural communication is difficult for someone who enters a particular culture and wants to rely on information accuracy without understanding its variation and texture. It is akin to someone in a choir who has the correct pitch without the right tonal quality to blend with the rest of the choir. Sometimes, it is easier to work with someone without pitch or, in this case, no knowledge of the culture, than to work with someone who has all the information without the knowledge or ability to offer the appropriate tonal quality. In music, one speaks of someone with a "tin ear," unable to hear the pitch, but the real difficulty for a choir is a person with pitch and no sense of the appropriate tonal quality needed to be a member of a given choir. Finding the right language to explain how being correct can still be wrong requires a textured understanding that comprehends being on pitch and simultaneously hurting the overall sound of a choir. Such demanding moments take one into the home of the inarticulate.

The Inarticulate

It is the realm of the inarticulate that often governs movement from book knowledge to genuine participation. It is within the realm of the inarticulate that one understands the bodily connections of communicative life within a culture. It is within the inarticulate that one finds direction that guides without dictating—such is the home of culture, an invisible house that guides activities within it through its unique architecture. Using the example from earlier in this chapter, in the home of the inarticulate lies the answer to, "Why do we have a '*Fiddler on the Roof*'?" Tevye's reply might be as follows: "I cannot tell you why, but I can tell you that without the '*Fiddler on the Roof*,' we would not be who we are today."

Charles Taylor (1989) frames for us the power of the inarticulate. The inarticulate is the home of meaning that points without clarity of detail. In the book *Sources of the Self*, Taylor provides an analysis of "The Ethics of Inarticulacy" central to this discussion of culture. He begins by suggesting that qualitative distinctions are the foundation for moral and ethical beliefs; they form our identity. Qualitative distinctions shape our view of the good. These distinctions only make sense when held up against a given background; we make "sense of our lives in narrative" (p. 53). A cultural background works as an anchor for understanding the "good" and the "right." The background or the inarticulate functions "as an orienting sense of what is important, valuable, or commanding" (pp. 77–78). The orientation, the sense of guidance, rests largely in the inarticulate that makes practical reasoning in a given culture possible. It is the background that speaks loudly without clarity of voice.

The power of the inarticulate permits us to see public agreement on a given law and yet sense that it is wrong, beginning the movement toward change. It is "the understanding of the strong good central to much of moral life [that makes decisions possible]" (Taylor, 1989, p. 87). It is this form of background in a relationship that permits a friend to say the "wrong" words and, yet, for us to understand the "correct" meaning. The inarticulate of a culture works in the same fashion, permitting us to make sense of the unclear and to challenge the unjust, often without clarity of why such a position is in need of change. Taylor ends by suggesting that it is an uphill battle in modernity to reclaim the "qualitative distinctions [that] have an inexpugnable place in our moral life and thinking" (p. 87). His suggestion is that culture matters so much that it ultimately remains within the inarticulate, just as do the reasons for a great friendship or relationship—finally, the words fail, and one trusts in a vague sense of a power just out of reach of the right word.

The power of the inarticulate faces the danger of trying to speak prior to its readiness for utterability. In the inarticulate lives the saying of a culture that resists our moving all data into an information format for all to understand and list. The inarticulate resists modernity's demand for more efficiency, progress, and individual autonomy and withholds knowledge and insight that, if given up into a list, would destroy its power. Within the inarticulate rests the necessity of poetry and the heart of a culture.

Culture lives most often in the land of the inarticulate. The notion of gestalt is difficult to explain; the particulars are clearer—yet in the gestalt there is a resounding voice that appears, at first blush, inarticulate. Traditions live by a sense of gestalt—gestalt implies that something is greater than the sum of its parts. The gestalt of a culture lives in the whole; such is the reason Tevye can make mistakes and still be a major figure or representative of the culture. The meaning of events emerges from cultural background, telling us how to interpret and make sense of communicative action. Sometimes the words fail, and the answers emerge in the grace of the hands.

Watching the Hands

The question for intercultural communication ethics is how to learn from the inarticulate. For example, one of the authors grew up in a blue-collar family in which all the men worked on car engines. When one asked one of them about an engine, little information emerged. It was as if there were no knowledge of the engine, only wisdom in the hands of the mechanic. They could not tell you how to work on the engine, and, often, they could not even show you how to work on a given problem, but, somehow, they were able to fix the problem and make one engine after another work again. Indeed, the wisdom was in their hands. The learner, at times, can engage a culture by watching the hands, attending to the inarticulate, giving up, momentarily, the demand for analytic description. In the watching and the doing, one begins to feel the information—culture lives in the doing, not in book knowledge.

© Ivan Kulikov/Shutterstock.com

Such is the reason for language immersion programs. The key is to learn the grammar, to watch and takes notes, but, ultimately, being bilingual has little to do with notes taken as a student. The language lives in the doing of it—in writing, in speaking, in the meeting of the Other. If one has studied in an immersion program in another language, one begins to understand the inarticulate—such is the reason that some jokes are only funny in that language and the reason that some ideas only make sense within that language and in the manner of the body of the Other when speaking. After an extensive immersion program, there are moments in which one begins to think in the other language and then, eventually, to dream in that language. One begins to situate one's life within the articulate and, perhaps more importantly, the inarticulate of another communicative home. The reason that it is not possible to translate another language into English and understand its complexity is that the inarticulate refuses to give itself up for our analytic investigation—it lives beyond our reach, asking us to watch the hands of another.

The Guest

The phrase "to watch the hands of another" suggests that intercultural communication requires one to be more than an onlooker. One can use three terms to offer insight into engagement of a given culture. The first term is "stranger." This person refuses guest status and wants another culture to adapt to the self. This person works with conversation that wonders why people from another culture do not pay more attention to "my" own needs, the needs of the stranger. The person remains a stranger because the focus of attention is not on the Other, but on the self. The position of stranger is common to a culture where individualism functions. The focus on the self prevents one from learning from another—this philosophy has pragmatic consequences; it keeps one on the outside, not as a learner, but as a disgruntled consumer.

The alternative to the role of "stranger" is that of "guest." Both the stranger and the guest are on the outside; they are both onlookers. However, the line of demarcation between the roles of stranger and guest is the difference between an onlooker wanting another to conform to "me" and an onlooker seeking to appreciate and learn from difference. The role of a guest is no more or less lonely than that of a stranger; the significance comes not from being a part of another culture, but from learning. The focus on learning moves the stranger to the guest, invested with a spirit of appreciation and gratitude for the differences. Meeting another culture requires us to take on the stance of guest; we are not in the center or even on the periphery.

If one works within the guest role long enough, one begins to understand some of the communicative patterns and habits that shape a given culture. Such learning permits one to join the culture every now and then as a participant; such moments are akin to learning another language and beginning to think in that language rather than translate in one's head. As the role of participant becomes increasingly familiar, it is possible, though unusual, to become assimilated into a culture as an "indweller." The difference between a converted indweller and someone born into the culture is that the former will often have better articulate knowledge of the "why" and the actions of a culture than the person who was born into the culture and lives within the depths of the inarticulate. For intercultural communication ethics in a changing world, the metaphor of guest is central. We are onlookers trying to learn, with a basic assumption that our best approach to intercultural communication ethics lies within the pragmatic humility of the guest.

Pointing to a Dialogic Ethic in Intercultural Communication

Intercultural communication ethics points to a dialogic ethic in the manner of listening, attentiveness, and negotiation. The following model summarizes a dialogic ethic for intercultural communication, highlighting major points in this chapter.

1. *Listening—without demand: What is happening in a given moment? Whether we like or dislike that moment, we must engage the question(s) of a given moment.* Intercultural communication ethics is wary of demand, attested to by the importance of the role of guest as learner, which transforms one from the role of stranger to an onlooker with the possibility of increased participation.

2. *Attentiveness: What are the coordinating grounds upon which stand the self, the Other, and the historical moment?* Attentiveness to the embedded nature of being human within this living background called culture keeps the impulse toward a fictional version of autonomy at bay.

   a. *The ground of self (the ethical/narrative commitments that guide us) and*
   b. *The ground of Other (the ethical/narrative commitments that guide the Other).* The ethical ground that shapes intercultural communication ethics for self and Other is a commitment to something beyond the immediate communicative partners; it often rests in awareness of the importance of the inarticulate and in our patience in watching and learning from the communicative actions of another.
   c. *The ground of the historical moment (elements of the time in which we live, including "relational time" of the persons in conversation).* A culture is not static; it changes with shifts in the ongoing questions that move us from one historical moment to another. Culture carries both a resistance to change and adaptability through responsiveness to eventual changes.

3. *Dialogic negotiation: What temporal communicative ethics answers emerge "between" persons, pointing to communicative options for action, belief, and understanding?* Intercultural understandings negotiated again and again create a circle of understanding in which more knowledge of another culture assists insight into one's own, which then assists insight into another culture. As this circle of learning continues, intercultural and local understandings find more depth and texture.

4. *Listening, attentiveness, and dialogic negotiation constitute temporal dialogic ethical competence. What worked, and what changes might now assist?*

   a. *Evaluation/self-reflection (reflection upon one's own ethical/narrative commitments).* Attending to the question of what we do in intercultural communication ethics requires constant attentiveness due to an ongoing circle of learning that navigates between the articulate and the inarticulate, the local and the unknown.

   b. *From knowledge to learning (the key is not to "tell," but to learn from the Other, the historical moment, and reflective understanding of communicative action).* There is no intercultural communication ethic that is set in stone, but our responsibilities to engage both the local and the unknown do not lessen.

5. *Dialogic ethics listens to what is before communicative partners who are culturally different from one another, attends to the historical moment, and seeks to negotiate new possibilities. Dialogic ethics is a conceptual form of marketplace engagement, ever attentive to conversational partners and their "ground," the historical moment, and the emerging "possible" that takes place in the "between" of human meeting.* Intercultural communication ethics attends to a world of diversity and difference, learning from Others different from oneself. As the good of culture finds protection and promotion, so does the good of learning about other cultural practices and habits. Devoted engagement with the unfamiliar, whether across the sea or right next door, requires, as Kim (2005) reminds us, that we remember that intercultural engagement is the place of learning. Intercultural communication ethics begins learning by watching the communicative behavior of the Other and resisting the initial impulse to tell—"This is not how we do it at home"—and, in the words of Arendt and Kant, invites an "enlarged mentality" that moves from unreflective critique to the role of guest.

COMMUNICATION ETHICS: REFLECTION AND ACTION

1. Think back on the transition from high school to your entrance into the college or university environment. What changes did you experience? Would you describe them as culture shock? Why or why not?
2. How does "comfort" relate to culture shock?
3. What advice would you give someone encountering difference, whether through a study abroad program, moving to a different location, or entering a new organization?
4. Discuss the difference between a stranger and a guest. What implications does this difference hold for communication ethics?

ENGAGING COMMUNICATION ETHICS THROUGH LITERATURE: *LES MISÉRABLES*

In *Les Misérables*, intercultural communication arises within national boundaries. A culture of poverty continues to clash with a culture of privilege. Marius, son of a baron, engages life as a pauper to honor his father's loyalty to the French revolution upon expulsion from his grandfather's house for such loyalty. He learns what it means to have almost nothing, to work hard to make ends meet, and to live outside a life of privilege. He lives through the culture shock of leaving a life of comfort for a life of "never enough." Jean Valjean, likewise, enters a new culture of a respectable life. He changes his engagement of the world from that of a convict to that of a mayor and protector of a town. His care for the town and its people illustrates responsibility in communicative action; he does not make this responsibility explicit in his words, but lives it through his deeds, making visible the inarticulate commitment to the good into which the bishop had invited him.

Javert, the police inspector who hounds Valjean throughout the novel, also moves from one culture to another. Born in a prison himself, he enters a society whose margins he expected to inhabit, finding, instead, a place within a culture strange to his birth through participation in law enforcement. He embraces the culture of the police force fully. At the tale's end, he encounters one last culture shock when he understands Jean Valjean, a criminal in the eyes of police culture, to be a just and generous man. This unexpected encounter is too much for him; he cannot adapt to a new, changed world, a world with destroyed foundations, vanished from under his feet. He becomes a guest in Valjean's world, just for a moment, only to have his own world changed from the meeting. Intercultural communication ethics begins with the guest and continues with the courage to meet what the guest finds in the encounter with the unknown. The role of the stranger offers protection from a new culture that one does not really engage. The role of the guest takes us to a vulnerable stance—in *Les Misérables*, it is the guest who finds his life changed forever. The vulnerability of the guest emerges with learning, learning that transforms, that never leaves the learner untouched or unscathed.

Business and Professional Communication Ethics

Direction and Change

> Core values are the organization's essential and enduring tenets—a small set of timeless guiding principles that require no external justification; they have *intrinsic* value and importance to those inside the organization. ... The key point is that an enduring great company decides *for itself* what values it holds to be core, largely independent of the current environment, competitive requirements, or management fads. Clearly, then, there is no universally "right" set of core values. (Collins & Porras, 2004, p. 222)

Jim Collins and Jerry Porras (2004) end their best-selling book, *Built to Last: Successful Habits of Visionary Companies,* with simple, straight-forward advice—have a plan and be ready to change it the very moment that plan no longer meets necessary objectives and goals. In short, one must change what no longer works, no matter how well it once assisted. They remind us that there is absolutely no "cookbook recipe for success" (p. 248). Collins and Porras point to a basic ethical assumption for profit and nonprofit organizations—continue to last, providing goods and services that meet the needs of a given moment, keeping people employed. The goal of "continuing to last" is the "good" that requires protection and promotion in business and professional communication ethics. When people depend upon a given organization for their livelihood, continuing existence of the company becomes the baseline good. To keep a company going requires attention to the ongoing dialectic of direction and change; they work together as a unified guide for communication ethics action. After reading this chapter, you will be able to demonstrate the following learning objectives:

- Define business and professional communication
- Justify the importance of the dialectic of direction and change
- Create various opportunities for public testing

Introduction

Business and professional communication ethics literacy requires us to read the public direction of the organization as defined by its mission and purpose and to discern necessary moments of change. Keeping the focus of attention on core values permits clarity of vision to guide enduring public direction while permitting innovation to renew products, services, and persons. It is the dialectic enactment of direction of a company and change that announces the character, the identity, and the company type of a given business. The baseline good is survival that is attentive to the manner of protecting and promoting the distinctive character of a company.

This chapter connects the study of business and professional ethics to communicative practices with attention to the following three metaphors of communication ethics praxis:

1. **Business and professional communication**—the study of communication within particular business and professional settings, defined by participation in the public square of competitive economic exchange. Nonprofits must take the market and its demands seriously, just as a competitive business does; today's marketplace requires both types of business and professional settings.
2. **The dialectic of direction and change**—willingness to follow a particular path with the courage to move in a different direction when necessary.
3. **Public testing**—the good of continuing to last rests with a public testing responsive to both known and unforeseen demands of the market.

Student Application: Finding Direction

As one prepares to enter the marketplace, **business and professional communication** ethics assists understanding of various work settings. Graduating seniors are often concerned about making good first impressions on resumes and in job interviews. The goal is to gain entrance into a professional community where one can grow and acquire further experience. Of course, one's first job is not that of

▶

▶ CEO of a company, but through the communicative unity of **direction and change**, the path to leadership can emerge. For persons and for organizations, direction and change "push the envelope" in the marketplace, keeping people and organizations competitive in a context where **public testing** of direction, ideas, products, and services occurs on a day-to-day basis. Public testing keeps you and the company in step with the recognition that consequences occur as a result of our actions, keeping the ongoing reality of direction and change at the heart of business and professional communication.

Business and Professional Communication

Business and professional communication addresses form and style of communication—discourse protocols—in business and professional settings. Business communication shares some common ground with organizational communication, managerial communication, and corporate communication, but with significant areas of distinction (Shelby, 1993). Organizational communication, for example, addresses the entire scope of organizational action, including the macro or structural level of communication processes. Business and professional communication works at the micro level of organizational action, addressing issues of written persuasion, including routine letters, memos, and email correspondence, public presentations, and professional forms of discourse in the workplace. It deals primarily with specific written and spoken task-related communicative activities and emerges pedagogically in courses such as Business and Professional Communication (see Arnett, McKendree, Fritz, & Roberts, 2006), Communication for Business and Industry, Professional Presentation Skills, and Communication in the Workplace. Research in business communication spans a number of areas, including characteristics of business letters (e.g., Tebeaux, 1999), performance evaluations (e.g., Gueldenzoph & May, 2002), interviews (both hiring and exit) (e.g., Mandel, 1974; Marks & O'Connor, 2006), and supervisory discourse style (e.g., Jameson, 2001). Scholarly work in professional communication examines discourse from a number of perspectives—as messages produced by and to professional groups (Freed, 1993), as manifestations of professional culture or identity (Berkenkotter & Huckin, 1994), as rhetorical practices for legitimating professional identity (Day, 2000), and as oppressive or hegemonic practices (Wall, 2004).

Our approach acknowledges these perspectives and employs a communication ethics standpoint to highlight protection and promotion of a particular good that underlies the practice of business and professional communication as a public communicative act. Currently, questions of public virtue yield increasing discussion of human flourishing. Various versions of virtue ethics emerge in the work of Janie Harden Fritz (2013), Surendra Arjoon, Alvaro Turriago-Hoyos, and Ulf Thoene (2018), and a recent publication by Alasdair MacIntyre (2016). In earlier work, two of the authors framed professional civility as a good for business and professional communication (Arnett & Fritz, 2001, 2003; Arnett, 2006a; Fritz, 2013). This chapter takes a more baseline view, assuming the good of survival and competitiveness with the caveat that *how* one protects and promotes this good makes all the difference in the identity of a company and the character of a given business and professional communication ethics commitment.

Business and professional communication ethics assumes no one recipe for long-term success, only one truism—a business must embrace a unity of direction and change in the actualizing of the communicative goods of survival and competitiveness if it hopes to last. The title of *Built to Last* translates in this chapter as building, renovation, and constant improvement (Arnett, 1999, p. 80) if one intends to protect and promote the goods of survival and competitiveness.

The Dialectic of Direction and Change

Commitment to direction and change assumes that the presumptuous belief that a given place will exist for all time is dangerous. Only attentive response to the interplay of direction and change assures such a chance for survival. Otherwise, only temporary market windows make a given business viable. Business and professional communication ethics works with the assumption that direction and change together make it possible to respond creatively to ever-changing market conditions. Such an understanding of communication ethics makes public the

© Delpixel/Shutterstock.com

nature of creative engagement with the product or service, keeping the interplay of direction and change an ongoing expectation of an innovative spirit that constantly realigns direction, ever recasting the identity of a given place of work. Business and professional communication ethics is communicative action that embraces and actualizes contraries.

A Unity of Contraries

Communication ethics in business and professional settings requires a commitment to two complementary communicative actions: (1) clarity of direction and (2) the courage to pivot and change direction if and when necessary. This chapter views the communication ethics good of business and professional contexts in accordance with Martin Buber's notion of the unity of contraries (Buber, 1948)—business and professional communication ethics protects and promotes the good of the unity of direction and change.

The union of direction and change protects and promotes the good of survival and competitiveness. This view of business and professional communication ethics offers clarity and insight into the unethical: an environment with an unwillingness or inability to change, on the one hand, and, on the other hand, a commitment to change that moves too easily in response to demands and pressures, unresponsive to a reflective tradition. Unethical business and professional communication ethics fails to acknowledge the dangers of both "full steam ahead," a tradition-saturated direction unresponsive to conditions for change, and a hyper-responsiveness that unleashes a chaos of change, unresponsive to and unaware of the substantive importance of a given direction currently in place.

A student government organization may run into trouble if the active leaders of the organization neither introduce necessary change nor cultivate prospective leaders knowledgeable about the institution's particular mission and culture. Two communication ethics principles emerge from attentiveness to these concerns: (1) do not waste people's time: have a direction; know where and why you are going, and (2) do not waste resources by unwillingness to change direction when needed. Each of these principles protects and promotes the good that one wants to last.

The metaphor of direction and change refers to assumptions underlying the forms of business and professional communication, recognizing that communicative forms may change when direction shifts. For instance, the adoption of more casual dress and informal interpersonal conversation accompanying shifts in management approaches and underlying assumptions about employees and the nature of work show a shift in discourse protocols in response to a change in organizational direction. The commitment to ongoing viability takes business and professional communication ethics from the realm of professional communicative forms, or "public manners," to something beyond manners—the how of protecting and promoting the existence of a company shapes the character of the company and its identity. Business and professional communication, in this view, moves the focus of attention to leadership responsive to both ongoing tradition and the need for change. Communicative protocol, the form and style of messages, and other communicative particulars of workplace life keep interaction smooth and functional, weaving together strands of coordinated interaction toward a productive and enduring future. Today's interdependent and globalizing economy requires attentive responsiveness in multiple areas.

Beyond Manners

Understanding business and professional communication ethics requires one to release a basic unreflective assumption—that a communication ethics commitment in business and professional environments is the equivalent of good manners and proper form. Our parents and our friends who deal with us daily want us to have good manners, and work colleagues hope that we exhibit public decorum in dress and interaction at work. In general, the good of manners provides a means of coordinating smooth lines of interaction (e.g., turn taking in public meetings, restraint in email messages, conversational tact), and the goods of survival and competitiveness provide a necessary heart for keeping a profit or not-for-profit company alive.

Our confusion about communication ethics in business and professional contexts begins when we situate "ethics" in a person rather than in the communicative call for public accountability. "Ethics in the person" suggests that if we have good people, we will have good business and professional communication ethics. In an era of narrative and virtue contention, such a strategy has limited pragmatic utility. At a base level of cooperation, business and professional communication ethics assumes a more modest stance, promoting the good of survival and competitiveness in the marketplace. Ethics is enacted in *phronēsis*, which discerns, in the midst of everyday life, correct decisions and directions with temporal truthfulness (Kopf, Boje, & Torres, 2011). *Phronēsis* assists one in navigating unknown problems in known localities.

The impulse to equate communication ethics with attributes of the individual, "me," walks us into a common temptation of thinking that only "good people," "people like me," can assist an organization. In a time of postmodern disagreement on what is and is not good, it is simply impossible to find enough good people who believe just as "I" do. The obvious example of this fallacy of agreement rests not in business contexts, but in church settings. All one needs to do is to attend to differences that pull members of a given church apart. In the words of a friend who works with churches: "It is difficult when so many 'good' people see 'good' only in themselves and in those who agree with them."

Additionally, there is a common temptation to list or describe all the behavior that "should" define communicating ethically in a business and professional setting. The reason for rejecting this temptation is that it does not give one communication ethics literacy. In fact, it takes one from being a reader of communication ethics in business and professional contexts to being a voyeur concerned about whether or not people abide by the code of manners that one has learned. The listing effort offers some, but ultimately very little, help in guiding genuine public business and professional communication ethics accountability.

Public Accountability: Plant and Pivot

Too often, a company can confuse public accountability with the listing of all the "shoulds"; such action is an epidemic in many magazines for the popular press, but such cataloguing has little benefit for real living and communicating within business and professional contexts. For instance, one of the authors responded to a request from a national magazine to provide 10 ethical statements that should guide behavior in a business and professional setting. The first impulse was to state that within at least one religious tradition there already exists such a list, and the followers are so contentious with one another that they have divided into numerous denominations and continue to divide to this day. This sense of contentiousness rests within not only the Christian tradition but within numerous belief systems and faith perspectives. The world displays daily the result of differences among varying religious commitments. It is important to note that the doing of ethics is not the same as the doing of religious communication, but both have in common the desire of many to use the terms as weapons against those opposed to "my" view.

The limits of a checklist, beyond the obvious assessment discussed in the previous paragraph, rest with a misplaced focus of attention. First, a list moves us to asking what persons are doing, not the direction the persons and the organization assume. Second, with the focus on individuals, the move to making ethics into a "fashion show" is but one short step away. A checklist can take away our responsibility for a communication ethics literacy that permits us to read and discern the good: What is the direction, and when and how should a given company change direction? The direction is the key to holding a given organization accountable. The notion of change tempers the assumption that any direction can remain unexamined and unchanged forever. Public accountability assists both internal and external constituents with ongoing learning about the changing demands, responses, and identity of a business and professional communication setting and its actors.

For there to be public knowledge of and accountability for the business and professional communication ethics of a given organization or company, one must provide a public map of how and why a given direction changed. Change indicates that a given direction is a penultimate, not the ultimate, good in business and professional communication. Business and professional communication ethics calls for public articulation of a given direction and the why for change of direction when called for. The importance of public articulation is most necessary in moments of pivot and change, when the direction moves differently.

The aim of a profit or not-for-profit company is to keep the direction clear and responsive to change; otherwise, those who demand the products and services and those employed by the firm find themselves undercut. If we go around the room, we will find numerous persons who watched a mom, a dad, a neighbor, or a friend lose a job after a profit or not-for-profit lost its way. Sitting in the city of Pittsburgh, we are witnesses to the collapse of steel mills, the demise of Westinghouse, and difficulties with one health care facility after another. When a company or service loses direction and no longer responds to change, the cost is immediate and long-term to individual people, to consumers, and to an economic region. In short, if one wonders whether direction and change are actually a communication ethics good, one has only to ask someone whose professional life confronted the following question: "Are there ethical consequences for a company losing its way, its sense of direction, its ability to be responsive to change?" The response may be, in the words of this section: "If only we could have seen it coming, planted, pivoted, and changed before this disaster. . ."

Martin Buber (1948) stated that a human being without direction falls prey to the demonic. This chapter assumes that business and professional communication ethics that adheres to a given direction without attentiveness to the importance of and need for change falls into a similar state, one of destruction. The livelihoods of many depend upon the practice of direction and change. Public accountability rests with the ability to offer a "why" for a given direction and the reasons for taking another course.

Public Testing

The first major test rests within a public account of the identity of a given business and professional context. A company without clarity of direction falls prey to atrophy and decline, unable to engage in self-critical examination and change. Business and professional communication ethics is the keeper of direction within a company, providing clarity for both internal and external constituents—offering a roadmap for direction and the why and how of change. A direction that frames a clear plan can and must change when tested in the marketplace.

A direction is a vibrant meeting of the marketplace, requiring vigilance internally and externally. Each engagement of business and professional communication requires connection to the ongoing direction of a company. For example, Alcoa is a leading manufacturer of aluminum products with origins in the Pittsburgh region. When Alcoa began to change its position from a regional to an international player, they chose a simple direction—safety. Every decision lived within the question of safety. The CEO at that time, Paul O'Neil, wanted Alcoa to be the safest company in its competitive area of expertise. Each decision had to increase a commitment to safety. The notion of safety sought efficiency and increasingly less risk for the company. The direction of safety was a form of communicative currency that shaped their business and professional communication. In this case, the direction worked and became the center of the company. "Safety first" was not a slogan—it was the direction that became the heart of the company. The successful business communicator must know that the key good for a company is its direction. The question that generated the change that brought about the focus on safety for Alcoa was not a lack of safety compared to competitors; the focus on safety was to garner evidence in the public arena of an ethic that would earn trust from both internal and external constituents.

The reason for the existence of Alcoa is to make a profit, primarily through aluminum, just as the task of a math teacher is to teach math. In both cases, what gives direction, offers a sense of heart, and shapes a given good that offers

identity is something unique and specific. The good is particular, not general—this insight works within the spirit of Benhabib (1992), suggesting the notion of the "particular Other" as an alternative to the George Herbert Mead's (1962) "generalized Other." What makes a heart, gives a direction, and shapes a given good is particular to a given place. Public relations, understood as global/local, is not provincial, but competes on a large scale while attending to the particular local manifestations of whatever one seeks to support (Kennedy, 2016). The legitimacy of "safety" as a direction for a company happens when it transforms a general direction of a company into a particular organizational identity that distinguishes it from other companies doing the same "general" thing. From this perspective, safety as a differentiating attribute is the heart, direction, and good of a given company.

To students who are seeking jobs, these insights suggest that one should know a company's direction—and when and how a company has pivoted and changed direction. One must ask, "What direction does the company have, and how is that direction compatible with the ongoing direction of my own career and work vision?" The test of a direction and of change begins with each hire and each person who decides to go to another company. The test is not in getting one's first pick for a job or in losing employees to another company, but in the "why" of the "lose"—a clear direction both brings people into a given workplace and moves them to another setting. The test of direction and change rests in public accountability for the direction and the change. In an age in which virtue and value agreement is difficult and all too often impossible, it should not surprise us that a clear direction united with a willingness to engage change will both attract and repel given employees.

© Fishman64/Shutterstock.com

Clarity of direction invites a particular group of persons and moves others to another place. One works with those who want to assist the direction with necessary change, encouraging others to find their way elsewhere. The day of pleasing all is no more, if it ever existed. The test is in the marketplace and begins with those hired at a given moment. The basic ongoing question is "Can you, with conviction, contribute to the direction of a given company?" As an executive from IKEA stated at an international conference on corporate reputation, in a world where companies hear so many calls to placate customers, IKEA moved in a contrary direction. The slogan in each store and factory is, "We do it our way." They have a direction that the market tests each year.

The pragmatic public test is in the market itself. Like an athletic contest, business and professional communication ethics must meet public testing. In this case, the good is not some aesthetic commitment to a series of ethics codes or guidelines, but the lifeline of a given organization in a dynamic and demanding market. Each year the former champions of given sports must prove themselves all over again before our eyes with public testing. Business and professional communication ethics works with similar assumptions—there is no good for a company that can stand for all time; it is the ongoing testing of the vitality of direction and change that will define the long-term success of a given enterprise in providing jobs, lives, and families with necessary support through success in the marketplace.

Public testing of direction begins with the demands of the historical situation of a company at a given moment. For instance, before the sport utility vehicle (SUV) was popular, International Harvester in Fort Wayne, Indiana, made an SUV and was committed to its success, only to confront the first major energy crisis in the late 1970s, which eventuated in the collapse of that company. If this company could have shifted direction with a small SUV that had great gas mileage, it might have made it to a time in which the SUV surpassed the van in popularity. They were very close to success, but failed because they were simultaneously ahead of the market and behind the market. Their timing was wrong, and people suffered. Now, we find that major manufacturers must pivot again with another energy crisis—asking anew, "What should the direction be?" The fundamental reason for housing a good within a direction consistently open to pivot and change is that some failures put at risk the health of industries and the many that count upon them for a livelihood. Without such a commitment, jobs and human lives suffer, going as the people at International Harvester did—from good jobs to looking for work.

Additionally, today, as commuters drive major roads into the city, they are amazed at the number of businesses, once vibrant, that are no more. If direction and necessary change fail to guide a company, then we have a violation of a good that was not protected and promoted, resulting in disrupted jobs, lives, and families of those who depend on clarity of business and professional communication ethics—direction and change. If you have ever been on a road trip, you probably know how easy it is to take a wrong turn and how hard it can be for the driver to admit the necessity of change. In order to stay on course, it is necessary to temper direction with change throughout the journey. The complementary coordinates in the good of business and professional communication ethics require communication ethics literacy that attends to direction and the "how," or way in which people pivot in the midst of change.

Temporal Direction

The unity of direction and change frames all direction as temporal; a given direction has a limited lifespan. Typically, a sense of direction goes unnoticed when all is going well in a company. However, in a time of change, attention to the direction of a company is essential for two reasons. First, direction shapes the use of energy and resources. Second, if one knows the direction, it is possible to engage necessary changes when and if needed. One cannot change what one does not know or understand. It is in the knowing engagement of a direction that the possibility of change is forever a companion.

Every athletic team needs to find its sense of direction. A team that finds its own unique direction will play beyond its ability, going beyond the skill level of the individual members combined. In professional athletics, we are now, more often than not, accustomed to watching individual players, not great teams. Yet, every now and then, a great team emerges with a clear sense of direction that permits excellence to emerge beyond the expectations of the talent level of the team members individually. Perhaps the possibility of a team's finding a sense of direction and working well beyond the addition of the talents of each individual member is what makes high school and college athletics attractive for viewers, whereas professional sports have moved to an increasing emphasis on individuals. A company, like any good athletic team, wants "stars," but finding "stars" who help define the direction and make others better is what moves a team or a company from the status of the ordinary to the status of excellence—from good to great.

Finding a direction for a company is more than simply discovering a market niche—it is the discovery of a way of interacting that offers shape to the products and the communicative form of an organization in a constructive fashion. This way of interacting includes and does not marginalize anyone who seeks to contribute to the work of the organization. Oppressive norms, immoral actors, and unethical imposition of ideas dehumanize and marginalize persons. Pragmatic communicative hope rests in the implementation of dialogue that seeks to learn while informing (Paquette, Sommerfeldt, & Kent, 2015). Imagine Devon and Daniel, who meet together to form a student association to volunteer at a local children's hospital. As they develop the constitution required by the student government association for this campus group, they work carefully to ensure a significant role for each member. They are committed to forming a group where everyone feels a sense of ownership for the work of the group. They believe that this way of structuring the association is consistent with the service-oriented purpose of the group.

The action of the group is intuitively consistent with communication theory understood by Calvin Schrag (1986), who articulated the notion of "communicative praxis." Understanding the good of direction in business and professional communication ethics requires the doing of direction as a form of communicative praxis. Schrag gives us insight into finding communication "on the move" with his emphasis on three prepositions that guide this work: doing of the "about," "by," and "for." Communication ethics in business and professional communication finds direction and the need for change when the doing of the "about," the "by," and the "for" no longer work in harmony with one another. For instance, when a company attempts to do what is beyond the reach of its expertise or mission—that is, when it fails to do what it does well (the "about")—it misuses those who must make the product (the "by") and it misinforms those who will use the product (the "for"). Of course, change must happen, but when it does, the "about," "by," and "for" must align; their alignment is the simple test of communication ethics seeking direction for an organization and its goods and services.

In the case of the student group seeking to serve the children's hospital, the "about" is service, the "by" is the student members, and the "for" is the children's hospital. If the children's hospital no longer requires the services of the student group, the "for" of the group will need to be revisited if the group is to last. They may discover that the new "for" focuses on children's concerns beyond the area of health care. On the other hand, an expanded "for" may direct them to other areas of the "about" of service related to health care, such as the elderly or the developmentally disabled.

Misalignment announces error and the invitation for decline, indicating that a real-life test is not calling forth a passing grade. Error rests with the unprepared and with the person who cares more for the preparation than for success. Take, for example, Company X, a long-time maker of baseball bats. Known for its outstanding craftsmanship with wooden bats, this company expanded with the American pastime of baseball. The company's plans were simple—do careful, consistent work with wooden bats, and the market will continue to assist your success. What the company did not expect was the shift in the interests of young people and the popularity of the metal bat. A business communication consultant offered them the following advice: "Keep your plan and grow smaller, or keep a part of your plan while also entering the metal bat market." The plan was careful and consistent; the change was from solely wooden bats to metal bats, plastic bats, and memorabilia. The change does not suggest that success is inevitable, but without the change, failure is likely. The business and professional communicator must know that only plans appropriate for the demands of today's market and a simultaneous willingness to change keep the possibility for long-term success. As change happens, the about, by, and for continue to work for alignment, co-informing one another. Business and professional communication does not walk away from responsiveness in product development or in communication ethics.

Communicative Responsiveness

The key to keeping a profit or not-for-profit company alive is responsiveness, defined by the test of direction and change in an increasingly competitive marketplace. Business communication tied to ethics dwells in overt codes, mission statements, and policies and procedures, but its primary power remains within habituated practices that guide daily interaction internally and externally in organizational life (Macklin & Mathison, 2017). Communicative excellence understood in terms of business and professional communication ethics requires public clarity that permits internal and external constituents to understand the identity of a given setting and persons working to propel a given public character

© garagestock.com

of that place. Communicative responsiveness begins with a plan that meets the needs of company and the market, a plan ever willing to shift, change, and reverse itself to meet the needs of success and excellence. The statement is that without a vision, the people perish. Business and professional communication ethics assumes that a plan and no inclination to stop and fix it when it does not work will assure limited life in a competitive market.

Each business and professional communicator must know the "about," "by," and "for" to understand the public importance of direction and change. Socrates discussed the unexamined life as not worth living (Plato, 1954). An unexamined communicative life of a person in business and professional communication in such a competitive environment is a sure recipe for failure. To fail to probe our communicative direction and discern the need for change is to live with the illusion that unexamined old methods or high school charm will propel long-term success. Such is simply no longer the case. Either know what you do, and why, or join the ranks of those no longer able to meet the competition that comes not just to one's own industry, but also to one's own neighborhood.

Communication ethics, in this case, walks hand in hand with a communicative excellence that must live or die in the marketplace. Business and professional communication ethics is not the same as our personal ethics. However, just as a personal ethic needs to protect the direction of our own lives, the same adage rests in a business and professional setting—protect and promote the public good of survival and competitiveness through public accounting for direction and change. Business and professional communication ethics rests in literacy attentive to one major demand—know the what, the why, and the how of the direction and reason for change in business and professional communication. Such knowledge does not ensure success, but it does enhance the opportunity to duplicate what works and evaluate the resulting communicative action, eventually changing it when success no longer follows.

Pointing to a Dialogic Ethic in Business and Professional Communication

Business and professional communication ethics points to a dialogic ethic in the manner of listening, attentiveness, and negotiation. The following model summarizes a dialogic ethic applied to business and professional communication, highlighting major points in this chapter.

1. *Listening—without demand: What is happening in a given moment? Whether we like or dislike that moment, we must engage the question(s) of a given moment.* Business and professional communication ethics rejects the demand of keeping a given direction forever in place. Direction is at best one concern, with the other being change; the ultimate goal is survival and competitiveness, assisting all those who depend upon the success of a given business and professional communication setting.

2. *Attentiveness: What are the coordinating grounds upon which stand the self, the Other, and the historical moment?* Attentiveness to survival and competitiveness as the good of business and professional communication ethics requires public accounting for how such a good guides a given set of people.

   a. *The ground of self (the ethical/narrative commitments that guide us) and*

   b. *The ground of Other (the ethical/narrative commitments that guide the Other).* The ethical ground that shapes business and professional communication ethics for self and Other is a commitment to something beyond the communicative partners, a good that keeps employment possible. Witnessing the financial and personal stress on a family and a community after a major business and professional setting has failed calls for the importance of this baseline good. The issue is not the survival of the fittest, but the survival of those with public accounting for the how and why of identity that permits internal and external constituents to support the project.

   c. *The ground of the historical moment (elements of the time in which we live, including "relational time" of the persons in conversation).* Business and professional communication ethics begins and ends with a commitment to a public relationship that requires public accountability.

3. *Dialogic negotiation: What temporal communicative ethics answers emerge "between" persons, pointing to communicative options for action, belief, and understanding?* The business and professional communication ethics understanding of how and why to survive and engage the market competitively requires constant negotiation through the ongoing communicative practices of

a unity of contraries of direction and change. We must negotiate the demands of the world before us, remaining attentive to a baseline good. Negotiation reminds us of the consistency of the interplay of direction and change.

4. *Listening, attentiveness, and dialogic negotiation constitute temporal dialogic ethical competence. What worked, and what changes might now assist?*

   a. *Evaluation/self-reflection (reflection upon one's own ethical/narrative commitments).* Attending to the question of what we do in business and professional communication ethics is a deliberate self-reflection that requires a public accounting for internal and external constituents.

   b. *From knowledge to learning (the key is not to "tell," but to learn from the Other, the historical moment, and reflective understanding of communicative action).* There is no business and professional communication ethic set in stone. The key is to link the baseline good of survival and competitiveness with the responsibility to account publicly for the how and the why of direction and change.

5. *Dialogic ethics listens to what is before business and professional communicators, attends to the historical moment, and seeks to negotiate new possibilities. Dialogic ethics is a conceptual form of marketplace engagement, ever attentive to conversational partners and their "ground," the historical moment, and the emerging "possible" that takes place in the "between" of human meeting.* Business and professional communication ethics listens to demands of the historical moment, providing a clear direction, accounting for change, and attending to a basic good—we keep people employed and are responsible for a public account of the manner of our so doing. In business and professional communication ethics, seeking a responsible good requires demanding and public action. Business and professional communication ethics does public relations with internal and external constituents, reminding all that what counts is not only what we do, but the public accounting for the how and why of the action. As 2006–2007 National Communication Association (NCA) president Michael Sproule (2007) suggested regarding the need for a discipline to pivot and change with public accountability as the historical moment changes:

> The majority of our forebears saw building the association as something ever primary. Beginning with our 17 founding members, whose mission was to carve out a new place hospitable to communication study, NCA continues as vital to protecting and advancing our particular epistemic. . . [As society changes and we feel] a call to address wider ideological currents in society, we project the life of reason outward along two lines; first, through engaged scholarship, and second, through research-informed commentary. (p. 3)

The dialectic of direction and change finds life in a commitment to research and development throughout a business and professional setting—making sure of the "why" of both direction and change.

COMMUNICATION ETHICS: REFLECTION AND ACTION

1. Identify a business or not-for-profit firm for which you could see yourself working. Locate its mission statement. What good or goods does this business or not-for-profit entity seek to protect and promote? What is its direction?
2. Many popular press books about change in business and professional settings address business practitioners. Locate one of these books and look through its contents. What recommendations does it offer for changing direction while maintaining consistency of a given mission?
3. Set up an interview with a manager or CEO of a local business or not-for-profit, educational, or religious association to discuss how this business or association has adapted to change over time, how it has provided "public accountability" for its actions, and how each change has maintained consistency, or lack thereof, with its guiding mission or narrative. How has the "product" of the enterprise reflected change and continuity over time?

ENGAGING COMMUNICATION ETHICS THROUGH LITERATURE: *LES MISÉRABLES*

In *Les Misérables*, multiple examples relevant to the good in business and professional communication emerge. If we consider French government as a business, we can see the metaphors of direction and change quite clearly. In prerevolutionary France, it was evident that life could not continue in the direction in was currently heading. The calling of the Estates General took place in order to locate means of change for a government rapidly losing money, credibility, and power. The public testing of the previous regime had failed. The good was no longer enacted, and new voices arose in protest. The latter years of the 18th century and the first half of the 19th witnessed attempt after attempt to locate the good within some means of government that would meet a "public test" with success. Progressive succession through monarchy, republic, empire, and restoration of monarchy marked the country's attempts to set a direction for improvement in society through change after change.

Considering the town of Montreuil-sur-mer as a business offers additional insights. Jean Valjean, as mayor or "CEO" of the town, pivoted and set a new direction for the town by enacting a number of changes: building a home for the elderly, setting up a free drugstore for the people of the town, and constructing new schools for the town's children. The public testing of these enacted goods brought forth results of increased health and prosperity for the town; these public outcomes confirmed the responsiveness, change, and subsequent clarity of direction under the mayor's leadership. Business and professional communication ethics lives in public communicative accountability—in the doing and the describing of the "why" of direction and change.

Integrated Marketing Communication Ethics

Coordinating Difference

An understanding of branding that absolves us of any responsibility as consumers does not fit into the metaphor of obligation as a guiding concept in IMC. Similarly, the negotiation of meaning of a brand or commercial narrative is a communication activity that requires participation from both parties. The metaphor of obligation includes the ideas of stewardship and the culture of discipline and guides us as consumers and producers, as buyers and sellers, and as managers and workers, all participating together in the branding narratives of IMC. (Persuit, 2013, pp. 47–48)

Integrated marketing communication is inherently ethical. This volume defines communication ethics as that which we attempt to protect and promote. There is perhaps no other communicative structure more designed to protect and promote a given good than integrated marketing communication. That is its task. The objective of this chapter is to explicate and illuminate the implicit in integrated marketing communication. The protection and promotion of a given good, a communication ethic, is not explicitly articulated but performatively engaged repeatedly in the enactment of integrated marketing communication. Protecting and promoting a given good requires ongoing integration in content, channels of communication, and responsive engagement with stakeholders and customers. Marketing presupposes a promotion of this good. Communication assembles integration and promotion of a given good or goods internally and externally recognized and engaged. This public presentation gives identity to an implicit good that drives the heart of any integrated communication enterprise. Note: integrated marketing communication does not presuppose one good. It presupposes a structure in which various goods are protected and promoted within an integrated marketing communication framework that yields public clarity about what is important to a given organization. After reading this chapter, you will be able to demonstrate the following learning objectives:

- Define integrated marketing communication
- Assess the public clarity of an IMC campaign
- Articulate the importance of integration for IMC

Introduction

Integrated marketing communication begins the moment an organization discerns what it seeks to protect and promote in a comprehensive marketing communication effort. The coordinates of integrated marketing communication involve content, stakeholders, and channels. The content is the carrier of a particular good that an organization seeks to protect and promote through integrated marketing communication. Channels carry that information to multiple constituencies, both internal and external, and customers in particular. In this historical moment, integrated marketing communication represents a tacit explication of communication ethics in the marketplace. From the perspective of this particular text, our objective is to make this knowledge publicly accessible and clear.

This chapter connects the study of integrated marketing communication ethics to communicative practices with attention to the following three metaphors of communication ethics praxis:

1. **Integrated marketing communication**—the study of communicative content that is engaged from a number of differing vantage points within the marketplace, incorporating the functions of advertising, public relations, marketing, promotions, interactive strategies, and all functions relating to an institution's audience.
2. **Public clarity and caution**—integrated marketing communication works to make the purpose and objectives of a business or nonprofit organization public, or, in other words, make transactions and opportunities in the marketplace transparent. IMC seeks to protect and promote the "good" of integration with

▶

▶ an implicit communication ethics assumption—integration makes the choices of market participants public and visible.

3. **Integration**—the importance of diverse ideas that come together to create a unique whole that is more than the combination of its parts—the whole is greater than the sum of its parts.

Student Application: Consistency of Message

Theo is the publicity chair of a student leadership organization. He is planning to send letters out to prospective members, recruiting from sophomores and juniors who meet the organization's grade point average requirement. He mentions to his advisor that he wants to use the school's logo on the letter. "Theo, that's a great idea," his advisor remarks, "but we need to get permission from public affairs." Theo asks why, and the professor explains: "The job of public affairs is to make sure the logo and any images associated with the school appear in a consistent fashion everywhere. They must also make sure that whatever goes out under the school's name reflects the mission of the school." Theo is now an account executive with an integrated marketing communication firm and recognizes the importance of having a consistent brand and image. He takes particular note of the alumni magazine he receives regularly from his alma mater and notes, with approval, that even though his school has moved from a college to a university, the image is consistent with the one he remembers as an undergraduate.

Integrated Marketing Communication

This chapter examines how the "good" of integration protects and promotes the careful use of communicative resources: keeping communicative content clear, inviting dialogue between parties, emphasizing the importance of the specialist–generalist, and inviting a sense of professional community. Integration unites

© Matej Kastelic/Shutterstock.com

communicative engagement with communicative content. The content emphasis of integrated marketing communication (IMC) lessens the possibility of IMC being a mere technique. IMC unites multiple content perspectives; it pragmatically textures communication information and action. IMC functions as a communication ethic that clarifies organizational discernment about the good or goods protected and promoted. Consider the case of GoPro, one of the fastest growing camera companies in the world. Its remarkable success is due to its integrated marketing communication campaign in which the consumer promotes the product. GoPro involved its customers by getting them to shoot footage with their GoPro cameras and posting it on YouTube. Thousands of videos are posted each day on YouTube with the word "GoPro" in their title or description (such as "Look what I shot with my GoPro!") (Landau, 2014).

Integrated marketing communication is not a form of second-order change that completely alters the structure of an organization. IMC engages first-order change, or what Karl Popper called "piecemeal" change (1957, pp. 64–70). IMC is not a structural revolution, but a pragmatic way to mobilize limited resources. A small company needs to marshal its funds and its energy in a directed manner. IMC permits and shapes clarity of direction. IMC offers a communication strategy for leveraging one's resources in a manner that makes the individual parts of an organization larger, verifying in action the influence of the gestalt, where the whole is indeed greater than the individual sum of the parts. IMC is a pragmatic communicative effort to enhance one's resources with clarity of direction.

The history of IMC centers on the communicative mobilization of information and organizational direction. A succinct and cogent introduction to the history of integrated marketing communication frames Chapter 2 of Jeanne M. Persuit's *Social Media and Integrated Marketing Communication: A Rhetorical Approach* (2013, pp. 31–52). Persuit begins her historical summary with the origin of integrated marketing communication, which emerged from Northwestern University, the Medill School of Journalism, in the late 1980s. She discusses the classic work in this area, *Integrated Marketing Communications*, authored by Don E. Schultz, Stanley I. Tannenbaum, and Robert F. Lauterborn (1993). The authors emphasized the four Ps (product, price, promotion, and placement), with a shift to four Cs (consumer wants and needs, cost to satisfy, convenience to buy, and communication) (Lauterborn, 1990). Integrated marketing communication unites the communicative enterprise with product access (convenience), product expense and value (cost), and finally, with the recognition that each of these three major considerations of cost, convenience, and communication are always evaluated within the eye of the customer.

IMC continued to develop theoretically and practically, incorporating use of digital technology throughout the business enterprise and pinpointing branding as essential for differentiation and recognition in a global marketplace (Persuit, 2013, pp. 54–56). Implementing IMC as a technique is unwise; nevertheless, IMC functions as a formula that yields the necessity of ongoing attentiveness to emergent results, both intended and otherwise. Results connect to the audience, the customer. The value of IMC pivots on public recognition and integrated use of communication processes that yield clarity and direction for brand, product, and organization.

Additionally, Persuit emphasizes the contributions of Tony Proctor and Philip J. Kitchen, who explicate the importance of IMC with an emphasis on four basic questions: What does the company stand for? What values character-ize the company? What are the performative accomplishments of the company? Who manages and leads the company (Proctor & Kitchen, 2002, p. 151)? These four questions frame articulately the significance of unification and integration of messages and all actions internally and externally relevant to a given company. Integration functions as an ongoing mantra, connecting all aspects of an organiza-tion. This integration announces an ethical obligation to discipline the doing, the conceptualization, and the iden-tity of a product, both internally and externally. Consider Chipo-tle, a popular fast-food Mexican grill that uses responsibly raised meat and organic tofu. The com-pany stands for bringing healthy food into the fast food restaurant mix. One of their values is acces-sibility of their food to everyone. Chipotle supports local farmers and plans to commit $10 million to help farmers meet their food and safety standards through education and training, financial assistance, and partnerships. Steve Ells, the founder and executive chair, focuses on high quality ingredients and excellent cooking techniques. He notes that these original aims have expanded to include concerns for where the food is grown and the social and environmental impact of the business—their vision is "food with integrity" ("Corporate Profile," 2017). Persuit's conception of IMC offers a profound reminder that organizational iden-tity emerges from practices, patterns, and consistency of product design and expli-cation. The goal of IMC is descriptive articulation of performative identity that emerges in the making, delivery, and discussion of all aspects of an organization.

© Studio Barcelona/Shutterstock.com

IMC has significant outreach and a continuing legacy in the communication field. We now turn to two essays, one from 2016 and the other from 2017, that describe the impact of integrated marketing communication in the United States and in Europe. Rajeev Batra and Kevin Lane Keller (2016) discuss integrated marketing communication as central to the unification of customer, brand, and media in a manner that articulates a "path to purchase" (p. 122). In their review essay of IMC, Batra and Keller detail multiple ways IMC has matured in use. The initial implementation of IMC was "top-down," imposed by executives (p. 132). A "bottom-up" emphasis on IMC starts with the very doing of life within the organization. The shift from a "top-down" to a "bottom-up" perspective brought IMC into every aspect of an organization (p. 123). Both models emphasize com-munication integration, and each centers on customer characteristics, context, and communicative necessity in framing direction. A "bottom-up" orientation expands the influence, and ultimately the power, of IMC within an organization, stressing the goal of learning from customer satisfaction and/or dissatisfaction in the discovery, use, and reflection on brand quality. IMC coordinates use of media, technology, and brand, being ever attentive to persuasion while one engages the particularity of customer responses, from initial glances to long-term product use.

The task of leadership is to learn from and respond to ongoing insights emerging from comprehensive engagement of integrated marketing communication. IMC assists with the marketing of a brand, but more importantly, performative action integrated throughout the organization and understood and identified by customers. IMC recognizes that direction comes from the product and the doing. Means and ends both count. Brands communicate; customer use communicates; delivery systems communicate; and organizational direction communicates. Leaders throughout the organization must attend to feedback emerging from IMC implementation and consequences recognized internally and externally.

IMC constantly evolves. Manfred Bruhn and Stefanie Schnebelen (2017) connect integrated marketing communication to the development of new media. The authors emphasize the linkage between IMC and new media in an era in which this channel of communication continues its key role in the marketplace. Social media calls forth an even more attentive customer-centric view of IMC capable of addressing ever-emerging social media markets. Bruhn and Schnebelen begin with a basic assumption: IMC is a fundamentally important communicative act that includes "integration, coordination and unification of communication instruments" (p. 464). And it is much more—IMC must link the customer to its ongoing concerns for integration. The emergence of the Internet necessitates increased alertness to a consumer-centric framework, as choice with social media facilitates customer knowledge about brand, industry, and purchases. The core of IMC in action includes two basic values: coherence and consistency. The customer is both a critic and a shaper of coherence and consistency. To ignore the results of data gathered on the Internet invites organizational peril. The authors contend that traditional IMC has moved from an emphasis on internal stakeholders to an increasing focus on external stakeholders. Their suggestion is that the origin point for IMC in a media-centric moment is the customer, which, of course, continues to include internal and external stakeholders. This understanding of IMC situates the customer as the pulse of IMC research and development. Ultimately, the task of IMC is to persuade, and the customer is the ultimate audience for this commercial rhetorical form. Persuit explores some of the problems that can accompany a corporation that ignores its publics (2013, pp. 77–93). User-generated content educates a company.

IMC traditionally attends to content, networks, and multiple stakeholders, moving from the heart of an organization to its exterior commitments. The additive dimension of a customer-centric IMC model uplifts the importance of relationships that shape insight and awareness about content, networks, and process. The customer-centric model offers another set of eyes on the content and networks that give rise to the implementation of integrated marketing communication. Linking

IMC to social media and to customers emphasizes the performative essentials of IMC, which functions as a fluid structure. This flexibility releases some control and gains creativity of insight, as multiple stakeholders from differing standpoints examine content and networks. The metaphor-in-action of fluidity emphasizes a relationship orientation that guides changes in perception and insight, ever fueling new ideas that can alter the implementing of IMC. The customer is not merely a link in the IMC chain, but the fulcrum point upon which new integrations in structure commence. Customers provide an outside glance that yields innovation through de-specialization. The expert can no longer constrain the movement toward excellence. The expert, just as the customer, is just one part of a process in creative flux that embraces one major objective: Integrate in a manner that invites success and does not fear the unexpected.

Public Clarity and Caution

The market makes knowledge of goods possible; the first introduction of ethics into this equation begins with discernment of whether or not we should buy. What permits this selectivity is careful attention on the part of the consumer, aided by clarity of IMC direction and messages. Integrated marketing communication begins with an implicit communication ethics commitment—make the message clear and coherent through multiple venues. IMC offers coherence and intelligibility, extending opportunity to customers to enact thoughtful product judgment.

Communication ethics literacy requires choosing to answer a fundamental question raised by Jacques Ellul—not whether a particular action *can* be done, but whether it *should* be done (1954/1964, p. 436). Integrated marketing communication helps us detect the answer to such a question. The communicative result of integrated messages in and through multiple channels offers more coherence and clarity of idea and product. Consider the case of a county facing a high number of feral animals. A no-kill shelter facing the problem of overcrowding and lack of space for animals brought to its doors knows that the easy solution would be to euthanize animals after a short period of time if no one adopts them. The shelter's mission, however, moves it to work harder to find homes for the animals. The shelter's answer to the question, "Should it be done?" is "No." Other shelters without this mission may answer the question differently.

Ideas Matter

IMC does not automatically ensure success. Ideas matter. Doing IMC well infused with a bad idea can result in the collapse of a company. IMC makes the message clearer, giving the consumer greater opportunity to recognize the core significance of a communication campaign. IMC offers public clarity to the fundamentals of a product line, and without genuine commitment to research and development, IMC brings customers into the reality of inattentive quality control. As information

becomes integrated ever more thoroughly, central product issues become visible in two ways: (1) what the company deems as important; and (2) whether the integrated message connects with product performance. Even dishonest messages open a communication ethics door for public evaluation and testing. Take, for example, the Volkswagen emissions scandal. Volkswagen wanted to sell diesel cars with enhanced fuel efficiency, but this enhanced efficiency came at a cost of high pollutant emissions. The manufacturers put a device in the car that, upon emissions testing, would shift the engine into a "test mode," during which the engine would meet EPA standards. However, when the car was on the road again after the test, the engine would move out of test mode and emit pollutants up to forty times above the acceptable U.S. standard. Subsequent tests of emissions under road conditions on a sample of diesel vehicles from multiple manufacturers, including Volkswagen, revealed the true emission levels. Now, the question people had begun to ask about how these vehicles could get such amazing gas mileage was answered (Hotten, 2015). In this case, IMC successfully articulated corporate character, which logically encouraged consumers to investigate other car manufacturers. Bringing ideas together in a concerted IMC campaign aids public protection of consumers, permitting the testing of claims with data from marketplace performance.

Once again, IMC does not curtail bad products or ideas. It works in a manner akin to free speech. The answer to bad free speech is not censorship, but speech that counters with the hope of the best insights emerging in the marketplace of ideas. As Arnett (1990) states, a commitment to free speech involves "the conviction that the best and brightest ideas can be discovered together in conversation" (p. 216). The lucidity of IMC permits ongoing debate and discernment. There is no assurance that we as consumers will make the "right" decision in a given moment, but IMC assists in the rendering of judgment as one connects clarity of message with marketplace performance.

Collaborative Attentiveness: A Scarce Commodity

Making correct decisions requires ongoing attentiveness, which all too often is a scarce commodity. Richard Lanham (2006), for example, argues that attention, not information, is the currency of the digital economy, opening a need for skilled communication practitioners capable of assisting consumers with their choices. For example, the Super Bowl generates millions of dollars in advertising revenue. A 30-second commercial costs at least $5 million (Michaels, 2018). The goal is to keep people watching, so companies have become more and more creative in their attempts to secure viewers' attention. Even in an age of social media, marketers recognize the importance of paying the high sticker cost for a Super Bowl ad that will reach over 100 million viewers who have come to expect interesting and compelling advertisements during this event (Disis, 2018). Attentiveness begins first with a recognition that an organization can and must learn from its public relations, advertising, and marketing. These communication functions inform those outside and inside a given company about what matters and how it performs. One may not know the specifics of a company, but one can sense its character from tone, direction, and performance. Message content persuades with its salience and its testability in the marketplace.

IMC assists product marketing and communication with internal and external stakeholders in an era of increasing diversity of constituents and market environment. Engaging diversity separates IMC as a communication ethic from a communicative lone wolf—acts of "bowling alone" (Putnam, 2000). IMC necessitates collaboration, which functions as its first ethical principle. It is not possible to enact integrated marketing communication in environments of communicative isolation. The cooperative nature of integrated marketing communication rejects the assertion, "Do not ask for permission, ask for forgiveness." This perspective represents the lone wolf and misses the integrative and cooperative heart of IMC. IMC questions communicative practices and actions that promote persons and ideas in isolation. IMC is the practical home of a communication ethic that walks into the marketplace and interprets otherwise than the convention of individualism.

IMC is cooperative and attentive, responsive to content, stakeholders, customers, and the marketplace itself. Apple, for example, is responsive to the dynamic technological environment and consumers' changing needs within that context. This company comes to mind

© Novikov Aleksey/Shutterstock.com

quickly as a prototype of IMC responsiveness. IMC not only seeks to integrate, but attends to learning as ideas are tested within the marketplace. IMC functions as an ongoing research and development site for creativity and pragmatic responsiveness to and with the marketplace.

Integration

IMC meets the marketplace as a pragmatic communication ethic, bringing philosophy of communication into practical application. Integration is a creative idea equivalent to fusion. Fusion happens when two hydrogen atoms are forced together with great pressure to form a different atom—helium. Something new and creative emerges from two formerly separate entities. Fusion is the practical metaphor for the conviction that the whole is greater than the sum of the parts. Such a practical philosophy guides research for a major energy alternative; this perspective drives IMC as a practical philosophy with communication ethics implications for the marketplace.

Integration provides coherence for messages and direction, unleashing unexpected creativity. IMC invites clarity of direction, frankness of response, and attentiveness to an emerging rationale for change. Such forthright communication permits admission of error in an IMC environment, calling forth a concentrated response to mistakes and insights not yet envisioned. No matter how many problems confront a company, success is likely if honesty in integrated response becomes a normative feature. IMC cannot assure success, but its commitment to direction and responsive meeting of the unwanted ever fuels the creativity of this communicative enterprise. IMC generates energy with direction and responsive change, working as a pragmatic unity of contraries.

IMC protects and promotes the good of the unity of contraries, recognizing that excellence emerges from creative tension, not seamless agreement. In this historical moment, integration continues to gather depth, breadth, and texture, moving far beyond the assumption of unreflective agreement. Content, brand, stakeholders, and customers shape direction and response to the marketplace, recognizing that IMC dwells within art that unites emotion and some rational allegiance to a given brand. A brand's involvement in the environment, reputation, image, and ethical issues—the list goes on—offers a fjord within which emotive integration enters the conversation. Tony Proctor and Philip Kitchen (2002) question a direct examination of brand without attentiveness to emotional allegiances outside the product itself. They connect an emphasis on emotion to a postmodern world of fragmentation. The authors suggest that integrated marketing communication must lean into the fragmentation and discover ways to add and clarify the *why* of brand loyalty continually.

Appropriately, as IMC continues in its influence, it must answer the challenges of questioning voices. For example, Lars Thøger Christensen and Simon Torp provide a critical counter to the integration theme (Christensen & Cornelissen,

2011; Christensen, Firat, & Cornelissen, 2009; Christensen, Morsing, & Thyssen, 2017; Torp, 2009). In an essay that they co-authored with A. Fuat Firat, they claim that the ongoing mantra of the importance of integration requires some resistance (Christensen, Torp, & Firat, 2008). Their primary caution centers around a basic organizational observation: When integration equates with consistency and smoothness of flow of communication, and organizations seek to quell or abolish the notion of barrier, fears about integration require attentive response. The authors articulate this historical moment as composed of fragmentation, identity confusion, and limited loyalty. Integration must address a jagged, fragmented, and uncertain world, taking organizations beyond a product, image, the company, and reputation into issues of responsibility and social issues, moving perhaps from a concentration on brand to an understanding of IMC as story, moving behavior in the marketplace into story-centered action. This understanding of IMC links well with the work of Hannah Arendt, a political theorist who described the difference between behavior and action. Behavior is isolated, but when behavior is told and understood within a public story, it takes on the realm of action (Arnett, 2013).

IMC is story-responsive, attending to context and creativity of application. IMC is a marketplace form of *phronesis*, or practical wisdom, that unites integration, learning, and flexibility of engagement. Integration has long-term staying power when attentive to context and ongoing enactment of *phronesis*. IMC protects and promotes the good of integrated creativity that does not presuppose ongoing imitation. IMC can shift and change. IMC embraces flux, flexibility, change, and responsiveness, because the customer, the environment, and the context provide important information that requires ongoing recalculation. IMC

© Mathias Rosenthal/Shutterstock.com

is a communication ethic in an era of narrative and virtue contention that both integrates and shifts with ongoing novel insight. IMC frames the importance of difference by bringing together integration and responsive change as a unity of contraries. IMC as a mere technique loses touch with this unity of contraries, but when engaged with integration and responsive change, IMC is a guiding commercial light for an organizational structure. IMC engages difference, the reality of no one answer, and the necessity to integrate that which will necessarily change. The unity of contraries of integration and responsive change forges the reality of difference into the performative heart of IMC. No one can utilize this perspective in the marketplace in this manner as a targeted-message campaign. IMC pivots upon reciprocal attentiveness to integration and shifting needs and characteristics of context and customer. In this historical moment, IMC functions as a dialectic, not as a uniform, reified voice.

IMC's concentration on integration maximizes the importance of content. In 1960, David Berlo framed a significant book, *The Process of Communication*. Integrated marketing communication remains for many primarily a process orientation; we understand IMC as principally the integrating of content. Of course, process is part of IMC. But, the conceptual core of IMC is not process but the gathering of content. Integration brings together content and attends to changes in context and marketplace, yielding an ongoing commitment to difference and change in the doing of integrated marketing communication. IMC understood as a communication ethic is fundamentally dialogic. New insights emerge between integrated content and continual responsiveness to the marketplace. In the "between" of a unity of contraries, creativity emerges as a natural outcome of IMC in action.

Pointing to a Dialogic Ethic in Integrated Marketing Communication

Integrated marketing communication points to a dialogic ethic in the manner of listening, attentiveness, and negotiation. The following model summarizes a dialogic ethic applied to integrated marketing communication, highlighting major points in this chapter.

1. *Listening without demand: What is happening in a given moment? Whether we like or dislike that moment, we must engage the question(s) of a given moment.* IMC assumes the importance of implementation and learning in the process of performative engagement. Listening without demand occurs as one learns from content, structure, networks, stakeholders, customers, and the marketplace. The task of IMC is not to force ideas, but to recognize and respond. Listening propels constant innovation in IMC.

2. *Attentiveness: What are the coordinating grounds upon which stand the self, the Other, and the historical moment?* Learning requires attentiveness to all dimensions of implementation. The goal of IMC is to pay attention before implementing, during implementation, and in response to the marketplace and all dimensions of IMC.

a. *The ground of self (the ethical/narrative commitments that guide us) and*

b. *The ground of Other (the ethical/narrative commitments that guide the Other)* in the engagement of IMC emerge from the unity of contraries of the integration of content and ongoing responsiveness to insights from the marketplace.

c. *The ground of the historical moment (elements of the time in which we live, including "relational time" of the persons in conversation).* IMC has a fundamental charge to market a given product and direction. This task requires knowledge of the historical moment—the questions relevant to a given period of time that lead what we conventionally understand as popular culture. Popular culture imitates emerging historically relevant questions. IMC, if it is to be highly successful, cannot imitate, but must respond creatively.

3. *Dialogic negotiation: What temporal communicative ethics answers emerge "between" persons, pointing to communicative options for action, belief, and understanding?* IMC is a particular ethic that seeks insight from the interplay, or the "between," of integrated content and marketplace shifts and changes. Attending to the "between" is an ongoing process of negotiation. IMC is a performative marketing vehicle in which creativity of direction emerges ever anew, negotiated again and again.

4. *Listening, attentiveness, and dialogic negotiation constitute temporal dialogic ethical competence. What worked, and what changes might now assist?*

a. *Evaluation/self-reflection (reflection upon one's own ethical/narrative commitments).* Attending to the question of what we do in integrated marketing communication is a deliberate self-reflection that the gathering of content and listening to the marketplace are two competing and ever relevant actions that permit self-reflection on IMC direction.

b. *From knowledge to learning (the key is not to "tell," but to learn from the Other, the historical moment, and reflective understanding of communicative action).* There is no integrated marketing communication ethic set in stone. IMC, properly understood, unites order and constant change. It is a learning model that yields clarity of direction.

5. *Dialogic ethics listens to what is before those in charge of IMC implementation, attends to the historical moment, and seeks to negotiate new possibilities. Dialogic ethics is a conceptual form of marketplace engagement, ever attentive to conversational partners and their "ground," the historical moment, and the emerging "possible" that takes place in the "between" of human meeting.* One cannot impose upon the market; one must respond to it with the uniqueness of one's product and direction. IMC requires listening, attentiveness, responsiveness, engagement, conversation, and a willingness to embrace the unity of contraries. The dialogic space of the "between" is the fulcrum that extends IMC into new ideas and creative options, keeping it ever responsive and changing. IMC manifests the intelligence of responding to difference in order to recast and reshape one's participation in the marketplace.

COMMUNICATION ETHICS: REFLECTION AND ACTION

1. Identify two companies or organizations that have been successful in their public messaging. What strategies did the companies use for promoting their brand and/ or product(s)? Compare and contrast these two organizations' strategies in terms of effectiveness in promotion.
2. Develop an integrated marketing strategy for an on-campus student organization that is struggling to recruit members. Identify the group's mission and generate a consistent, coherent approach that reflects the principles of this chapter.
3. Research a nonprofit organization (such as the March of Dimes) that had to change elements of its mission in order to adapt to a new historical moment. Assess the extent to which the organization maintained its long-term purpose and focus and the methods it employed to do so.
4. Identify an organization that is in decline (or has already ceased to exist). Using material from this chapter, explain its decline (or demise). What actions could organizational leaders have taken to prevent its decline or failure?

ENGAGING COMMUNICATION ETHICS THROUGH LITERATURE: *LES MISÉRABLES*

Jean Valjean arrived at the town M. sur M. and changed its fortunes by an ingenious idea that revolutionized the way imitation lignite, or black jet, was manufactured. Once the new method was in place, the products sold well, and the benefits became clear. The cost of raw material decreased tremendously, which allowed greater focus on manufacturing, increased attentiveness to workmanship, and a lower price for the product. Increased quality and decreased price benefited the consumer. As Jean Valjean, now known as Father Madeleine or Monsieur Madeleine, grew in wealth, he used his wealth to assist the town. He poured funds into the hospital. He renovated one school and built another. He opened a home for retired factory workers. He gave a job to anyone who needed it; his only requirement was that everyone be honest.

If we consider Monsieur Madeline as an entrepreneur, his integrated message was to do as much good as possible. In fact, it was his desire for a consistent, coherent, integrated message that finally convinced him, after many offers from the king and continued refusals on his part, to accept the appointment as mayor of the town. What changed his mind? An old woman reminded him that a good mayor could do much good—why was he shrinking back from the good he could do? This reminder brought his eventual acceptance of the office of mayor into integrated alignment with his prior actions for good to the people of the town.

Health Care Communication Ethics

Responsive Labor

> Health care is grounded in caring. It arises from a sympathetic response to the suffering of others. The humble fact of human frailty, of the inevitable brokenness and brevity of human life, shapes the range and depth of needs to which health care is a response. . . . The hallmark of health care need, at its most basic level, is therefore human vulnerability. (Dougherty, 1996, pp. 51–52)

M ost of us have been ill at some point in our lives, followed by the struggle of the rigors and demands of recovery on the way back to health. Additionally, we have witnessed illnesses of others, watching the emergence of good and, at times, painful resolutions of their struggles with declining health. Optimism urges us to assume that all gallant efforts toward the reclaiming of health will secure success. However, the human condition does not support such unfounded optimism. To understand health care communication ethics is to broaden our understanding of the notion of health, taking it beyond obvious optimism to an active place of communicative response, a place of hope. Health care communication ethics protects and promotes the good of responsive hope and the good of care for the Other in meeting moments of robust heath, normal difficulties, the tragic, and the inevitable. After reading this chapter, you will be able to demonstrate the following learning objectives:

- Define health care communication
- Assess your response to the experience of health and illness
- Apply responsive care with contextual and relational sensitivity

Introduction

Christopher Lasch (1991) differentiated between hope and optimism. Optimism falls prey to a consumer mentality of demand for life to conform to one's wishes; hope rests in the same desire, but, additionally, possesses a gritty sense of work and conviction situated within a realization that not all hopes actualize themselves. The key to hope is responsiveness, and the demand of optimism is expectation. For Lasch and this chapter, hope and optimism are as different as night and day. Hope endures even in the face of disappointed expectations; optimism fades when faced with the reality that life does not grant one's demand.

This chapter connects the study of health care ethics to communicative practices with attention to the following four metaphors of communication ethics praxis:

1. **Health care communication**—the study of communication practices within the broad domain of health care, from patient–professional interaction to institutional communication about health.
2. **Health**—the interplay of communicative responses to conditions of mind, body, and soul, from the beginning to the end of a life.
3. **Responsiveness**—responsibility that meets the call of the Other, even when the call is unwanted.
4. **Care**—a human answer to the call of the Other; a willingness to meet and attend to someone other than oneself.

Student Application: Responding to the Other

College and university students face the demand of balancing academic, social, extra-curricular, and internship experiences. These demands invite reflective consideration of **health care communication** in many domains, ranging from physical to mental to social. The issue of **health** focuses on how our physical, spiritual, and mental communication engagements meet particular standards of wellness. Our

▶

▶ health and the health of others matters. **Responsiveness** points to the way we engage others and ourselves in times of health-related need. For instance, a group of college students may engage in a weekly commitment to working out at the gym, renting movies for relaxation, and taking occasional road trips to experience the refreshment and renewal of "getting away." Responsiveness to situations such as a parent's life-threatening illness, a close friend's weight loss that jeopardizes her health, or a fraternity brother's all-consuming focus on grades to the point of exhaustion and irritability are all central to health care communication. As human beings face issues of health care encountered by friends and loved ones, we want to **care** for the Other. We do not want to see the Other experiencing pain and physical suffering. We want to assist but may not have the words to make things better. The key is to find ways to enact, in word and deed, responsive hope for another without falling into the abyss of optimism and demand.

Health Care Communication

As human beings age, issues of health care increasingly come to the forefront of our everyday lives. Gary Kreps (2006) comments on the importance of health communication: "Health communication performs a central role in the delivery of health care and the promotion of public health" (p. 768). Health care communication emerged as a distinct field of study in the 1980s, foreshadowing the debut of the *Journal of Health Communication* in 1996. The domain of this area is large in scope, extending from health communication campaigns in mediated contexts to patient/consumer–physician/provider communication. The *Handbook of Health Communication*, edited by Alicia Dorsey, Katherine Miller, Roxanne Parrott, and Teresa Thompson (2003), defines the scope of communication inquiry in health-related areas, identifying research in this expanding area of the communication field. The work of Lewis Donohew (Ray & Donohew, 1990), Athena du Pré (2016), Vicki Freimuth (1995), Patricia Geist-Martin, Eileen Berlin Ray, and Barbara Sharf (2002), Gary Kreps (Kreps & Thornton, 1992), Kim Witte (Witte, Meyer, & Martell, 2001), Michael J. Hyde (2005, 2012, 2016), and others has served to bring issues of health communication into the classroom and public square.Questions surrounding insurance availability and regulation, for instance, continue to provoke discussion among lawmakers as well as concerned families and individuals. The rising costs of medical supplies and life-saving drugs such as epinephrine injections require thoughtful attention to communicative responses regarding health. In this chapter, we turn attention to what we consider the heart of health care communication ethics—a responsive sense of hope in the ongoing meeting of questions of human health.

© Valeri Potapova/Shutterstock.com

Health

To be human requires acknowledgment of a basic assumption—health is a term that accounts for beginnings, endings, and intermediate moments, some of which are seemingly long and others short in duration. This convoluting of time is akin to thinking one will never get out of high school, only later to think that those years flew by. Additionally, as our days increase in number, our memories take us back to past journeys with questions of health—demanding moments with others in the final years, months, weeks, days, hours, and minutes of a life. Health care communication ethics, at its best, finds a way to respond to what Viktor Frankl (1967) called the final freedom, "the stand we take toward a fate we no longer can change" (p. 15). The goal of health care communication ethics is to protect and promote a sense of gratitude and knowledge of a final freedom—our response to health, its absence, and the eventuality of death.

This chapter connects health care communication ethics to an understanding of health that, in its fullness, points to what it means to be human—health care communication ethics assumes a life that includes vigor, its lack, and the inevitability of death. Lynn M. Harter and Arthur P. Bochner (2009) explicate questions of health care and issues of meaning of life and death within narrative rationality. They propose additional research in communication that examines and explores the notion of "narrative medicine." Health is a term that requires an adjective for us to know what kind or state of health is present at a given moment. To respond to the question, "How is your health?" requires some sense of what it means to be in "good" health, a narrative that defines health quality and permits us to report on our health with a modest degree of interpersonal accuracy.

At a social function for a not-for-profit organization, we witnessed such clarity of response in communicative exchange. A major benefactor must now carry oxygen with him wherever he goes. A young man came up to him and inquired, "How are you?" The man laughed and said, "How do you think I am? I must carry my own oxygen and answer questions like this." The benefactor laughed again and said to the young man, "Do something with your life. If this happens to you, then you, too, can provide responses that invoke guilt in the young to do something with their lives." The benefactor walked off into a meeting to assist an organization that would never function as well without him. The exchange was not a glib version of "nice," but rather an honest response that brought insight and laughter. In the presence of a physically ill member, one could sense health of spirit that inspired. As we walked away, we wondered whether this young man would remember that exchange when age no longer met him with grace. The young man had met health that defied the status of decline before him.

Responsiveness

The importance of describing one's state of health as a response makes all the difference—health care communication ethics rests in the response. Health care communication ethics understands health not in what happens to us, but in our *response* to that which meets us. Frankl's reminder of the notion of final freedom is central to health care communication ethics. When it seems that all roads that we seek to follow remain closed, our final freedom rests in our stand against the inevitable. Put differently, when life seems to offer no way out of a bad moment, apparently offering only a sense that we must swim with no dry land in sight, our final freedom frames a pragmatic question: "What do we do in those moments of treading water that seem to last forever, while we wait for the end—or until an unexpected rescue saves us?" The emphasis upon responsiveness as the final freedom identifies a pragmatic sense of tenacity that defines the best of the human spirit. The importance of response emerges from a pragmatic realization—when there is no longer an easy answer given to us, we must find a creative response that breaks free of our demand for options no longer available. At such a moment, we choose the manner in which we meet the inevitable.

Health care communication ethics is a dialogue with life, an ongoing set of responses that shapes our living as we prepare for our end. Within the communicative action of response rests the good of health care communication ethics. The action of response is the antithesis of equating health with a "demand" for life on our terms. As Martin Buber (1970) stated, dialogue necessitates response, as does our effort to invite a more comprehensive view of human health. Health care communication ethics is a call to responsibility defined not by demand or acquiescence, but by responsiveness.

The key for a health care provider, the patient, and the family is responsiveness. To engage health care communication ethics, one looks for ways to respond to the illness in the larger context of a life, not just for answers to "fix" ill health. For example, it is different to take medicine in a way responsive to illness than it is to take medicine with the assumption that it will fix the problem. We have more than one diabetic friend or family member who takes medicine to fix the problem and then eats large amounts of sweets. The medicine ceases to be a response and becomes an excuse that permits them to avoid taking responsibility for their health. The medicine taken with exercise and eating correctly moves the person to a sense of concern for health that requires—in fact, demands—responsiveness.

Nahum Glatzer (1966) edited a series of Martin Buber's writings/sayings in *The Way of Response: Martin Buber*. This title is illustrative of the heart of Buber's understanding of dialogue. The writings in this collection end with a short fragment, "Thanksgiving." There is one line that seems to capture the moment of a responsiveness that takes gratitude one responsive step farther—"This is the hour of Thanksgiving." Yes, this is the hour, the moment, the time of thanksgiving—when a human being steps forth in response to meet existence on its own terms—whether joy, sadness, or sorrow. Uniting final freedom and the notion of response begins to define an action-framed understanding of health care communication ethics. From one of the writing fragments, we find the following call to response:

> The kindling of the response in that 'spark' of the soul, the blazing up of the response, which occurs time and again, to the unexpectedly approaching speech, we term responsibility. We practice responsibility for that realm of life allotted and entrusted to us for which we are able to respond, that is, for which we have a relation of deeds which may count—in all our inadequacy—as a proper response. (Glatzer, 1966, p. 19)

Responsiveness is the responsibility for doing the task of health care communication ethics.

We have read about and witnessed celebrities' struggles with health and its absence within the public view, providing for us clarity of response that reminds us of an enduring human dignity under demanding life conditions. Accounts from the lives of Helen Keller and Lou Gehrig join the courageous actions of Christopher Reeve and Michael J. Fox to place front and center the fragile nature of what we deem good health and the importance of human response. Their public engagements with health and its absence display to us the power of response, permitting us to understand an expansive view of health befitting what Kant and Arendt termed an "enlarged mentality" (Arendt, 1982).

These public figures' responses are but tips of a human iceberg; they point to untold numbers of persons who live outside the public eye as unknown exemplars of human responsiveness, offering responses that display human courage, finding freedom in options apparently unseen by others. Such responses live in the actions of neighbors, family members, friends, and colleagues without fanfare or notice.

© rweisswald/Shutterstock.com

As lesser-known persons display responses of courage that go without public acclaim, they often rub shoulders with us. They remind us of the multitude of responses constituting this iceberg of human courage—our glimpses offer insight into the human spirit, health care communication ethics lived out in the domain of ordinary life. They remind us of the importance of responsiveness as a pragmatic move that meets not a fork in the road, but an opportunity for response that somehow creates a road not seen before.

On a daily basis, human beings engage courage to fight against and respond to the unwanted—the inevitability of decline. Our final freedom of response begins not in the moments before death, but in daily living, in repeated practice. Each time health not wanted by us meets us in our lives, we have the opportunity to practice the pragmatic necessity of response, readying ourselves for the final freedom—our response to the inevitability of death.

Health care communication ethics is no stranger to the demands placed upon us in our final freedom, an unwanted and unchangeable interruption that meets us all too often. Today, we write one day after the death of a colleague. One of the authors, in his role as department chair, sent a note to all faculty members about our colleague, ending that message with the only freedom available, a reminder of a long parade of persons working to make places better:

> This is a sad day. Yet, as I returned from the hospital Sunday night a student and parent wrote a note stating that the decision to come to Duquesne University came after visiting the campus—a campus that many lives who are no longer on this earth helped build. Clark is now part of that community. I will follow this student's career. At the right time, I will tell the student about Clark. The parade continues.

The words were not elegant, but, like those of Robert Bellah and colleagues (Bellah et al., 1991), sprang from a commitment to a *Good Society* that keeps before it the reality of a final freedom for those left behind—in this case, helping another in the memory of a colleague and friend. This chapter rests within that memory of a colleague, reminding the writers—perhaps more than the readers—of a final freedom that finds some way to invite a good health, seeking to build from the ongoing ashes around us. As put by a farmer colleague, we are called to build, and life on the farm reminds us of the hard work of building and the importance of what at first looks like bad stuff (manure) from which good growth comes. Our final freedom is to find a way to build when life before and around us refuses to conform to our demands. From such human tenacity grounded in gritty realism our responsive understanding of health care communication ethics springs. At its most graphic, the responsiveness of health care ethics is for the student whose younger sister is unlikely to recover from childhood leukemia, another whose beloved grandmother suffers from Alzheimer's disease, the student whose uncle is dying of AIDS, all of whom struggle with events that refuse to conform to their hopes for a life—and for all of us when existence simply reminds us that in such moments, our final freedom rests with how we respond.

The notion of a final freedom is not played out once, but one time after another. Human life has no replay, no reverse. We play out the notion of a final freedom day in and day out. Sadly, many of us miss the power and the necessity of understanding life as a meeting of final freedoms. Some of these moments are clearly more important than others, but each unredeemable moment requires our response. It is, indeed, accurate to view life as "play forward." There is no rewind, just our human response to that which meets us and in a blink of an eye is no more, calling forth a response from us that continues a constructive building activity, "playing life forward."

In an essay entitled "Administration as Building and Renovation," Arnett (1999) outlined the final freedom of an administrator as trying to find ways to build and renovate when all the obvious presenting paths remain blocked. Such a view separates leadership from management. Our final freedom in issues of health can build and renovate a life when a response finds a new path when the hoped for or demanded is no more. Bryonna, who is just finishing her junior year in college, is working to complete her classes while worrying about her 3-month-old daughter, who is still in the neonatal intensive care unit. Born prematurely, the infant shows very slow growth and development. Bryonna knows that her daughter is receiving the best possible care and recognizes that her own success in school is one of the best responses to this moment that she can enact—for herself and her child. In our response to a final freedom, we meet irredeemable moments that call forth a response, inviting our engagement of health care communication ethics.

No matter what meets us—whether joy, sadness, or sorrow—the human being has one final freedom: our response. Responsiveness is central to Buber's dialogue, inherent to Frankl's understanding of human meaning, and tied ever so closely to human health. Response is the active reaching out to another and to one's own problems. Responsiveness leads to communicative action that, when directed toward another, outlines the necessity of human care.

Care

What drives the communication ethics of health care is the word "care." Health care communication ethics seeks to protect and promote care—care is the communicative action or practice that links to the good of responsiveness to the Other. Health care communication ethics does not pivot upon the question of information; it stands firmly on the question, "How do we provide communication that cares for another?" Health care communication ethics points to an active, caring responsive to all stages of life, offering meaning through the doing of human assistance. Health care communication ethics protects and promotes care, human caring of one for another, in a professional context and in all contexts where decisions affect the quality of life and, all too often, life itself.

The importance of responsiveness points to a particular view of caring, one that calls forth our engagement with the human condition, requiring something of us—care. Lauris Christopher Kaldjian (2017) frames the importance of decision making in health care as a landscape that gathers the following coordinates: (1) patient centeredness; (2) evidence-based analysis; and (3) ends-based/purpose. A flourishing life requires health care attentive to patient evidence and the trajectory of a life. Simply put, health care communication ethics begins with a basic assumption about the human condition: we fall ill and lose, temporarily—and, someday, forever—our sense of robust health. Rejecting health as physical alone, health care communication ethics works with our final freedom, whether in practice or in the final moments of a life, keeping before us the importance of our response. This focus on responsiveness in practice and in the final freedom of humanness defines "care" as understood by health care communication ethics—care becomes the protection, the promotion, and the facilitation of human responsiveness as the defining characteristic of the good of health care communication ethics.

The temptation we seek to bypass is the question, "Why others do not care, and why is caring so difficult a response in health care?" There are a million answers to this sad question and one unfortunate reality: too much focus on this question moves us away from our own responsibility to respond and back to demand and consumption of what we deem as good. Our responsibility to care begins with a responsive first principle, foregoing the impulse to blame those who do not meet our standards of care. In essence, the emphasis upon responsiveness opens the conversation about what it means to be a doer of care, not a consumer of care.

We all benefit from care as consumers, and this work does not want to minimize the importance of campaigns that seek to assure proper care of the disenfranchised and those without necessary support (e.g., Kreps, 2006). Such work is, indeed, a responsive view of caring and is important to a society's understanding of the good life. Yet, this work begins with the assumption that something odd happens when the demand for caring begins to eclipse our own sense of responsibility to respond for ourselves and for others. The responsiveness of health care communication ethics moves us to another metaphor that unites such action: "the labor of care," a term coined by Marie Baker-Ohler and Annette M. Holba (2009). Baker-Ohler and Holba point to the importance and the power of health care communication as a labor of care.

© Spiroview Inc/Shutterstock.com

A Labor of Care

Baker-Ohler and Holba's (2009) "labor of care" metaphor depends upon the work of Nel Noddings (1984, 2012) and Julia Wood (1994) on caring. What offers important texture to the literature on caring is Baker-Ohler and Holba's engagement with the insight of Hannah Arendt. Arendt (1958/1998) understands three major elements of life as defining characteristics of the human condition: labor, work, and action. Labor is a necessity; it is required doing. For Baker-Ohler and Holba, care is a necessity of the human condition. Even in daily discourse, we hear acts of not caring described as "inhuman." To be human is to care; the labor of care is a necessity of our identity. Health care communication ethics reminds us of this necessity. We can argue about what the "right" labor is, and we should, but the necessity of a labor of care defines our humanness and calls forth responsiveness to the world before us.

Health and its lack are part of the human experience—communication about such moments meets us many times over the course of our years. Conversation that helps us find our way to health again from surgery, from a heart attack, from a sports injury, from addiction to drugs and alcohol, or from severe depression functions like a ladder permitting us to climb one step at a time from the abyss. This sense of climbing points once again to the labor-of-care metaphor, reminding us of questions of health and calling forth response, a labor of care in the meeting of illness.

Today, a young graduate student called one of the authors, talking to him behind the ever-erupting noise of tears. The student is an instructor who was very sick and losing her voice—the sound of illness met the author's ear. The student was very conscientious and did not want to miss class, but for the health of many in the class, as well as her own, she had to leave and go to the doctor. The labor of care that claimed the attention of the student was not some grand disease or the loss of a loved one, but simply a moment of feeling so bad that her assigned duties were beyond completion. In this case, the labor of care required admission of the illness, then thinking of others and staying home, and then thinking of herself and going to the doctor. It takes the engagement of the labor of care to admit illness and then to take proper action. For someone very conscientious, the admission of illness, the canceling of class, and a visit to the doctor requires a labor that shifts the care from the doing of normal work to the task of attending to health, one's own and that of others.

To climb back to health from a moment of inconvenience or a deep abyss as a patient or as a caregiver requires more than physical strength alone. Again, Frankl reminds us of meaning that bears the unwanted—in the concentration camps of World War II, the bespectacled, physically unimpressive, and apparently frail lasted longer in such dire circumstances than those of obvious outward health. The unexpected survivor found a sense of "why" to bear any "how"—as Frankl (1963) reported a famous quote from Nietzsche:

> A man who becomes conscious of the responsibility he bears toward a human being who affectionately waits for him, or to an unfinished work, will never be able to throw away his life. He knows the "why" for his existence, and will be able to bear almost any "how." (p. 127)

Health care communication ethics finds responsiveness in a sense of "why" that gives one a reason to bear the "how."

From Technique to Tenacity

To accomplish the enactment of a labor of care in the midst of disappointment, pain, frustration, and fatigue, we must find an engine for the doing of this care. In essence, a labor of care depends upon a sense of "why" that gives one a reason propelling the human tenacity to engage the "how" of the doing of care for oneself and for others. A labor of care requires an engine that keeps one going when the routine breaks and the demands of the inconvenient or the frightening are before us. It is this attachment of a sense of "why" to a labor of care that keeps health care communication ethics from becoming a technique, a simple set of actions learned in the abstract and brought to communicative life without attention to the specific needs and the specific face of another. Health care communication ethics requires labor and a "why" for the doing of what is beyond our normative request for a good life.

The labor of care needs an engine. In the vernacular of a child's story, care is "the little engine that could" be powered with the communicative fuel of responsiveness. Following this metaphor, one may ask, "From where does the communicative fuel of responsiveness come?" The answer makes us backtrack and consider responsiveness as a form of communicative energy. Trains of old developed over time, moving through multiple forms of fuel, from coal to wood to electricity, but the objective was the same—energy. Human beings find the reason to respond from many sources, each giving a sense of energy. This chapter does not examine what makes a human being respond; our task is more straightforward—acknowledging the importance of whatever it takes to find a way to assist oneself and the Other in thoughtful response. Our response permits the activation of care.

This chapter privileges the importance of having a sense of "why" for a communicative labor of care over the exact details of the process. Jacques Ellul (1954/1964, p. 436) identified the problem of our time as seeking to find techniques that focus us on the "how" of a given communicative action and prevent us from asking difficult questions related to the "should" of that action. The first step toward asking a "should" question begins with a sense of "why." In order to discern what should be done, a sense of "why" must propel the asking. The simple question of "What should I do to assist my own health and that of others?" begins not with a technique, but with a "why" that makes the very asking of the question important.

Health care communication ethics works with a good that gives us reason(s) to pursue health, endure recovery, and meet the ongoing demands and repeated anguish of human life. Each human face in health care communication ethics must find a "why" to meet the inevitable challenges ahead—meeting a life of finitude with an abundance that continues to offer light when the carrier of a given lamp passes the task to another. The Holy Grail of health care communication ethics is a sense of "why" that permits us to bear any "how." Sean, a freshman, has begun to experience the repercussions of very late nights out on the town and rising early to attend class. He has nodded off while taking notes and lacks the energy necessary to complete assigned readings. He does not want to disappoint his friends, who encourage these late night excursions and whose earliest classes begin at 1:00 p.m. Over the past month, Sean has noticed a decline in his exam scores, and several friends have accused him of being grumpy for no reason. As the end of the semester approaches, Sean begins to think of his long-term future and career goals. This "why" prompts him to redirect his efforts away from conforming to his friends' late hours. He still sees them occasionally, but the "how" for his renewed health and energy sends him to bed at a more reasonable hour during the school week.

There is no magic in communication about health, but communication that inspires and guides us is powerful beyond description. Sometimes this sense of "why" comes from theories and ideas, but most often it comes from a human face that reminds us of the importance of finding the tenacity to meet the demands before us. The courage and the conviction of this sense of "why" dwells in the eyes of a loving parent caring for a sick child, in the eyes of a son or daughter by the side of a parent in hospice, and in the eyes of an ally working against all odds with a friend battling addiction. It is as if a human face were taking mere aphorisms and bringing them to life. The old cliché of "when the going gets tough, the tough get going" sounds only like an overused slogan until a young athlete lying on a bed of ill health looks into the eyes of a favorite coach, and a phrase heard much too often becomes a form of real human magic. In these human faces, we find the power of a communicative good greater than the obstacles before us.

One finds more than a technique in a labor of care that begins with a sense of "why" elicited by a place of illumination—the face of another. Emmanuel Levinas is correct—one finds the light of ethics in the face of another. Levinas tells us that humans find identity from the Other, that without the Other there is no "I." Thus, one must take care of the Other or lose one's own identity in relation to that Other. From such a view, Levinas alerts us that the human face reminds us that "I am my brother's keeper" (Cohen, 1998, p. xii; Levinas, 1998). Somehow,

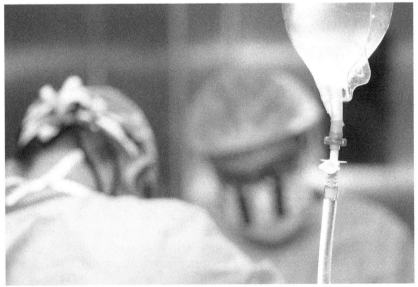

© sfam_photo/Shutterstock.com

some way, when a human face finds such a good, it becomes a sense of light that illuminates life for all those around—a light that offers a sense of "why" to enter a conversation that we do not invite. Health care communication ethics begins with human faces that remind us of the "why" of health and its end, offering hope for the dignity of life in the midst of a common cold and in what Martin Buber called the final moment in which one hand reaches out to another. Health care communication ethics is more than accuracy of information; it takes us close to the human heart, a heart that finds a "why" to carry on, somehow finding an antidote for our moments of loss, responding with tenacious hope to these words of despair: "I do not have the heart for this anymore." Into such a place one walks with care grounded in responsiveness with no answer in sight. Into such a place walks conversation about ends of lives, embedded in the fabric of family and directness of care. Sometimes deep concern for the Other calls forth the unwanted conversation made palatable by the thoughtfulness of those gathered in its delivery (Thompson, 2011). Health care communication ethics is a labor of care that propels us in moments of darkness and when a mist of confusion seems to greet us in our communicative life. Health care communication ethics carries a good that offers hope when there seems no hope before us, with a responsiveness that begins by getting out of bed, eating breakfast, putting one foot in front of another, and going through the paces of life—just because it is simply the next thing to do. Yet, in this "just doing" lie the seeds of health and hope in moments of despair and the loss of that which or whom we hold so dear.

In all cases, health care communication ethics centers on a good that gives us a "why" for seeking information, for seeking help, for a reason to fight, for a reason to think about others in the final moments of our own lives. Health care communication ethics protects and promotes the good of responsiveness that carries the possibility of hope in a discovered sense of "why" for engaging a situation that most of us do not want to encounter—the lack of one's own health, the illness of a loved one, or the terminal diagnosis of a friend. This understanding of a communicative good stands before us in a human face—the face of a child with asthma finding the courage of leadership in lack of breath, the face of a colleague living as a recovering alcoholic and survivor of two nervous breakdowns who finds the courage to change other lives, the face of a mother wanting to make one last trip to see a son just to say "adieu," the face of a father fearing old age and hanging on just to lessen the pain of loss in the family, and one friend after another with ghosts of ill health walking as shadowy companions—somehow all are sustained each day by work, by care for others, and by a responsive persistence best called a gritty sense of tenacity.

There is no technique for this understanding of care, just honest meeting of what is before us, a tenacious commitment to build and renovate in the midst of whatever is before us, a refusal to give in to what seems without hope, the practicing of one final freedom after another, a desire to respond, a recognition of the demands of this task as a labor of care, and, finally, a willingness to say that health care communication ethics lives not by technique, but by a tenacious response before the unwanted. Perhaps more than any other understanding or context of communication ethics, health care communication ethics reminds us of our humanness, a human face with a tenacious spirit, at its best unwilling to give up our fundamental human obligation—to respond, as Martin Buber would say, and to understand, as Baker-Ohler and Holba (2009) suggest, that human health rests with our responsiveness to a call to responsibility in an ongoing labor of care.

Pointing to a Dialogic Ethic in Health Care Communication Ethics

Health care communication ethics points to a dialogic ethic in the manner of listening, attentiveness, and negotiation. The following model summarizes a dialogic ethic applied to health care communication, highlighting major points in this chapter.

1. *Listening—without demand: What is happening in a given moment? Whether we like or dislike that moment, we must engage the question(s) of a given moment.* Health care communication ethics is wary of demand; the goal is to meet what is before us. The key is responsiveness to the "good, the bad, and the ugly" of life, fighting the common impulse for life to conform to our demand. Such a view is not the accommodation of resignation, but a constructive way of fighting to secure good health. The means of the engagement matter.

2. *Attentiveness: What are the coordinating grounds upon which stand the self, the Other, and the historical moment?* Health care communication ethics requires attentiveness to the nature of the response called for in the act of caring.

    a. *The ground of self (the ethical/narrative commitments that guide us) and*

    b. *The ground of Other (the ethical/narrative commitments that guide the Other).* The ethical ground shapes health care communication ethics for self and Other; it is a commitment to something beyond the communicative partners, a call to protect and promote human responsiveness, and a call to a labor of care.

    c. *The ground of the historical moment (elements of the time in which we live, including "relational time" of the persons in conversation).* The appropriate communication ethics response is not static and changes with the demands of the historical moment, finding reason for communicative action in a sense of why for maintaining a tenacious commitment to a labor of care

3. *Dialogic negotiation: What temporal communicative ethics answers emerge "between" persons, pointing to communicative options for action, belief, and understanding?* Health care communication ethics requires repeated negotiation in friendships, in relationships with significant others, within particular institutions and cultures, all working together to try to figure out the "best" response in a given historical moment for a particular person or persons.

Michael Hyde (2005) reminds us that discussion of the "post-human" is with us now. Change in what we consider human comes with altering what we define as outside the limits of our conception of humanness. There is no health care communication ethic that can offer answers to all the questions that confront us in the remainder of this century, but the keys of responsiveness and the labor of care for another will need to be dialogic guides.

4. *Listening, attentiveness, and dialogic negotiation constitute temporal dialogic ethical competence. What worked, and what changes might now assist?*

   a. *Evaluation/self-reflection (reflection upon one's own ethical/narrative commitments).* Attending to the question of what we do in health care communication ethics requires deliberation that embraces a "unity of contraries": the human face of a particular person and implications for a larger culture. Only constant monitoring of this dialectic will ultimately give us insight into the pragmatic consequences of our decisions.

   b. *From knowledge to learning (the key is not to "tell," but to learn from the Other, the historical moment, and reflective understanding of communicative action).* There is no health care communication ethic set in stone; as the historical demands change, so do our responses in health care communication ethics.

5. *Dialogic ethics listens to what is before communicative partners, attends to the historical moment, and seeks to negotiate new possibilities. Dialogic ethics is a conceptual form of marketplace engagement, ever attentive to conversational partners and their "ground," the historical moment, and the emerging "possible" that takes place in the "between" of human meeting.* Health care communication ethics listens for the call that invites a particular response, ever attentive to limits and demands that form responsibility for caring. Such caring, textured by the inevitability of changing health conditions and cautioned by doubt, alters one's view of health care and human possibilities. With so much before us in the way of demanding possibilities, our hope, which moves beyond an "optimism" that fails to take account of an unwanted reality, rests in the ability of human beings to continue to find ways to care linked to labor and human responsibility. Such hope links the "post-human" to the hand of those long before us in a continuity of caring as we seek to care when we do not know what the "right" answer should be in a given moment. Julia Wood (1994) asks the right question: *Who Cares?* The health care communication ethics answer is the communicator who is responsive, understands the labor of care, and is tenacious when optimism fails, taking up, instead, a gritty sense of hope that stands firm in a final freedom. There is no technique-driven answer, but there is much hope when caring finds response in health care communication ethics.

COMMUNICATION ETHICS: REFLECTION AND ACTION

1. Recall an experience of being ill. What responsive communicative actions from others were most helpful and most unhelpful?
2. Identify three different situations related to health, broadly considered (e.g., physical or mental illness, nutrition, exercise, or something else). What messages of care and responsiveness might assist someone engaged in these health-related concerns?
3. Bring to mind and reflect on two different friends or relatives who have experienced illness. How did their differing needs call for different types of care and responsiveness in those around them?

ENGAGING COMMUNICATION ETHICS THROUGH LITERATURE: *LES MISÉRABLES*

Health care communication ethics, with its focus on health, response, and care, appears in a number of places within *Les Misérables*. The health of a human face, that of Cosette, in particular, finds nurture and protection when Valjean ransoms her from the Thénardiers. His rescue of Cosette was a response of a tenacious sense of care to the dying Fantine, to whom Valjean made a promise to care for her daughter. Valjean's concern for Cosette's education at the convent of the Petit Picpus encompasses care for her long-term future.

In terms related to physical health, we see a repentant grandfather caring for a wounded and hurting Marius. The constant vigil by his grandson's bed, his eagerness to bring Marius the smallest thing needed, and his attentive watchfulness for signs of returning health are the marks of responsive care not only to an individual, but to a restored relationship. When Jean Valjean lies ill and dying, Cosette and Marius cannot prevent his inevitable decline. They cannot return him to physical health, but their responsive care for him nourishes the health of his spirit and soul during those last hours. The entire book is a tribute to health care communication ethics in one caring response after another: the bishop's care for the health of an embittered convict's destiny; a reformed convict's care for the health of a town, responding to its need for education, health care, elder care, productive labor, and wise stewardship of even its nettles, seen as weeds by all except him. Jean Valjean manifests care for the life and health of Marius, a threat to Valjean's own happiness as a "father," as he carries Marius through the sewers of Paris to bring him home. He cares for even Javert, his arch enemy, in his release of Javert after feigning Javert's execution for infiltrating the revolutionaries' lair, finding meaning in acting otherwise than convention. Health care rests in response and in an ongoing labor of care—tenacious to the end, carried in the human face.

CHAPTER 13

Media Ethics

Communicative Responsibility in a Digital World

> As the media sketch out our world, organize our conversations, influence our decisions, and affect our self-identity, they do so with a technological cadence, massaging in our souls a technological rhythm and disposition—enabling us to adapt efficiently to a technological world. With moral and social values disrupted and reoriented in the process, the ethics of communication technologies are an important arena for examining everyday life in technological societies at present. (Christians, 2008a, p. 205)

Media ethics addresses the goods that we protect and promote through our use of electronic/digital, audio/visual, and print communication in personal and professional contexts. Many elements of our lives are mediated in some way, whether through the messages of friends or knowledgeable sources describing people, places, and events we have never experienced. Through our mediated relationships, we shape and influence the world as we engage it via the telephone, television, Internet, or portable electronic devices (Strate, 2017). Media ethics has been approached from several frameworks, including utilitarian/consequentialist and duty-based (deontological, or Kantian) ethics, which often find expression in the context of professional media practices in the form of codes, procedures, and standards. Since the start of the 21st century, communitarian, dialogic, and feminist approaches have emerged as alternative frameworks for global media ethics (Christians, 2011a). An approach growing in prominence for mediated communication practices is virtue ethics (Fritz, 2018). Virtues are character traits that incline persons toward right action. Virtues reside performatively within narratives that define particular goods or understandings of what is right to do or to be. The goods of a narrative give substance to virtues of character developed by persons embedded within that narrative. After reading this chapter, you will be able to accomplish these learning objectives:

- Define media ethics
- Identify professional and personal contexts requiring ethical mediated communication
- Analyze the elements in a mediated context that require ethical attentiveness

Introduction

This chapter addresses communication ethics in the broad context of mediated communication. What goods do we protect and promote through our use of communication technologies in professional and personal contexts? More specifically, what goods do media professionals, such as journalists, protect and promote through their work on behalf of citizens in a democratic society? How do information and communication technologies protect and promote goods of personal relationships? Mediated communication in today's historical moment enables information to travel quickly across huge networks of people and connects communities globally and interpersonally. The broad ethical focus of mediated communication, from the perspective of this text, is two-fold: (1) the good of information awareness, tied to the more specific good of participation within the larger public sphere, and (2) the good of relational connections with other human beings.

This chapter connects the study of media ethics to communicative practices with attention to the following four metaphors of communication ethics praxis:

1. **Mediated communication**—communication through channels other than face to face/body to body.
2. **The public sphere**—the arena in which citizens exchange opinions and make decisions.
3. **The private realm**—personal arenas of life calling for discernment in use of mediated communication.
4. **Digital responsibility**—protecting and promoting the good of persons and relationships in the use of mediated communication.

▶

▶ ## Student Application: Digital Engagement

This historical moment offers seemingly endless opportunities to engage in **mediated communication**. The Internet allows extensive access to **the public sphere** and enables connections across the globe, inviting the potential for "citizen journalism" as well as enhanced demand for ethical news reporting by professionals who have embraced journalism as a tradition of practice. Technology offers both benefits and drawbacks. Students connect with each other through social networking and educational technology. From coordinating a group project across multiple members to downloading a study guide from a learning management system such as Blackboard, Moodle, or Schoology, students make productive use of electronic communication and its affordances. Students navigate web sites devoted to internships and job opportunities. Since employers can locate information and images about potential employees, career counselors encourage students to be careful about posting compromising photos taken at parties and uploaded to social networking sites. Instructors tell their classes cautionary tales of high-level executives whose supposedly humorous tweets, intended for a small circle of friends, received national publicity and generated disastrous consequences. In the **private realm**, relational partners negotiate how available each person should be during the day to respond to texts or how quickly (or whether) each should react to an Instagram post generated by the other. Digital communication allows instant access to the latest news and events, increasing our ability to keep in touch with professional colleagues, friends, and current events around the world. With an increase in the amount of information and mobile connectedness available comes increased **digital responsibility**, asking us to reflect on the goods we protect and promote through our engagement with media in all its forms.

Mediated Communication

The study of mediated communication spans a broad range of phenomena ranging from print, broadcast, and digital journalism to computer-mediated and digital communication technologies. The explosion of communication technologies during the last two decades has reshaped the context of public and private communication, prompting renewed focus on the ethical implications of electronic and digital communication. Information and communication technologies (ICTs) and digital mobility through smartphones connect an ever larger portion of the world's population (Ess, 2011), expanding the reach of mediated messages. The availability of technologies for video and audio recording and dissemination has changed the landscape of professional journalism (Zion & Craig, 2015). Enduring issues of dissemination of political opinions and information privacy gain new currency in our increasingly connected landscape. Relational life is mediated in new ways, prompting concerns about what it means to be present with those both near and far

© Vasin Lee/Shutterstock.com

away (Baym, 2010; Turkle, 2011). The potential for constant connection through mobile communication devices brings new avenues for exploring the dialectic of autonomy and interdependence (Baxter & Montgomery, 1996).

The media have the potential to promote human flourishing or to compromise human wellbeing. The media are relevant to all contexts of human communicative experience. In the public/political sphere, we see implications across the globe of widespread ability to communicate. In increasing numbers, in country after country, citizens seeking fuller participation in political decision making coordinate their efforts via traditional and new media, resulting in movements such as the Arab Spring (Brown, Guskin, & Mitchell, 2012). On the other hand, terrorist groups can make use of the coordinating power of the Internet to plan attacks and recruit new members (Taylor, 2016). Digital communication affects the good of interpersonal relationships through instant access to communication (Duran, Kelly, & Rotaru, 2011). We can use technology to build relationships through supportive messages or to harm other persons through cyberbullying (Willard, 2007). Technology permits workers to telecommute, shifting the way patterns of interaction define relational culture in organizations (Fay, 2012). Our views of the culturally different come to us from the media; the history of media images reveals many problematic portrayals of minority groups and persons from other cultures (Dixon, 2015). The media have revolutionized the potential for organizations to shape their brands and identities and connect with stakeholders through integrated marketing communication and crisis communication (Arnett, DeIuliis, & Corr, 2017). The Internet provides access to support groups for those with life-threatening illnesses or chronic conditions and also challenges the authority of physicians, as patients seek information that confirms or contradicts what they learn from medical professionals (du Pré, 2016). Each of these contexts calls us to think about our practices and the goods we seek to protect and promote. This digital responsibility is particularly evident in the profession of journalism, a tradition devoted to equipping citizens with a basis for insights that inform decision making in the public sphere, and in the realm of private relationships.

The Public Sphere

Clifford G. Christians, John P. Ferré, and P. Mark Fackler (1993) provide historical context for the development of Anglo-American journalism ethics, noting its roots in the Enlightenment, in which "the notion of free self-determination of the human personality" was "the highest good" (p. 21). Journalism's rich history in the United States is tied to the good of participation in decision making in a democratic context. The role of journalists is to provide citizens with access to information about issues and events so they can make informed decisions. From this perspective, journalists have a duty to report the news in a manner that informs the public. Today, fair and accurate news accounts must offer public disclosure of journalistic perspectives and experiences. The tradition of practice in journalism continues to expand in creative response to everyday access to mediated communication and social media outlets.

A Tradition of Practice

A virtue ethics perspective suggests that journalists serve as representatives of a professional narrative or tradition of practice (Borden, 2007). As an example, the 1980 Hastings Center Report included journalism with other professions such as medicine and engineering (Callahan & Bok, 1980; Christians, 2008a). Ward (2011) identifies four levels of goods that journalism strives to protect and promote, each of which defines an area of human dignity. These goods include *individual goods*, which sustain a life with sufficient physical resources, such as food and shelter; *social goods*, which involve using our reasoning and moral capacities to participate in the world of friendship and social interaction; *political goods*, consisting of contributions to public decision making; and *ethical goods*, which consider the interests of others and of the larger world, including justice. Patrick Lee Plaisance (2015), for example, presents moral exemplars in journalism and public relations professions, basing his work on moral psychology, an integration of philosophical ethics and social science. These representative figures illustrate what is considered praiseworthy action in the practice of media, demonstrating virtues of courage and humility in various contexts of professional life. His position is one of "'pluralistic universalism,'" pointing toward central "ethical principles (such as integrity, responsibility, public service) that ought to drive the behavior of all media professionals while also acknowledging that the manifestation of those principles necessarily depend[s] on social, cultural, and professional contexts" (p. 9). Plaisance's commitment to pluralistic universalism represents a scholarly/practical category understood by Christians, who stressed the importance of protonorms (Christians, 2010, pp. 11–12).

Sandra Borden (2007) applies MacIntyre's theory of virtue ethics to the profession of journalism. Her work highlights virtues that enable journalists to pursue excellence, thereby protecting and promoting journalism as a tradition of practice. Journalists who have been educated in a tradition of practice continue to uphold the goods represented by that tradition, serving as role models for others (Borden, 2007; Plaisance, 2013). Borden's ethical theory for professional journalism identifies virtues that sustain the practice of journalism that emerged from the history and tradition of journalism and respond to conditions facing journalists in today's historical moment. Borden notes that courage and ingenuity are important protections against market competitiveness, which, for example, tempts journalists to pay more attention to sensational events that sell newspapers than to issues worthy of public deliberation. Journalists are responsible for carrying on the practice of journalism as an institution by protecting and promoting reporting excellence necessary for news organizations to endure. Journalists must enact virtues of justice, courage, and honesty in their dealings with one another; collegial relationships help attain the goals of journalism by providing a context for constructive criticism and mutual verification of information (Borden, 2007, pp. 66–80). Borden's work points to the importance of a narrative that houses practices that guide constructive journalistic action.

Borden's insights resonate with those of Nicholas Couldry (2010, 2013), who suggests that the good of media as a practice is to sustain individual and collective life. Accuracy and sincerity are functional communicative virtues in journalism. Without reliable information from others about the environment, human beings would experience a diminished quality of life. Journalistic practice involves assisting persons and communities by circulating information relevant to a particular domain and by providing opportunities for citizens to express opinions. Encouraging citizens to be visible to each other sustains "a peaceable life together," particularly during disagreements related to "conflicting values, interests, and understandings" (Couldry, 2010, p. 68). Journalism at its best enhances citizens conscientiously committed to building a public domain composed of differences, not simply alignment with their own positions.

A New Historical Moment

From the second half of the 19th century onward, the newsroom provided a context for socialization of journalists to the ethics of professional practice and development of professional identity (Wyatt, 2014). The advent of convergent journalism in a digital age points toward work that is often solitary and independent, a context quite different from the traditional context of journalistic work (Wyatt, 2014). Wyatt (2014) suggests journalists may forge new communities of connection with fellow journalists and the public. She recommends a revisioning of journalism education reflecting broad principles of ethics highlighted by the

Hastings Center Report. Zion and Craig's (2015) edited volume addresses ethics for digital journalists. Digital communication expands the potential for anyone with access to the Internet to become an information provider to the larger world. Journalists recognize the potential for partnership with communities and citizens as new understandings of journalistic work emerge.

Christians (2004) offers an alternative understanding of journalism and associated goods of professional practice derived from the African concept of *ubuntu*, a communitarian approach that understands the human person as an integral part of a community rather than an isolated, atomistic individual or as part of a monolithic political collective. From a perspective of *ubuntu*, journalists should take the perspective of the community of which they are a part, rejecting an objective perspective that places them beyond bias. Authentic disclosure, a hallmark of *ubuntu* journalistic practice, provides historical context and background for interpretation and understanding of reported information, with the goal of representing context and culture accurately (Christians, 2004, p. 247). News is local, resisting monolithic power structures that colonize and level particular communities.

From an *ubuntu* perspective, the community matters; we are not merely rational creatures, but embedded, bound with ties of affection and concern to particular localities. The good of human beings depends on connection to others and to communities, which is why we cannot be merely rational choosers when confronted with ethical issues. The particular matters; the human face is part of what moves us to action. Justice and ethics are intertwined as we consider the near and the far, the familiar and familial, and the distant, the stranger, and the neighbor (Plaisance, 2005; Arnett, 2017b).

Both an understanding of duties and the call for development of character traits that incline journalists to embody excellence of practice can be identified in professional standards and guidelines for ethical practices. These guidelines, developed over time, comprise a code of ethics specifying expectations for ethical professional behavior, providing a means for identifying violations of ethical expectations. The Society of Professional Journalists, for example, lists expectations for ethical journalistic practice (Society of Professional Journalists, 2014). Cases like that of Janet Cooke, in which a news reporter fabricated an eight-year-old heroin user, bring these guidelines to the forefront and prompt discussion about the role of journalism and the understandings of objectivity (e.g., Eason, 1986).

The Private Realm

Plaisance (2013), in his discussion of an ethic of digital flourishing, draws on the work of Goffman (1973). Plaisance addresses the manner in which digital technologies reconfigure regions relevant to the self. If every digital keystroke is recorded, leaving a digital footprint that can never be eradicated, there is no space for the "backstage" behavior typical of private moments with family and friends that is "off the record." The frontstage region is the only realm of interaction, which is typified by carefully planned messages that we know are likely to be viewed by multiple audiences. The issue of private and public blurring parallels the issue of dialectical tensions between connection and autonomy.

Digital communication and mobile devices offer the possibility of remaining connected with friends and family. When it is not possible to go home for the weekend, FaceTime or Skype allows communicative access to parents or grandparents. If a friend or romantic partner is away on a study abroad trip, technology provides the opportunity to catch up on each other's lives. Although not the same

as a hug or a human touch, the ability to hear or see a loved one provides reassurance and a sense that the relationship matters.

With the potential for connectedness, however, comes unintended consequences. For example, once digital communication devices such as cell phones are taken for granted, I may believe that I should be able to call or text my best friend at any time and get a response. If I do not receive an immediate response, I may become impatient. In other words, digital communication technology tempts us to believe that if we can stay connected, we should. As discussed in the chapter on interpersonal communication ethics, the technological imperative of "can" eclipses the "should" (Ellul, 1954/1964, p. 436).

Digital technology reveals our need to balance connection with autonomy, a theme examined in dialectical theory (Baxter & Montgomery, 1996). Constant connection leaves no room for personal space or time alone. Friends, romantic partners, and parents work out these challenges as they discern rules for cell phone use (Feiler, 2015) and participation in other communicative technologies such as Snapchat and Twitter. Protecting and promoting the good of relationship when partners disagree on how much connection is desirable requires communication to develop practices that will constitute and sustain the relational culture (Wilmot, 1995). Before the mobile communication revolution, communication media (such as telephone, letters, and even email) provided relatively broad margins for keeping in touch. Mobile devices, because of their portability, leave less margin or "buffer" for response time. The upside is the need to make expectations explicit, which can open opportunities for discussion of other areas of the relationship, thereby protecting and promoting relational health.

Digital Responsibility

Digital responsibility is more than following the digital laws that enforce copyright law, downloading standards, and privacy. Digital responsibility is being aware of why and what you are communicating in a global world. Technology has many purposes, such as to entertain, inform, and/or persuade, and reflecting on your words and your audience is critical. Once something is said or posted, it cannot be erased or taken back. Most people have heard the saying, "Never post anything that you wouldn't show your parents or future employer." Digital responsibility recognizes that there are both personal and public consequences of using technology. Technology is a part of our everyday interactions, and everyone has an obligation to use it and share it responsibly. Nancy K. Baym (2010) addresses the intersection of interpersonal communication, relationships, and digital technologies. She does not raise ethics explicitly as an issue, but throughout the volume, the good of persons and of relationships receives consistent attention. She notes that any new technology brings change and resulting anxiety (p. 2). She also notes that technology blurs the boundaries between public and private—for example, if one creates a YouTube video showing how to use a shoehorn to share with one's friends, those friends may send the link to their networks, and the video may eventually become popular with a much broader audience. Digital responsibility requires recognizing the impact that technology can have on our health, interpersonal relationships, environment, and society.

A 2018 study by the Pew Research Center suggests that although Americans recognize the benefits of the Internet, they are increasingly recognizing its affordances and shortcomings for society (Smith & Olmstead, 2018). While it is good to be connected to others and to have instant access to information, concerns about fake news, exposure of private data, and the potential isolating effects and overuse of digital communication devices temper enthusiasm about our digital age. The study also notes that 11% of Americans are absent from the online world, using neither the Internet nor email at all. The digital age involves the majority of Americans, but not all, with an increasing number no longer true believers in its value.

Consequences of Media Attributes

Baym (2010) suggests seven key themes or attributes of media that help us understand how media shape our relationships with others. These principles help us compare different media with each other and with face to face, or "body to body" (Fortunati, 2005, as cited in Baym, 2010, p. 6) communication in order to discern how to protect and promote goods of relationship and of persons. Although these attributes are not goods in and of themselves, they hold implications for relational practices and subsequent relational and personal well-being and flourishing, in virtue ethics terms, encouraging digital responsibility.

The first attribute is social interactivity, the ability to reach out and respond to others interactively. Can I respond to the person emailing, texting, videoconferencing, or speaking to me on the phone? If Elspeth and Renaldo are collaborating on a group project in an online class, they may choose to hold videoconferences rather than exchange text messages because of the high level of interactivity needed to generate a creative final product.

The second attribute is temporal structure, whether there is a time delay or the potential for a time delay—is the medium synchronous, with people connected at the same time, or asynchronous, with a lag between message and response? If Shanika needs to know what her roommates want from the grocery store, she will probably choose to call or text them rather than emailing because of her need for an immediate response. On the other hand, asynchronous media like email may work better for communicative exchanges that require time for careful thought and reflection.

The third attribute is the presence or absence of social cues, the vocal and nonverbal signals that offer interpretive clues to the meaning of messages. Without visual cues and only text, it may be difficult to discern whether a comment is meant as a joke or as a serious comment. "Emojis" and "emoticons" may provide limited clues regarding the intended meaning of a text message, but they can never replace the rich inflections of face-to-face speech that Bakhtin (1998) identified as "intonation." Moreover, in text-based media, the identity of a communicative partner may not be readily available. The potential for anonymity in the online environment may prompt less inhibited communication, which could be either beneficial or problematic.

Storage and replicability of messages are two additional features of mediated communication. Can the message be saved, archived, and searched, or does it disappear forever? Snapchat is one example of a social media platform designed to resist storage and replicability, which can be especially appealing for teens and young people seeking total freedom of expression online. However, the knowledge that one's words will not be permanent generates its own possibilities for unethical and dangerous communicative behavior.

The reach of a medium refers to the number of people to whom the message can be distributed. One message can reach hundreds or thousands of people locally or globally, depending on the particular technology or application. For example, Facebook provides its users with extensive controls over who can see posts and personal information—"friends," "friends of friends," and "public" are some possible options. Other platforms such as Twitter are designed for public and global distribution and offer less control over one's audience.

Finally, mobility refers to whether the medium can function regardless of one's location. Cell phones are portable; desktop computers are not. The general shift in the last two decades has been toward increasing mobility in all communication channels. At first, many technology users were excited about the possibility of greater connectivity and productivity when traveling or waiting for a meeting to begin. Now, busy professionals may long for the days when one's email could only be accessed at one's desk. This is just one example of the unforeseen societal consequences that accompany all technological development.

© Rawpixel.com

Incivility and Cyberbullying

Shelley D. Lane (2017) explores the rise of incivility, which she connects to differing norms across generations as well as to greater informality prompted by digital technologies. The potential for instant sending of messages leaves little room to reflect about whether I "should" send this text or email or Snapchat to others or to an entire group. We cannot predict the unintended consequences that our digital actions may bring about; the best we can do is to reflect and consider carefully whether the content of the message is one that we would be willing to share with a larger group and whether the comment would contribute to the good of a group or person.

In an extensive review, Robin M. Kowalski, Gary W. Giumetti, Amber N. Schroeder, and Micah R. Lattanner (2014) note that cyberbullying can take place through "instant messaging, e-mail, text messages, web pages, chat rooms, social networking sites, digital images, and online games" (p. 1074). Kowalski and colleagues draw on the work of Willard (2007) to describe the many forms cyberbullying can take—for example, engaging in an online fight (flaming), sending offensive messages repeatedly to another person (harassment), tricking someone into sharing personal information and then distributing that information, cyber-stalking, and sending offensive messages under another's name (p. 1074). Cyberbullying diminishes the integrity of other human beings, detracting from the good of human flourishing.

A controversial example of cyberbullying in action revolves around the once-popular social media app Yik Yak (Safronova, 2017). This platform, launched in 2013, allowed users to post anonymous, location-based messages. As Yik Yak gained popularity among college students, however, it soon became a site for expressions of bullying, racism, and threats of violence. Some universities responded by disabling access to Yik Yak's platform on their WiFi networks, and the cyberbullying that took place on the platform has spawned at least one lawsuit. By 2017, the founders of Yik Yak decided to close down the app. Because of their new affordances of anonymity and instantaneity, platforms like Yik Yak challenge our understanding of the traditional "good" of freedom of expression, especially when placed in contact with the conflicting "good" of protecting individuals from bullying and harassment. The ever-broadening potential for incivility in cyberspace reminds us again of the need for a dialogic ethic in mediated communication.

Pointing to a Dialogic Ethic in Mediated Communication

Mediated communication points to a dialogic ethic in the manner of listening, attentiveness, and negotiation. The following model summarizes a dialogic ethic applied to mediated communication, highlighting major points in this chapter.

1. *Listening without demand: What is happening in a given moment? Whether we like or dislike that moment, we must engage the question(s) of a given moment.* Mediated communication ethics requires thoughtful engagement of communicative technologies in multiple spheres of life. Journalists protect

and promote human flourishing through the good of information provision, maintaining a tradition of practice while responding to audiences who are now participants in the news gathering process as well as consumers. Increased opportunity for connection in relationships requires us to listen to the dialectic of closeness and distance to protect and promote relational health. Digital responsibility is needed more than ever in this historical moment.

2. *Attentiveness: What are the coordinating grounds upon which stand the self, the Other, and the historical moment?* Attentiveness and learning work together in professional and personal engagement of digital communication in all its forms.

   a. *The ground of self (the ethical/narrative commitments that guide us) and*
   b. *The ground of Other (the ethical/narrative commitments that guide the Other).* Journalists stand in a tradition of practice defined by ethical standards; citizens seek information that helps them make wise decisions in the public sphere as part of the democratic tradition. Relational partners seek common ground to define closeness and distance in relationships.
   c. *The ground of the historical moment (elements of the time in which we live, including "relational time" of the persons in conversation).* This historical moment presents media professionals and relational partners with multiple opportunities for information and connection; mutual responsiveness between journalists and their audiences and between partners protecting and promoting a personal relationship ensures flourishing in public and private spheres.

3. *Dialogic negotiation: What temporal communicative ethics answers emerge "between" persons, pointing to communicative options for action, belief, and understanding?* There is no one answer for how to engage media ethics in this historical moment—only the call to reflect and consider whether professional or personal communication sent through print, email, text, a social networking site, or other media channel will protect and promote human flourishing.

4. *Listening, attentiveness, and dialogic negotiation constitute temporal dialogic ethical competence. What worked, and what changes might now assist?*

   a. *Evaluation/self-reflection (reflection upon one's own ethical/narrative commitments).* Attending to the question of how to engage mediated communication requires thoughtful deliberation on the topic, relationship, and purpose of a mediated message.
   b. *From knowledge to learning (the key is not to "tell," but to learn from the Other, the historical moment, and reflective understanding of communicative action).* In the face of an ever-changing digital media landscape, relational responsibility requires learning from ongoing experiences and consequences of communicative practices in professional and personal spheres of life.

5. *Dialogic ethics listens to what is before one when considering employing mediated communication, attends to the historical moment, and seeks to negotiate new possibilities. Dialogic ethics is a conceptual form of marketplace engagement, ever attentive to conversational partners and their "ground," the historical moment, and the emerging "possible" that takes place in the "between" of human meeting.* One cannot escape the reality of a digital world; one must respond to it with consideration of the potential unintended consequences of engaging mediated communication in professional and personal contexts, ever aware of the need for negotiating expectations on the part of media audiences and relational partners. Media professionals bear a tradition of practice into a mediated public square; relational partners respond creatively to new forms of technology and monitor effects on the relationship. In public and private spheres of human life, digital responsibility guides engagement of mediated communication to protect and promote social and personal well-being.

COMMUNICATION ETHICS: REFLECTION AND ACTION

1. Interview a journalist who has been a part of the profession for at least twenty years. What changes has this media professional witnessed?
2. Do a search to locate web pages of three or four departments of journalism in institutions of higher education. How do the web sites portray the profession of journalism? What is the role of ethics in journalistic practice, according to these web sites?
3. Make a list of three or four films that focus on personal relationship development. How is digital communication technology portrayed as a contributor to—or detractor from—the good of relationship?
4. Consider conversations you have taken part in or overheard over the last few days, either face to face or mediated. To what extent did the issue of digital or mobile communication as a point of concern emerge? In what ways?

ENGAGING COMMUNICATION ETHICS THROUGH LITERATURE: *LES MISÉRABLES*

Although set in a historical moment two centuries ago, mediated communication is a part of everyday life in both public and private spheres in *Les Misérables*, just as it is today, with similar implications. One of the primary contexts of mediated communication in the novel is the exchange of letters. Fantine and the Thénardiers communicate about Fantine's daughter, Cosette. The Thénardiers deceive Fantine about her daughter's health, leading to great sacrifice on the part of Fantine in order to provide the money they demand for medicine. Jean Valjean presents a letter on Fantine's behalf to secure Cosette's release, leading to freedom for Cosette. Newspapers, books, proclamations, and other print media of various sorts are integral elements of the public world of that era. Marius reads histories of the Republic and the Empire, and he sees his father's name in the bulletins of the army. Characters in the story make decisions about the good they will protect and promote in each engagement with mediated communication.

If we step back from the action of the novel and take a view of the book itself in the context of our own lived experience in the world, we see how media carry the message Victor Hugo articulated. The book *Les Misérables* became a musical and a movie. Images from the musical abound, and the novel's characters appear in various locations within the culture. The translation of the message of *Les Misérables* into different mediated forms illustrates the way a story representing a narrative standpoint embeds itself within the larger culture. Audiences respond by attending the musical and purchasing the soundtrack, keeping the story within the horizon of public awareness and appreciation. The contribution of Victor Hugo to the public imagination of many cultures and nations is carried forth by the mediated form of a wonderful story through the centuries.

CHAPTER 14

Communication Ethics
Literacy and Difference

Dialogic Learning

> For Levinas, the Other comes from up high—the Other is teacher before part-
> ner. There is no symmetry in being responsible, that is, in being answerable and
> addressable. Since responsibility as response-ability is the very beginning of
> subjectivity, I am always already answerable to the Other's call, always already
> approachable, open, predisposed toward the Other. (Pinchevski, 2005, p. 75)

Communication ethics in an era defined by difference, disagreement, and lack
of concurrence requires two pragmatic moves. First, cease using ethics as a
weapon; disagreement should not immediately move us into referring to an opponent as unethical. Second, embrace the necessity of learning as we meet diverse
ethical positions contrary to our own, with the assumption that learning does not
necessarily suggest agreement. We will not and we should not agree with all ethical positions that we encounter. The first step in an age of difference is to *learn*
about the alien, the different, and that which we do not know. The second step
begins with *discernment* about the interplay of our own position and that which

▲ **233**

we learn. *Learning* and *discernment* put in place a natural dialectic, reminding us to check our own position with new insights and to permit our own ideas to function as a check against unreflective acceptance of that which is new. This chapter centers communication ethics on the good of learning as the constructive, pragmatic response to an era defined by difference. After reading this chapter, you will be able to demonstrate the following learning outcomes:

- Describe the importance of communication ethics literacy
- Recognize the pragmatic need of communication ethics
- Identify the need for crisis communication

Introduction

This chapter connects the study and practice of communication ethics to the following three metaphors of communicative praxis:

1. **Pragmatic**—the need for practical engagement of ideas responsive to a particular historical moment.
2. **Crisis communication**—an increasingly relevant metaphor for today's postmodern moment of virtue contention; the unexpected emerges and requires discernment and action as we encounter differing particular "goods" in the public domain.
3. **Communication ethics literacy**—identifies the good in the interplay of self and Other and the particular historical moment, attending to what requires protection and promotion.

Student Application: Understanding the Other

When students come to the end of a course, they typically sit for a final exam or prepare an extensive course paper. In either case, they must master a great deal of material, doing the work of learning that takes them away from friends and recreational activities. This learning, however, is essential for content literacy in the course. Without knowledge of the content, one cannot move ideas into **pragmatic** application. Likewise, learning about difference in today's world presents similar challenges. To work with others in community, marketplace, public, and personal contexts requires engaging multiple viewpoints and, at the same time, taking a stance on a variety of issues related to our life together. For example, on a college or university campus there are many options for dorm life. Some residence halls are smoke free and alcohol free; the good of substance-free living protects and promotes such spaces. Others may reside within dorms that protect and promote academic excellence by enforcing extended quiet hours. The existence of "dedicated" residence halls is one result of negotiating competing goods. The clashing of multiple goods calls forth an understanding of **crisis communication**, where one finds the need to respond with care and discernment in order to address the unexpected that

▶

emerges between and among persons of difference. This type of engagement points to the heart of **communication ethics literacy**: working from one's own position, learning from that of the Other, and interpreting that material for the task of the moment in pragmatic engagement with the Other.

Pragmatic

The pragmatics of dialogue unites *learning*, *discernment*, and *difference*, requiring one to learn from the Other and, additionally, from one's own ground, with each checking and texturing the other. Jason Hannan (2011) cites Richard Bernstein's *The Pragmatic Turn* (2010), which makes a case for the emerging renaissance of pragmatic thinking. Multiple authors represent pragmatism in action. The principal uniting force questions the dominance of analytic philosophy and its method, opening American philosophy to its own tradition. Hannan also explicates a basic reality about pragmatism: the term dwells within multiple and differing schools of thought. However, each embraces "the indeterminacy, open-endedness, plurality, and sociality of the world" (p. 109). This unity of learning, discernment, and difference affirms multiple views of the good, neither ignoring nor concurring unreflectively with the new. Unlike modernity, postmodernity offers no advantage to the new; our obligation rests with learning about and discernment of both the new and the time-tested.

Postmodernity finds definition in difference and incommensurability of views of the good. Keeping the conversation going in such an era begins with meeting what we do not know, which permits learning and, ironically, sheds more clarity on the ground or position upon which we stand. Pragmatism works to engage and assist with the unexpected and the problematic in everyday existence, unlike the metaphysical impulse to align one's ideas with reality. Mats Bergman (2016) suggests that pragmatism begins with existence itself and attempts to address its needs rather than demanding that existence conform to "my" preconceptions and pet projects. In essence, communication ethics takes on pragmatic currency; we must learn about other views of the good with recognition that, like it or not, multiple views of the good exist and contend for attention in the ongoing postmodern marketplace of ideas.

We are forewarned of the demand for learning differing views of the good and of communication ethics among cultures, nations, and religions by numerous mundane decisions such as holiday travel, the transporting of children from one parent to another, and the seemingly now common response, "Can you believe he did that?" "Can you believe she said that?" The banality of this historical moment finds definition in difference as the normative characterization of our lives together. Each of the previous chapters in this book has addressed a particular

© Pitsanu Kraichana/Shutterstock.com

communicative context that calls for recognition of and learning about multiple goods in a time of difference.

In this concluding chapter, we move communication ethics to the forefront of discussion with its companion application of crisis communication. This work assumes that the presence of differing views of the good requires the study and practice of crisis communication; this communication area is a central issue in every curricular reform in our discipline that engages the question of competing goods in our communicative work with one another. The major root of difference is differing views of the good. This contention over the notion of the good is at the heart of crisis communication, which reminds us not to assume that the Other will think as we do or value what we hold dear. The pragmatic demand is to learn and to investigate ways of negotiating contending goods, which leads to the ongoing rise of crisis communication studies in this historical moment.

Crisis Communication

The person many consider the founder of crisis communication is Ian Mitroff, who has authored numerous books and articles on crisis communication since the turn of the 21st century. Thirty years ago, he foreshadowed the reason for crisis communication emergence in an era of difference. He first examined the work of Carl Jung and reminded us that people have diverse means of engaging data and new ideas. Some work from sensation and others from intuition; some make decisions from thinking and others from feeling (Mitroff, 1978). A combination of these approaches defines the matrix from which the Myers-Briggs personality inventory finds theoretical support. Jung, along with Adler and Freud, brought conversation about psychological difference to the foreground. The early work of Mitroff recognized and highlighted the importance of diversity of persons' responses to given events.

Mitroff's next step was diversity of methodological approaches to gathering and understanding data (Mitroff, 1978), which was an outgrowth of the diversity of ways in which persons meet and understand data or events before them. He stated that bias of person and methodology colors what we see and understand, discussing the differences among the "analytic scientist" wanting to understand causal connections, the "conceptual theorist" seeking to understand multiplicity of positions, the "conceptual humanist" asking how these differences affect others, and the "particular humanist" proclaiming the power of the particular and the normality of difference. Mitroff laid the groundwork for understanding crisis communication and the meeting of difference that has personal and methodological origins; today, scholars add differences of gender, class, religion, culture, ethnicity, and nationality to the mix. Pragmatically, ever-increasing differences invite crisis in contention over the good. It is our position that increasing frequency of ongoing crises generated by competing views of the good makes communication ethics literacy a pragmatic necessity.

Mitroff (1978) quotes both Dewey and James on the pragmatic admission of position taking, another way to stress the importance of learning from difference. In our terms, to ignore the diversity of goods is to miss the communication challenges and opportunities before us. Pragmatically, learning begins with difference. Mitroff draws upon John Dewey (1953), who, in *Essays in Experimental Logic*, responds to charges of subjectivism levied against William James as follows:

> Because Mr. [William] James recognizes that the personal element enters into judgments . . . he is charged with extreme subjectivism, with encouraging the element of personal preference to run roughshod over all objective controls. . . . [T]he question raised . . . is primarily one of fact, not of doctrine. Is or is not a personal factor found in truth evaluations? . . . [T]he moment the complicity of the personal factor . . . is recognized, is recognized fully, frankly, and generally, that moment a new era in philosophy will begin. We shall have to discover the personal factors that now influence us unconsciously, and begin to accept a new and moral responsibility for them, a responsibility for judging and testing them by their consequences. So long as we ignore this factor, its deeds will be largely evil, not because *it* is evil, but because, flourishing in the dark, it is without responsibility and without check. The only way to control it is by recognizing it. (pp. 326–327)

Communication ethics is the call to learn about differing views of the good assumed by differing positions. Communication ethics begins with literacy, learning tied attentively to the question, "What good is protected and promoted in a given communicative act?"

Crisis communication begins with the contention of goods that disrupts the public sphere. Kathryn Anthony and Timothy Sellnow (2011) explicate the importance of "first and second things," underlining the need to keep them separate. For instance, in the issue of organizational crisis, a "first thing" is safety, which must assume priority over secondary objectives of financial gain and reputation enhancement. Our discipline, following the lead of Mitroff and others, has taken up the charge to understand and engage crisis communication, exemplified by the work of Matthew W. Seeger, Timothy L. Sellnow, and Robert R. Ulmer (Seeger, Sellnow, & Ulmer, 2007; Ulmer, Sellnow, & Seeger, 2007; Seeger & Griffin Padgett, 2010). The rise of crisis communication is not only a way of assisting needed negotiation between contending views of the good; it is an indicator of the defining shape of this historical moment as marked by a contentious understanding of the good.

A Historical Moment of Contending Goods

A historical moment finds definition in questions that shape the horizon of possibilities before us. One of the major questions of this era is, "How do we live constructively within an era of so many differing views of the good, a time of acknowledged different goods?" The importance of this moment finds shape and clarity in the desire to understand (learn and discern) "communication ethics" rather than to prescribe "the" communication ethic. Just as there is no longer an expectation of finding one good that will unite us, there should be no expectation that one communication ethic can and should govern all communicative life.

In short, there is one major point of agreement in this historical moment: do not expect the Other to endorse your understanding of the good. It is possible to ask another to seek to understand our position as we seek to understand another's position, but agreement and endorsement are no longer a sure bet. Difference is what fuels the dialogic call of this historical moment. Learning and discernment, on the one hand, need to guide; the reality of crisis communication, on the other hand, continues to warn us that we cannot assume that the Other will necessarily think or act as we deem correct.

This historical moment of contending goods plays its way out in daily communicative interaction. At one university, a faculty member wrote the president to ask for help, making a plea for regular cleaning of the stairwells. The note referred to the stairwells as "filthy." The president, a published philosopher, decided to walk over to the building to see for himself. The president wanted to see what definition of "filthy" might prompt a faculty member to send such a memo. In the words of the president, "I did not want to forward an email on behalf of a person with undue standards for institutional tidiness." After the president's investigation, he forwarded the email, thereby securing attention to the need for more cleanliness.

The person doing the cleaning was not pleased. There are many senses of the good in relation to cleanliness—not just whether something is clean, but what is most important to keep clean. With limited time and personnel, if the stairwells are cleaned regularly, what gets less attention? Are the stairwells more important

© Quality Stock Arts/Shutterstock.com

than the classrooms? The president's action revealed that we cannot assume the same good about cleanliness standards, and the worker's response displayed the power of differing goods in decision making—offices, classrooms, and stairwells were, for him, in competition for attention and energy. The clashing of goods is an ongoing part of contemporary life, even in the cleaning of stairwells.

Such innocent differing views of the good give way to larger questions that will shape the remainder of the 21st century. Take, for instance, the example of what Michael Hyde (2004, 2016) calls the "posthuman." The clashing of goods related to whether and how to assist longevity and whether and when to end life are just beginning. Early in 2007, for instance, we witnessed an example of such a clashing of goods in a medical journal report on the case of "Ashley X," which made national headlines (Gunther & Diekema, 2006). At the age of nine, she underwent an operation to halt her physical growth. The rationale was two-fold: to keep her physical size in agreement with her mental aptitude, giving the parents a greater chance of caring for her with her disabilities, and to prevent discomfort to her that would have resulted from puberty and its associated physical changes. The controversy about such an act was and is loud on both sides of the question. Some say that growing in size is part of the human experience, regardless of one's mental abilities, with others understanding the difficulty before the parents and the reason for the choice. One of the emerging questions before us in this historical moment, like it or not, is, "What is the posthuman?" What happens when we can and do engage in serious manipulation of what has historically constituted a "normal" human being?

Communication ethics takes on both philosophical and practical challenges when met with increasing diversity of competing views of the good; the narrative within which we situate ourselves as communicators takes on increasing power and significance. Arguably, one of the most important philosophical and pragmatic contributions to communication in our lifetime has been the work of Walter Fisher (1987), who brought narrative theory into conversation in the discipline. Narrative theory gives us a way of explaining the notion of ground under one's feet that is idea based and not simply the soil of unexamined tradition. For example, it is possible to engage a tradition thoughtfully, as a narrative or story based on reflective content. We can follow that same tradition unthinkingly, without consideration of its content or coherence. Narrative theory encourages us to be reflective about the traditions that embed us and the goods that those traditions carry. Both dialogue and communication ethics owe much to the work of Walter Fisher, who reminds us of the importance of narrative ground under our feet, even in an age of increasing difference. As Dietrich Bonhoeffer (1981) suggests, taking the narrative ground from another is an immoral act. Many live in a time of "existential homelessness" (Arnett, 1994), and Fisher was insightful enough to follow the work of MacIntyre, Hauerwas, and Arendt, who called forth discussion of narrative ground. The loss of a metanarrative—one universally acknowledged position—makes discussion of multiple narratives essential.

Fisher and others suggest that the question of difference and competing goods has a narrative answer, which Ana Smith Iltis (2003) provides for us in her overview of *Institutional Integrity in Health Care*. She suggests that there are so many understandings of the good that the word "integrity" has more pragmatic utility in this moment than ever before. Integrity suggests that an organization do what Fisher called for in narrative discourse: work at telling a story supported by practices. Iltis elaborates:

> The importance of institutional integrity is underscored by the fact that we face the task of morally evaluating health care organizations in a society in which we lack a single, thick understanding of morality. The circumstance of moral pluralism complicates efforts to evaluate or assess health care organizations because we do not have a shared, robust concept of the right and the good that can guide our evaluations. It is because of this post-modern reality that we must turn to the concept of integrity. Integrity makes it possible to evaluate the extent to which health care organizations live up to their obligations regardless of what those obligations are. There are, in fact, two different kinds of obligations under consideration in this volume. Some obligations, it is argued, are borne by all health care organizations regardless of their moral commitments or identities. Because they are health care organizations, they are obligated in particular ways. Other obligations, however, may not be justifiably attributed to all health care organizations. These are the obligations grounded in an institution's moral commitments, and the ramifications of this are especially poignant in discussions of religious health care institutions. (p. 2)

Questions of integrity become constitutive byproducts of a narrative supported by practices that protect health and attend to issues such as death by infection contracted at the hospital; integrity will depend upon an institution's ability to align its story about health with the assurance and practice of health in the hospital itself.

In such a moment of difference, we must look for one way after another to unite the philosophical and practical, the story with the communicative practices. Fisher's view of narrative and that of many other scholars point us to a rationality situated within a given narrative view of the world, not a universal presupposition of the good or right for all time. When we cannot expect the universal to guide us, we cannot expect our own position to meet with agreement from all. Confidence must rest in the public disclosure of communication ethics with a public recording of the congruence between the story and daily communicative practices. Communication ethics theory becomes a form of spectacles that provide a particular view of the world; the key is not just in the theory, but also in the telling about the particular way of looking—a public display of the spectacles that govern our insights.

In Need of Glasses

Communication ethics theory is a form of optical lenses necessary for engaging and understanding the complexity of issues involved in discerning the good. To wear glasses is to understand the power and importance of peripheral vision and how glasses do not lend themselves to such peripheral looking and seeing. Additionally, it is important to understand that not just any pair of glasses will assist one's looking and seeing. One must obtain the right prescription in order to assist one's vision; otherwise, one will actually see less clearly.

Literacy requires having the proper lenses with which to read, whether they are part of one's physical makeup at birth or obtained through an optometrist's prescription. One engages the seeing with either natural ability or with assistance that has constructed limitations. Our vision has limits, and whatever we use to aid us has limits, as well. Another way of understanding this limitation of vision is to think of wrapping presents with children in the house. The long tubes that hold the wrapping paper become great telescopes. When one looks down the tube all is clear within that limited scope, but one misses the periphery completely.

The introduction to theory in communication ethics requires a stress upon the good that finds protection and promotion in a given communicative environment. This book has examined theories that act as "eye glasses": (1) democratic, (2) universal-humanitarian, (3) codes, procedures, and standards, (4) contextual, (5) narrative, and (6) dialogic communication ethics. The differences in the good protected and promoted find definition through the looking or the theory engaged. We privilege a dialogic communication ethic for this historical moment—an appropriate prescription for seeing in a postmodern age of difference and multiplicity. The goal is to learn from alterity, from that which is outside us, outside what we expect to understand within conventional expectations.

Dialogic theory based upon standpoint, the ground or narrative from which the communicators stand and meet the world, moves ethics from the private to the public domain, permitting debate over which theory to use, how to use it, and what emerges from the looking. Arnett, Arneson, and Bell (2006) suggest that Fisher's notion of narrative permits dialogue to mature philosophically. A continental view of dialogue, particularly that of a Buber or a Bonhoeffer, begins before the conversation begins. The narrative or ground of meaning upon which a person stands is a gestalt collection of voices before "I" and "we" enter "this" conversation. Habermas (1984) is correct in suggesting that the most important element of the Enlightenment was making public a given way of looking. Without theory, we succumb to the whim of the looker and to our using of junior high vocabulary: "You are wrong, and I am right." The use of theory takes us into a public arena of examination and testing. Theory does not stop conflict, but permits the looking and the examination to take on a public dimension that lessens our tendency to look only to find what we want or demand to see.

The use of theory counters the impulse of "individualism," the thought that one can stand above history and render an accurate assessment (Arnett, in press). Theory moves one into the public, away from undue confidence in one's private looking. Ian Watt (2002), in *Myths of Modern Individualism: Faust, Don Quixote, Don Juan, Robinson Crusoe*, reminds us of the limits of individualism as he examines these stories. Selling one's soul for knowledge, ignoring change because it does not fit one's demands or hopes, exploiting others, and taking for granted the person who assists you all have one common feature—a looking at and seeing of what is good that begins and ends with oneself, forgetting the otherness of work and limits, changing historical circumstances, the feelings of others, and the importance of others.

© REDPIXEL.PL/Shutterstock.com

We live in a time of general approval of individualism in which concern for one's own view or looking takes precedence over a tradition that embeds a particular human being. Theory is a form of embedded looking and seeing, making public the limits of what one can see. Theory fights against the silo of myopic individualistic insight, a nearsightedness that makes what is close appear clear and blurs what is far away. Watt (2002) comments on the rise of individualism: "Our four myths, then, were historically new; and in this they reflected their period's new emphasis on the social and political primacy of the individual" (p. 242). Theory brings us into the public domain, providing an alternative to individual looking, providing temporal ground for common sense in a postmodern culture. In this historical moment, we begin with the assumption that common sense is not common, making individualistic efforts even more reckless in this historical moment as we live without an agreed-upon set of common sense restraints.

Communication Ethics and the Public Domain

In addition to the pioneering insights of Hannah Arendt, two major voices keep before us the importance of the public domain in this historical moment: Seyla Benhabib (1992) and Jürgen Habermas (1996). A robust public domain requires attentiveness to some organizing communicative agreement that offers a minimal sense of the common. For Arendt (1958/1998), the minimum was the necessity of honoring the natural dialectic of public and private; for Benhabib and Habermas, it is a commitment to discourse ethics. These minimal agreements work to counter unreflective acceptance of individualism with little commitment to public engagement as the norm. The importance of public engagement meets us daily in issues ranging from school safety to air travel.

Take, for instance, the danger of guns in high schools across the country. Twenty years ago, who would have expected the routine need for devices to check for guns before going to a party or, in some cases, before going into the school itself? Shootings in high schools continue to happen much too regularly, and students are showing their frustration with gun violence by walking out of classrooms in protest (Grinberg & Yan, 2018).

One can turn to less catastrophic events by asking the question, "Can you depend on your friends to have public agreement on what is ethical in their dealings with you?" For instance, if you need time to do work, is such time possible with these particular friendships? If you are going to the airport and need a ride, does someone offer to assist? If you are sad and fighting melancholy, does someone "hang close" during such moments? Or are your friends friendly to you as long as you make their days better and more entertaining? The definition of friendship implies assisting the Other without constant regard for oneself.

The insight about the diversity of this historical moment with the loss of public agreement is central to Habermas's (2003) *The Future of Human Nature*. This work is a series of reflections begun while receiving major awards, including the

Peace Prize of the German Book Trade on October 15, 2001. Habermas makes his case simply, with an emphasis on the focus on the "me" of our historical moment. Pragmatically, we cannot escape the moment before us:

> What ought I, or what ought we, to do? But the "ought" has a different sense once we are no longer asking about rights and duties that everyone ascribes to one another from an inclusive we-perspective, but instead are concerned with our own life from the first-person perspective and ask what is best "for me" or "for us" in the long run and all things considered. Such ethical questions regarding our own weal and woe arise in the context of a *particular* life history or a *unique* form of life. They are wedded to questions of identity: how we should understand ourselves, who we are and want to be. Obviously there is no answer to such questions that would be independent of the given context and thus would bind all persons in the same way. (p. 3)

Habermas reminds us of a communication ethics reality—the public domain consists of the obscure, the unduly certain, the lost, and the exhausted. The move to "me" is one of the pragmatic alternatives of our time, and this move eclipses the natural complexity of human insight, missing the natural dialectic of public and private life.

Habermas suggests that the public domain rests within a commitment to discourse ethics. Consistent with Habermas's contention, we add literacy to communication ethics; communication ethics literacy assumes the necessity of "reading" the protected and promoted good of a given communicative event. With such an understanding of communication ethics, it is necessary to discern both individual and collective actions in the reading of a given good that is protected and promoted. The diversity and difference before us takes us to a public sphere of required communication ethics literacy as we seek to read and understand a good protected and promoted by a group or an individual person.

Communication Ethics Literacy

Questions about religion, race, gender, and ethnicity now join questions about the environment, crisis communication, and issues of language and science literacy. We are no longer in a time of information increase alone, but in an era of responsibility increase, as well—a time to learn and engage information that we do not know and would not even care to know. The banality of our time resides in new information. The ethical edge rests with a communication ethics *responsibility to learn and discern*. Communication ethics does not rest comfortably in passive listening to a teacher who tells, but, instead, walks in agitated demand, calling out both teacher and student to learn.

Communication ethics committed to learning suggests that the defining characteristics of unethical communicative acts are twofold: (1) assuming that you know everything and (2) assuming that what the other knows is not worth knowing. The joy of learning is the communication ethics burden of this moment.

Learning and discernment, attending to the reading of the good, lead to communication ethics. Sandra Harding (1991) outlined the importance of standpoint of position; in communication ethics, one must ask, "What is the good protected and promoted by a given communicative action and position?" In this historical moment, communication ethics becomes the pragmatic unity of *learning* and *discerning* of differing views of the good, standpoints that carry value-laden implications.

One of the authors sits on a civility committee for the entire campus. He was asked, "Do you think the campus could agree about importance of a campaign about civility?" The answer was not what the person wanted to hear: "I am confident we can agree upon one major issue—there will be no agreement on what civility is and what constitutes civility in all settings." In this historical moment, we suggest, one must define civility with the beginning assumption that we live in a time of normative disagreement. Later in the meeting, when asked if we should have a moratorium on cursing, the answer continued in similar spirit. "Of course, and do not expect all to consider this a good idea. In this historical moment, it is important for those who do not want a moratorium to recognize that some are so committed to such a moratorium that they are willing to endure comments from those that consider such an action short sighted and culturally chauvinistic."

Haiman's (1967) "Rhetoric of the Streets" continues to warn us of such cultural dangers after its publication more than thirty years ago. Additionally, Janie Harden Fritz's book *Professional Civility* (2013) notes that some scholars view the term "civility" as more oppressive than liberating (pp. 4–5), which Shelley D. Lane (2017) also highlights in *Understanding Everyday Incivility: Why Are They So Rude?* These scholars are both correct and incorrect, in that those calling for civility and those questioning civility are both right—to displace telling makes space for learning that looks not to one idea but to ideas held in dialectical tension. This insight guides the crisis communication work of Mitroff, mentioned earlier in this chapter. Additionally, the importance of dialectical tension defines the central insights of Arendt in her commitment to both public and private domains of communicative life. The "existential" legacy of Heidegger, Arendt, Bonhoeffer, Jaspers, and Buber was the connection of dialectic to everyday life, taking it out of the realm of idealism into the arena of identity. Simply put, it is only through darkness that light offers meaning, and vice versa—the dialectic is a defining sense of identity for all existence.

This historical moment asks us to take a modernist understanding of truth off the table. We sit between the hope of learning and the demand of imposition. We contend that the greatest danger rests in a telling/imposition with conviction that takes the Other off the conceptual map of influence. Learning does not presuppose agreement or commonality; neither does it discount another's standing or register automatic disdain for the unfamiliar or for a good or goods we do not accept or find attractive.

With differences on issues such as civility, one must fall to one side of the conversation more than to the other—otherwise, the notion of dialectic morphs into relativism, the view that anything goes or that all goods are equally valuable in human life, losing the necessity of conviction in a postmodern age of narrative and virtue contention. This book project falls to the side of the pragmatic necessity of learning that begins with a willingness to respect the Other enough to learn about what is important to the Other. Richard Bernstein (1989, 1992) refers to a form of "engaged fallibilistic pluralism" that seeks to meet our fragmented moment with respect and full knowledge of the fragility of the learners and the world before us:

> But the question becomes how we are to *respond* to this pluralism. There are powerful centrifugal tendencies toward fragmentation. But there are also counter-tendencies—not toward convergence, consensus, and harmony—but toward breaking down of boundaries, "a loosening of old landmarks" and dialogical encounters where we reasonably explore our differences and conflicts. In this situation, the pragmatic legacy is especially relevant, in particular the call to nurture the type of community and solidarity where there is an engaged fallibilistic pluralism—one that is based upon mutual respect, where we are willing to risk our own prejudgments, are open to listening and learning from others, and we respond to others with responsiveness and responsibility. I conclude with a citation from John Courtney Murray, who eloquently expressed the *ethos* of an engaged fallibilistic pluralism. "Barbarism . . . threatens when men cease to talk together according to reasonable laws. There are laws of arguments, the observance of which is imperative if discourse is to be civilized. Argument ceases to be civil when it is dominated by passion and prejudice; when its vocabulary becomes solipsist, premised on the theory that my insight is mine alone and cannot be shared; when dialogue gives way to a series of monologues; when the parties to the conversation cease to listen to one another, or hear only what they want to hear, or see the other's argument only through the screen of their own categories . . . When things like this happen, men cannot be locked together in argument. Conversation becomes merely quarrelsome or querulous. Civility dies with the death of dialogue." (1992, pp. 338–339; see Murray, 1960, p. 14)

Communication ethics learning is situated within the same pragmatic spirit; our moment offers many potential dangers, but there is one guaranteed danger—an unwillingness to meet and learn from the unknown. Just as Bernstein makes the pragmatic move to dialogue, so does this work on communication ethics in an age in which difference is our defining common center in the public arena.

The Pragmatics of Dialogic Ethics

The pragmatic move to dialogue emerges first and foremost from a content view of communication ethics. Dialogue requires that one know the ground from which one speaks, meet the Other with a willingness to learn, and learn about the ground from which the Other's discourse emerges. This view of dialogue begins with the importance of content—privileging content over style. The task of dialogic ethics is to meet whatever is before us—the good, the bad, and the ugly. The banal impulse of our time is to reject another's ideas because that person does not "do" dialogue as we demand. The move to demand transfers the communication from the possibility of dialogue to monologue in its most negative sense.

During a conference, a young scholar presented an essay on his faith position related to communication. The presentation was clear (some might go so far as to suggest the word dogmatic) in reference to the delivery and the perceived truth of the discourse. A thoughtful scholar of dialogue had the courage to raise the question, "How does the firmness of your belief open any space for dialogue?" The question needed attention, and the young scholar was unsure of an appropriate response. One of the authors of this work sat in the audience and thought, "I would not know how to answer that question, either." The question got at the heart of what might be the central dialogic question of an era of difference: "How is dialogue possible when one speaks from a position of confidence and conviction?" Only after more thought—as usual, days later, and long after the chance to assist the conversation—did the following insight emerge. It is not the space for dialogue that begins the conversation; it is our willingness to engage our own ground and meet that of another, no matter how much we contend with a given stance. If we are to address the authentic differences between persons in this age of recognized difference, we must begin with what Buber recommended a half century ago, the ground upon which we stand. Such is the reason that Bonhoeffer considered it immoral to expect another to refute or forsake a given ground of meaning in order to enter a conversation. Writing from prison, Bonhoeffer (1981) highlights the significance of ground:

> Heinrich: And if, then, death sits in your breast in the shape of a piece of shrapnel, grinning at you every day—and you don't know for what purpose you are alive and for what purpose you are dying—yes, then it's a miracle if you don't go mad with the urge to live and with despair, with hatred of all that lives, and with craving for wild pleasure. Give me ground under my feet, give me the Archimedean point to stand on—and all would be different.
>
> Christopher: Ground under your feet—I have never understood it like that. I believe you are right. I understand—ground under your feet, to be able to live and to die. (pp. 46–47)

Dialogue hides when we demand that another vacate the ground that offers meaning and vision for a given standpoint. However, when the request is more modest, dialogue has a chance to emerge. Perhaps a question of dialogic invitation begins with this question: "How and what can I learn from and about the Other's position when I am in disagreement, and how does this insight add texture to my own standpoint?" The difference in the two interpretive entrances into dialogue is that the conventional position begins with communication process and the latter question begins with content/ground and our responsibility to learn that content. Dialogic ethics begins with a content question and a responsibility to learn.

We cannot control dialogue, and our demand for it actually removes from us the likelihood of its emergence. Working from the ground or content of given positions is the first ethical mandate, which opens the door to the potential for new insights to emerge between oneself and the alterity or difference that meets one in a given moment. Such a view of dialogue is akin to practicing the "content" of a musical instrument; one cannot force oneself to be a good musician, but if one continues to play and learn content, every now and then emerges a moment between the player and the content that takes the music to a place not known before. One cannot demand such revelation, but without the hard work and practice on the content, no revelation will happen.

A "content beginning" of dialogic ethics rejects what Dietrich Bonhoeffer (1955) called "cheap grace." In the book *Dialogic Confession: Bonhoeffer's Rhetoric of Responsibility* (Arnett, 2005), the task was to learn how one could meet and learn from a position that is different from one's own. Dialogic confession uses content as a central pragmatic metaphor; one begins with confession of the ground upon which one stands, a statement about content that one takes ever so seriously, and then attends to the Other as the Other does the same. Such a view of communication ethics privileges content, learning, and discernment for self and Other. Arnett (2005) states:

> Bonhoeffer's interpersonal ethic of dialogic confession reaches out to others while firmly surrounded by a story that connects one to others through the "bridges" of service and awareness of other perspectives. His interpersonal ethic is neither an absolute unleashing of individual liberty nor a desperate clinging to an old moral system, but an interpersonal life guided by a center that reaches out to others, supported by conviction and extended by the cautionary act of lowering "bridges." This "unity of contraries" approach that guides his interpersonal ethic requires the strength and courage to know where one stands and to reach out to others, offering "bridges" where persons of difference can meet for conversation and work together. In a postmodern age, Bonhoeffer offers the following confession: begin with a position, walls that sustain ground for narrative life, and then reach out to the Other in this historical moment of diversity, of a "world come of age." Bonhoeffer offers insight into the "how" of taking walls into a world of diversity only to discover the pragmatic necessity of learning, which offers the bridge for the twenty-first century. (p. 219)

The work understands dialogic ethics as a communicative bridge pragmatically necessary for the 21st century.

An era of difference brings forth a view of dialogue situated in content and learning as the companions to a dialogic ethics first principle. We listen without demand, attending to what is before us—appreciated or not. Such attentiveness permits us to meet the historical moment before us, not that which we demand. Attending to the ground/content of self and Other calls forth a natural act of dialogic negotiation, necessitating a dialogic ethical competence that requires us to walk with knowledge of temporality and inaccuracy, requiring us to privilege learning over telling propelled by conviction.

Dialogic ethics listens and meets what is before us, attending to the historical moment and seeking to negotiate new possibilities through attention to content via listening, attentiveness, and negotiation of difference, inviting new insight through the "between" of persons and historical moment, ever protecting and promoting the goods of interpersonal relationship, dwelling places, a sense of welcome and home in organizational life. Dialogic ethics works with the dual importance of public and private communicative spheres in order to maintain the natural dialectic that makes questioning and critical engagement possible, culture as a primary carrier of standpoint, which lends itself to learning from difference, and the unity of direction and change. Dialogic ethics works with responsiveness to health of self and Other, recognizing the frailty of human life and the hope of the possible. Dialogic ethics engages a digital world with thoughtful care, resisting the equivalence of information and wisdom and connectedness with intimacy. Dialogic ethics that begins with content and learning finds goods that others find worthy of protecting and promoting. Learning is the needed response to what Seyla Benhabib and Fred Dallmayr (1990) have called the communicative ethics controversy of our time.

The controversy that this book has addressed is lack of agreement about the good. Turning to narrative, communicative practices, learning, difference, and negotiation in the dialogic meeting of this moment as an alternative to prescriptive telling is key to a postmodern world of difference. We may not be able to agree upon the good, but perhaps it is this fact that carries with it a pragmatic sense of hope. Look at all the problems around us. We have few answers to increasingly troubling questions. Honesty registers the reality of confusion. Learning and discernment, avoiding the danger of telling with a conviction that disregards the Other, is not a communicative "morsel" but a communicative "feast." We live not in a moment of fear or loss, but in a time of responsibility to learn, in a time of meeting ideas that we might want to dismiss, but cannot.

We live in a time that calls us to negotiate temporal agreement, in a time of competing views of the good that presents a sumptuous spread, a proverbial *Babette's Feast* (Axel, 1988) before us. *Babette's Feast,* set in the 19th century, tells the story of a Parisian chef, Babette, who flees France to seek refuge in Denmark. She lives with two elderly sisters, cooking for them and eventually running their household with grace and efficiency, retaining from her past life only a lottery ticket that a friend in Paris renews for her annually. One day, news comes that she has won the lottery. In a response of gratitude, Babette spends the entire sum on a lavish, extravagant meal that she prepares and serves to the small church congregation to which the elderly sisters belong.

In our historical moment, contending views of the good offer a banquet of possibilities, and within that lavish extravagance there is hope in moments of celebration from the learning, the meeting, and the negotiating of difference. Dialogic ethics ultimately views this moment as a "Babette's Feast," not a moment of despair and loss, but an urging of responsibility that rests in the hope of a human

© Kondor83/Shutterstock.com

condition in which the first communicative act is to learn, followed by a willingness to take a stand without losing our sense of "maybe" and pragmatic caution—
dialogic ethics lives within the pragmatic hope of learning and discernment ever
negotiated anew among self, Other, and the demands of the historical moment
before us. This moment is not a moral crisis, but a historical demand for us to
step up to the responsibility of meeting, learning, and negotiating differing views
of the good. A dialogic rendering of communication ethics begins with meeting
the world as it is before us—whether we concur or not, whether it is in agreement
with us or not—whether deemed by us as good, bad, or ugly. Now, we can learn
and work our way to temporal agreements engaged in a dialogue that begins and
ends not in despair, but in celebration of a moment of lavish extravagance for all
who want to learn. Communication ethics in this era is an open table, calling us
to gather at "Babette's Feast." As students, as participants in the marketplace of
an ever-increasing difference of ideas, as members of communities and families,
all of us are called to invite others to this table of learning, of difference, and of
conversation that, in turn, invites unexpected dialogic meeting as we engage this
historical moment together.

Communication ethics, as understood in this book, reminds us to learn from
difference. As stated by Lisbeth Lipari (2004),

> In my dialogic encounter with you, I will not only listen for your radical alterity
> but I will open and make a place for it. It means that I do not resort only to what
> is easy—what I already know, or what we have in common. It means that I listen
> for and make space for the difficult, the different, the radically strange. (p. 138)

Of course, we must choose upon which side to land in an argument. This communicative gesture defines the fallibility and the necessity of what it means to be human. We learn, then we do our best, and, perhaps, in the model of a Dietrich Bonhoeffer, we take temporal conviction into human life with its restless companion, doubt. A commitment to learning never permits the smugness of assurance to eclipse the necessity of learning and the possibility of new insight to offer a corrective. Such commitment reminds us of a basic communication ethics conviction in an age of narrative and virtue contention—learn from difference and, as one chooses, do not lose the pragmatic necessity of doubt and "maybe" in a time of change and recognized difference.

COMMUNICATION ETHICS: REFLECTION AND ACTION

1. What issues require you to think carefully and take action with a pragmatic understanding of communication ethics? For example, what issues emerge regularly in relationships with friends, parents, and significant others that require discernment and reflection in order to take constructive action?
2. Locate three significant current issues that have emerged in the past months on your campus that required crisis communication— for instance, what unexpected events have emerged that called for your educational institution's reflection upon and articulation of the good it protects and promotes in order to address those events in a manner consistent with the mission of the institution?
3. What steps can you take to increase your communication ethics literacy as you take your education into the marketplace, community settings, extended family contexts, and personal life?

ENGAGING COMMUNICATION ETHICS THROUGH LITERATURE: *LES MISÉRABLES*

In *Les Misérables*, Jean Valjean works with pragmatic action to protect and promote the goods of the lives and happiness of many throughout the story. In each situation, he engages crisis communication to protect and promote those goods. A number of days after his meeting with the bishop, he springs into quick action, entering a burning house to save the life of a child. While serving as mayor of Montreuil-sur-mer, he moves without hesitation, risking recognition of his true identity due to his prodigious strength, to save the life of Fauchelevent. When pursued by Javert, Valjean acts rapidly to scale the wall of the Convent of the Petite Picpus, moving Cosette to safety. Finally, Valjean responds to the crisis of revolution by saving the lives of his two worst enemies: Javert, the law officer who seeks to take his freedom, and Marius, who seeks to take from him his only joy in life, Cosette. As each unexpected crisis emerges, Valjean engages communication ethics literacy, honoring the good of the Other with whom he is in disagreement. He works from his own ground of hope and conviction, learns from the ground of the Other, and listens to the historical moment in each instance. This pragmatic engagement of communication ethics literacy moves him to engage his final moment of life with a reflective response to the inevitable, the meeting of death, offering a legacy of hope to those he leaves behind.

Valjean offers a dialogic ethic that begins with a pragmatic meeting and learning of what is before him, wanted or not, while doing the best he can to connect communicative action to a narrative structure that infused his life at the hands of Monseigneur Bienvenu, the "Bishop of Welcome." When the authorities caught Valjean with the silverware and brought him back, the bishop uttered a statement that acted as an ethical guiding echo for the remainder of Valjean's life—"Oh, thank you for bringing him back—he forgot the candlesticks." Sometimes narrative ground comes when least expected, and one's communication ethic becomes informed by engaging the face of another who has us meet the world otherwise, inviting change through learning, and is later tested through additional learning that no one would voluntarily accept. Hope comes in the strangest forms, sometimes in a gesture that changes lives—"Oh, thank you for bringing him back—he forgot the candlesticks." As Emmanuel Levinas reminds us over and over again, ultimately, it is not theory that calls us to responsibility for another, but a human face. The face of the Other offers the "why" to bear any "how," offering meaning through an inescapable burden—communication ethics literacy that seeks to learn about competing goods, never forgetting the "why" for such learning: our responsibility to and for the Other.

Glossary of Terms

Applied communication—the "how" of communicative doing tests any philosophy or theory and ultimately is the laboratory of communication ethics. Communication ethics does not live in the abstract, but, in the words of Willie Nelson, understands the necessity of being "on the road again," making a difference through action. Application is the place where communication ethics comes to life (ch. 2).

Business and professional communication—the study of communication within particular business and professional settings, defined by participation in the public square of competitive economic exchange. Nonprofits must take the market and its demands seriously, just as a competitive business does; today's marketplace requires both types of business and professional settings (ch. 10).

Care—a human answer to the call of the Other; a willingness to meet and attend to someone other than oneself (ch. 12).

Codes, procedures, and standards in communication ethics—defines communication ethics guidelines to evaluate appropriate ethical conduct, protecting and promoting the good of corporately agreed-upon practices and regulations (ch. 3).

Common sense—the commonly understood, taken-for-granted assumptions about the way the world works and expected communicative behaviors one will meet in navigating that world in daily life. The taken-for-granted in this historical moment is that common sense is no longer common. Theory provides a form of public common sense that drives ideas and communication ethics engagement (ch. 4).

Communication ethics literacy—identifies the good in the interplay of self and Other and the particular historical moment, attending to what requires protection and promotion (ch. 14).

Community of memory within organizations—the pragmatic equivalent of an organizational conscience, providing a reminder of what has and has not worked and what particular actions did and continue to do for communicative life together, shaping a given dwelling place in a particular fashion (ch. 8).

Contextual communication ethics—recognizes communication ethics variations across differing cultures, persons, and settings when applying communication ethics principles, protecting and promoting the good of the particular (ch. 3).

Crisis communication—an increasingly relevant metaphor for today's postmodern moment of virtue contention; the unexpected emerges and requires discernment and action as we encounter differing particular "goods" in the public domain (ch. 14).

Culture—consists of communicative practices, traditions, and stories that give identity to a group of people. Culture is a communicative background that provides meaning and stability

▲ **253**

to human life, providing an often unexamined sense of ground that makes foreground implementation of given communicative actions sensible within a given culture (ch. 9).

Culture shock—a feeling of disorientation experienced when encountering communicative events disruptive of one's expected routine (ch. 9).

Democratic communication ethics—a public communication ethics process for discussion of ideas, customs, and rights, protecting and promoting the good of collaborative decision making (ch. 3).

The dialectic of direction and change—willingness to follow a particular path with the courage to move in a different direction when necessary (ch. 10).

Dialogic communication ethics—acknowledges communication ethics as attentive to the emergent, not owned by either party in the conversation, responsive to multiple goods that give rise to and emerge in ongoing conversations, protecting and promoting the good of learning (ch. 3).

Dialogic coordinates—suggest communicative elements needed to invite dialogue; these five coordinates are learning from listening, refraining from the demand that dialogue take place, acknowledging bias, recognizing that not all communication is or should be in the form of dialogue, and keeping content and learning foremost. Invitation guides the basic assumption of dialogic ethics (ch. 5).

Dialogic ethics—assumes the importance of the meeting of communicative ground that gives rise to a particular sense of good and is simultaneously open to learning and emergent insight that belongs to an ontological reality between persons, not to any one person in a conversation. Dialogic ethics begins with meeting what is before us—the good, the bad, and the ugly. Such an ethic rejects demand and the occasionally heard comment, "We need more dialogue." This statement only assures the impossibility of dialogic ethics, which hides from the ongoing demand made by oneself or another (ch. 5).

Dialogic theory—situates background assumptions about dialogue in three major elements of human meeting: the different grounds/narratives from which self and Other begin the conversation and the emergent temporal answer given life by the meeting of such difference (ch. 5).

Dialogue and difference—begin with the ground under our feet, the narrative that gives shape to what we consider good, and learning from the ground of the Other, calling us to attend to the meaning emergent in the meeting of a given historical moment. Difference is the key to learning and living well in a postmodern culture. Difference is the energy that makes dialogue possible (ch. 5).

Differentiation of public and private space—identifies two spheres of life that shape and inform each other by maintaining their separate identities. The key to this differentiation is the reclaiming of a natural dialectic of accountability where one can call one dimension of communicative life into question by the other, texturing a clear understanding of one's public and private positions (ch. 6).

Digital responsibility—protecting and promoting the good of persons and relationships in the use of mediated communication (ch. 13).

Distance—provides necessary space for each communicative partner to contribute to the relationship (ch. 7).

Dwelling place—the type of communicative home a given organization invites by its communicative practices. The notion of home does not suggest all warmth and care; indeed, there are homes that are far from this reality. A dwelling place is a gathering of communicative practices and stories that gives an organization a sense of uniqueness, separating a specified organization from others within the same industry (ch. 8).

The good—describes a central value or set of values manifested in communicative practices that we seek to protect and promote in our discourse together (ch. 1).

Health—the interplay of communicative responses to conditions of mind, body, and soul, from the beginning to the end of a life (ch. 12).

Health care communication—the study of communication practices within the broad domain of health care, from patient/professional interaction to institutional communication about health (ch. 12).

Historical moment—announces a question relevant to human existence that we must engage; our manner of engaging this question announces the good we seek to protect and promote. We may agree on a given question announced by a historical moment and find significant disagreement on what communicative action should follow (ch. 1).

The inarticulate—refers to goods that one is unable to define or pinpoint with precision, but that, nevertheless, shape and nurture a culture's communicative life and practices (ch. 9).

Integrated marketing communication—the study of communicative content that is engaged from a number of differing vantage points within the marketplace, incorporating the functions of advertising, public relations, marketing, promotions, interactive strategies, and all functions relating to an institution's audience (ch. 11).

Integration—the importance of diverse ideas that come together to create a unique whole that is more than the combination of its parts—the whole is greater than the sum of its parts (ch. 11).

Intercultural communication—the study of differences and similarities of cultural content and its influence on persons within and across different cultures (ch. 9).

Interpersonal communication—works with the good of the relationship between and among a small number of people (two to four) (ch. 7).

Interpersonal responsibility—begins with each person's commitment to active care for the interpersonal relationship, owned by neither and nurtured with or without the support of the Other. Interpersonal responsibility adheres to the insight of Emmanuel Levinas, abandoning the expectation of reciprocity for attentiveness to a call to responsibility with or without the approval of the Other (ch. 7).

Learning—is the communication ethics good of this era; we begin with learning our own framework for what is good to be and to do, and then we learn about the framework of others, meeting the different or strange with a pragmatic desire to learn, not necessarily to agree (ch. 1). Without a single understanding of common sense, learning and understanding differing standpoints is a pragmatic communication ethics act (ch. 4).

Mediated communication—communication through channels other than face to face/ body to body (ch. 13).

Multiplicity of communication ethics—we cannot assume that each good that we seek to protect and promote and that shapes the heart of a given communication ethic finds support from others (ch. 2).

Narrative—a story agreed upon by a group of people that provides limits within which we dwell as embedded communicative agents. Communication ethics philosophy and application are foreground issues for this chapter, but it is the background narratives of what groups of persons know and do that put limits and shed light on the knowing and doing of communication ethics. Narratives can and do change from the actions of communicative agents and shifts in the historical moment—narratives change, ideologies resist alteration from the outside, and stories sometimes fail to move people to the point of active support (ch. 2).

Narrative communication ethics—assumes that a communication ethic begins with persons' lives guided by stories about the way the world is or should be, protecting and promoting the good residing within given narratives. Recent discussion on virtue ethics includes recognition of public virtues that guide the coordinates of a narrative ethic (ch. 3).

Organizational communication—the orchestrating of communicative practices through formal and informal structures of events and persons in a given organization to accomplish a given purpose or purposes (ch. 8).

Organizations and institutions—formations working together to establish a gestalt identity, with the latter providing a background identity that guides and shapes the horizon of possibilities played out in a particular fashion within a particular organization (ch. 8).

Philosophy of communication—having a "why" for the doing, for communicative action, is pragmatic in an era defined by difference. To understand what one does and to discern the communicative action of another opens the door to communication ethics assessment and change; a communication ethic finds shape in the ongoing conversation of "why" in interplay with the demands of a given historical moment (ch. 2).

Postmodernity—identifies our current historical moment and announces narrative and virtue contention as normative (ch. 1).

Pragmatic—the need for practical engagement of ideas responsive to a particular historical moment (ch. 14).

The private realm—personal arenas of life calling for discernment in use of mediated communication (ch. 13).

Public clarity and caution—integrated marketing communication works to make the purpose and objectives of a business or nonprofit organization public, or, in other words, make transactions and opportunities in the marketplace transparent. IMC seeks to protect and promote the "good" of integration with an implicit communication ethics assumption—integration makes the choices of market participants public and visible (ch. 11).

Public decision making—involves discerning a course of action with full recognition that other alternatives exist. The standard for public decision making is not one's opinion, but an idea, theory, story, or action known by a group of persons and offered as a public decision making map. For instance, calling someone to account for plagiarizing requires that there be a public standard that roots the decision making/judgment in a public evaluative base (ch. 6).

Public discourse—conversation about ideas in civic/community contexts marked by diversity of perspectives requiring thoughtful public engagement. It is not the notion of one to many that makes discourse public, but confidence that one has a public audience who will listen, agree, and/or contend with ideas delivered in the public arena. Public discourse examines differing insights that shape our public engagement with one another (ch. 6).

The public sphere—the arena in which citizens exchange opinions and make decisions (ch. 13).

Public testing—the good of continuing to last rests with a public testing responsive to both known and unforeseen demands of the market (ch. 10).

Responsiveness—responsibility that meets the call of the Other, even when the call is unwanted (ch. 12).

Standpoint communication ethics—suggests that the ground upon which one stands and meets the Other shapes one's perspective through differences in gender, race, ethnicity, affectivity, and culture (ch. 3).

Theories—public common sense, a public road map of a way to see, know, and understand that both broadens and narrows our insight (ch. 4).

Universal-humanitarian communication ethics—assumes one guiding communicative ethical principle of reason from the Enlightenment, protecting and promoting the ability of the human to discern the good through a rational process (ch. 3).

References

Adams, R. (1972). *Watership down*. London, UK: Rex Collings.

Alidou, O. A. (2002). A "Cinderella" tale in the Hausa Muslim women's imagination. *Comparative Literature, 54*, 242–255.

Allen, B. J. (2005). Social constructionism. In S. May & D. K. Mumby (Eds.), *Engaging organizational communication theory and research: Multiple perspectives* (pp. 35–54). Thousand Oaks, CA: SAGE.

Alpers, B. L. (2002). *Dictators, democracy, and American public culture*. Chapel Hill: University of North Carolina Press.

Andersen, K. E. (2000). Developments in communication ethics: The Ethics Commission, Code of Professional Responsibilities, Credo for Ethical Communication. *Journal of the Association for Communication Administration, 29*, 131–144.

Andersen, K. E. (2003). Recovering the civic culture: The imperative of ethical communication. *Carroll C. Arnold Distinguished Lecture, National Communication Association, November 2003*. New York, NY: Pearson.

Anderson, R., Baxter, L. A., & Cissna, K. N. (Eds.). (2004). *Dialogue: Theorizing difference in communication studies*. Thousand Oaks, CA: SAGE.

Anderson, R., Cissna, K., & Arnett, R. C. (Eds.). (1994). *The reach of dialogue: Confirmation, voice, and community*. Cresskill, NJ: Hampton Press.

Anthony, K. E., & Sellnow, T. L. (2011). Beyond Narnia: The necessity of C. S. Lewis' first and second things in applied communication research. *Journal of Applied Communication Research, 39*, 441–443.

Appiah, K. A. (2006). *Cosmopolitanism: Ethics in a world of strangers*. New York, NY: W. W. Norton & Co.

Appiah, K. A. (2007). *The ethics of identity*. Princeton, NJ: Princeton University Press.

Appiah, K. A. (2010). *Experiments in ethics*. Cambridge, MA: Harvard University Press.

Appiah, K. A. (2017). *As if: Idealization and ideals*. Cambridge, MA: Harvard University Press.

Arendt, H. (1963). *Eichmann in Jerusalem: A report on the banality of evil*. New York, NY: Viking Press.

Arendt, H. (1978). *The Jew as pariah: Jewish identity and politics in the modern age*. R. H. Feldman (Ed.). New York, NY: Grove Press.

Arendt, H. (1982). *Lectures on Kant's political philosophy*. Chicago, IL: University of Chicago Press.

Arendt, H. (1998). *The human condition* (2nd ed.). Chicago: University of Chicago Press. (Original work published 1958).

Aristotle. (1948). *The politics* (E. Barker, Trans.). Oxford, UK: Oxford University Press.

Aristotle. (1962). *Nicomachean ethics* (M. Ostwald, Trans.). Indianapolis, IN: Bobbs-Merrill.

Aristotle. (1995). *Treatise on rhetoric* (T. Buckley, Trans.) Amherst, NY: Prometheus Books.

Arjoon, S., Turriago-Hoyos, A., & Thoene, U. (2018). Virtuousness and the common good as a conceptual framework for harmonizing the goals of the individual, organizations, and the economy. *Journal of Business Ethics, 147,* 143–163.

Arnett, R. C. (1986). *Communication and community: Implications of Martin Buber's dialogue.* Carbondale: Southern Illinois University Press.

Arnett, R. C. (1987). The status of communication ethics scholarship in speech communication journals from 1915–1985. *Central States Speech Journal, 38,* 44–61.

Arnett, R. C. (1990). The practical philosophy of communication ethics and free speech as the foundation for speech communication. *Communication Quarterly, 38,* 208–217.

Arnett, R. C. (1992). *Dialogic education: Conversations about ideas and between people.* Carbondale: Southern Illinois University Press.

Arnett, R. C. (1994). Existential homelessness: A contemporary case for dialogue. In R. Anderson, K. N. Cissna, & R. C. Arnett (Eds.), *The reach of dialogue: Confirmation, voice, and community* (pp. 229–248). Cresskill, NJ: Hampton Press.

Arnett, R. C. (1998). Interpersonal praxis: The interplay of religious narrative, historicality and metaphor. *Journal of Communication and Religion, 21,* 141–163.

Arnett, R. C. (1999). Metaphorical guidance: Administration as building and renovation. *Journal of Educational Administration, 37,* 80–89.

Arnett, R. C. (2001). Dialogic civility as pragmatic ethical praxis: An interpersonal metaphor for the public domain. *Communication Theory, 11,* 315–338.

Arnett, R. C. (2002). Paulo Freire's revolutionary pedagogy. *Qualitative Inquiry, 8,* 489–510.

Arnett, R. C. (2005). *Dialogic confession: Bonhoeffer's rhetoric of responsibility.* Carbondale: Southern Illinois University Press.

Arnett, R. C. (2006a). Professional civility. In J. M. H. Fritz & B. L. Omdahl (Eds.), *Problematic relationships in the workplace* (pp. 233–248). New York, NY: Peter Lang.

Arnett, R. C. (2006b). Through a glass, darkly. *Journal of Communication and Religion, 29,* 1–17.

Arnett, R. C. (2012a). Biopolitics: An Arendtian communication ethic in the public domain. *Communication and Critical/Cultural Studies, 9,* 225–233.

Arnett, R. C. (2012b). The fulcrum point of dialogue: Monologue, worldview, and acknowledgment. *American Journal of Semiotics, 28,* 105–127.

Arnett, R. C. (2013). *Communication ethics in dark times: Hannah Arendt's rhetoric of warning and hope.* Carbondale: Southern Illinois University Press.

Arnett, R. C. (2014). Civic dialogue: Attending to locality and recovering monologue. *Journal of Dialogue Studies, 2*(2), 71–92.

Arnett, R. C. (2015). The dialogic necessity: Acknowledging and engaging monologue. *Ohio Communication Journal, 53,* 1–10.

Arnett, R. C. (2016). Educational misdirections: Attending to Levinas's call for ethics as first principle. *Atlantic Journal of Communication, 24,* 3–16.

Arnett, R. C. (2017a). Communicative ethics: The phenomenological sense of semioethics. *Language and Dialogue, 7,* 80–99.

Arnett, R. C. (2017b). *Levinas's rhetorical demand: The unending obligation of communication ethics.* Carbondale: Southern Illinois University Press.

Arnett, R. C. (in press). Individualism as a moral cul-de-sac. In E. M. Wąsik, J. Zaprucki, & Z. Wąsik (Eds.), *The semiotics of existentials: Between necessity and choice.* Karkonoska Państwowa Szkoła Wyższa w Jeleniej Górze.

Arnett, R. C., & Arneson, P. (1999). *Dialogic civility in a cynical age: Communication, hope, and interpersonal relationships.* Albany: State University of New York Press.

Arnett, R. C., Arneson, P., & Bell, L. M. (2006). Communication ethics: The dialogic turn. *Review of Communication, 6,* 63–93.

Arnett, R. C., Bell, L. M., & Fritz, J. M. H. (2010). Dialogic learning as first principle in communication ethics. *Atlantic Journal of Communication, 18,* 111–126.

Arnett, R. C., DeIuliis, S. M., & Corr, M. (2017). *Corporate communication crisis leadership: Advocacy and ethics.* New York, NY: Business Expert Press.

Arnett, R. C., & Fritz, J. M. H. (2001). Communication and professional civility as a basic service course: Dialogic praxis between departments and situated in an academic home. *Basic Communication Course Annual, 13,* 174–206.

Arnett, R. C., & Fritz, J. M. H. (2003). Sustaining institutional ethics and integrity: Management in a postmodern moment. In A. S. Iltis (Ed.), *Instituitional integrity in health care* (pp. 41–71). Dordrecht, Netherlands: Kluwer.

Arnett, R. C., Fritz, J. M. H., & Holba, A. (2007). The rhetorical turn to Otherness: Otherwise than humanism. *Cosmos and History: The Journal of Natural and Social Philosophy, 3,* 115–133.

Arnett, R. C., McKendree, A., Fritz, J. M. H., & Roberts, K. G. (2006). Persuasion in the school of business: Construction of a basic course in business and professional communication. In B. S. Hugenberg & L. W. Hugenberg (Eds.), *Teaching ideas for the basic communication course, 10* (pp. 17–24). Dubuque, IA: Kendall Hunt.

Asanti, M. K. (2002). *Handbook of international and intercultural communication.* Thousand Oaks, CA: SAGE.

Ashcraft, K. L. (2000). Empowering "professional" relationships: Organizational communication meets feminist practice. *Management Communication Quarterly, 13,* 347–392.

Ashcraft, K. L. (2005). Feminist organizational communication studies: Engaging gender in public and private. In S. May & D. K. Mumby (Eds.), *Engaging organizational communication theory and research: Multiple perspectives* (pp. 141–170). Thousand Oaks, CA: SAGE.

Ashcraft, K. L., & Mumby, D. K. (2004). *Reworking gender: A feminist communicology of organization.* Thousand Oaks, CA: SAGE.

Audi, R. (Ed.). (1999). *Cambridge dictionary of philosophy* (2nd ed.). New York, NY: Cambridge University Press.

Axel, G. (Director). (1988). *Babette's Feast* [Motion picture]. United States: MGM Studios.

Ayres, J. (1984). Four approaches to interpersonal communication: Review, observation, prognosis. *Western Journal of Speech Communication, 48,* 408–440.

Baker-Ohler, M., & Holba, A. M. (2009). *The communicative relationship between dialogue and care.* Amherst, NY: Cambria Press.

Bakhtin, M. (1998). Discourse in art, discourse in life. In F. Farmer (Ed.), *Landmark essays on Bakhtin, rhetoric and writing: Vol. 13* (pp. 3–10). Mahwah, NJ: Lawrence Erlbaum Associates, Inc.

Ballard, R. L., McManus, L. M. B., Holba, A. M., Jovanovic, S., Tompkins, P. S., Charron, L. J. N., . . . Swenson-Lepper, T. (2014). Teaching communication ethics as central to the discipline. *Journal of the Association for Communication Administration, 33,* 65–83.

Batra, R., & Keller, K. L. (2016). Integrating marketing communications: New findings, new lessons, and new ideas. *Journal of Marketing, 80,* 122–145.

Baxter, L. A., & Montgomery, B. M. (1996). *Relating: Dialogues and dialectics.* New York, NY: Guilford Press.

Baym, N. K. (2010). *Personal connections in the digital age.* Cambridge, UK: Polity Press.

Beatty, M. J., McCroskey, J. C., & Valencic, K. M. (2001). *The biology of communication: A communibiological perspective.* Cresskill, NJ: Hampton Press.

Bell, D. (1973). *The coming of post-industrialist society: A venture in social forecasting.* New York, NY: Basic Books.

Bellah, R. N., Madsen, R., Sullivan W. M., Swidler, A., & Tipton, S. M. (1985). *Habits of the heart: Individualism and commitment in American life.* Berkeley: University of California Press.

Bellah, R. N., Madsen, R., Sullivan, W. M., Swidler, A., & Tipton, S. M. (1991). *The good society.* New York, NY: Alfred A. Knopf.

Benhabib, S. (1992). *Situating the self: Gender, community and postmodernism in contemporary ethics.* New York, NY: Routledge.

Benhabib, S. (1996). *Democracy and difference: Contesting boundaries of the political.* Princeton, NJ: Princeton University Press.

Benhabib, S., & Dallmayr F. (Eds.). (1990). *The communicative ethics controversy.* Cambridge, MA: MIT Press.

Berger, C. R., & Calabrese, R. J. (1975). Some explorations in initial interaction and beyond: Toward a developmental theory of interpersonal communication. *Human Communication Research, 1,* 99–112.

Berger, C. R., & Gudykunst, W. B. (1991). Uncertainty and communication. In B. Dervin & M. Voight (Eds.), *Progress in communication sciences* (pp. 21–67). Norwood, NJ: Ablex.

Bergman, M. (2016). Melioristic inquiry and critical habits: Pragmatism and the ends of communication research. *Empedocles: European Journal for the Philosophy of Communication, 7,* 173–188.

Berkenkotter, C., & Huckin, T. N. (1994). Genre knowledge in disciplinary communication: Cognition, culture, power. Mahwah, NJ: Lawrence Erlbaum.

Berlo, D. K. (1960). *The process of communication: An introduction to theory and practice.* New York, NY: Holt, Rinehart, & Winston.

Bernstein, R. J. (1983). *Beyond objectivism and relativism: Science, hermeneutics and praxis.* Philadelphia: University of Pennsylvania Press.

Bernstein, R. J. (1989). Pragmatism, pluralism and the healing of wounds. *Proceedings and Addresses of the American Philosophical Association, 63*(3), 5–18.

Bernstein, R. J. (1992). *The new constellation: The ethical-political horizons of modernity/postmodernity.* Cambridge, MA: MIT Press.

Bernstein, R. J. (2010). *The pragmatic turn.* Cambridge, UK: Polity Press.

Best, S., & Kellner, D. (1991). *Postmodern theory: Critical interrogations.* New York, NY: Guilford Press.

Blau, J. R. (1993). *Social contracts and economic markets.* New York, NY: Kluwer Academic Publishers.

Bok, S. (1979). *Lying: Moral choice in public and private life.* New York, NY: Alfred A. Knopf.

Bok, S. (2002). *Common values.* Columbia: University of Missouri Press.

Bonhoeffer, D. (1955). *Ethics* (Trans. N. H. Smith). E. Bethge (Ed.). New York, NY: Macmillan.

Bonhoeffer, D. (1978). *Life together: The classic exploration of faith in community.* New York, NY: Harper & Row Publishers.

Bonhoeffer, D. (1981). *Fiction from prison: Gathering up the past* (U. Hoffmann, Trans.). R. Bethge & E. Bethge (Eds.). Philadelphia, PA: Fortress Press.

Bonhoeffer, D. (1997). *Letters and papers from prison* (Enlarged ed.). E. Bethge (Ed.). New York, NY: Touchstone. (Original work published 1953).

Bonhoeffer, D. (2005). *Ethics* (R. Krauss, C. C. West, & D. W. Stott, Trans.). C. J. Green (Ed.). Minneapolis, MN: Fortress Press.

Borden, S. L. (2007). *Journalism as practice: MacIntyre, virtue ethics and the press.* New York, NY: Routledge.

Bracci, S. L., & Christians, C. G. (Eds.). (2002). *Moral engagement in public life: Theorists for contemporary ethics.* New York, NY: Peter Lang.

Bridge, K., & Baxter, L. A. (1992). Blended relationships: Friends as work associates. *Western Journal of Communication, 56,* 200–225.

Brightman, C. (1995). Introduction: An epistolary romance. In Arendt, H., & McCarthy, M., *Between friends: The correspondence of Hannah Arendt & Mary McCarthy* (C. Brightman, Ed., pp. vii–xxx.). London, UK: Secker & Warburg.

Brown, C. T., & Keller, P. W. (1973). *Monologue to dialogue: An exploration of interpersonal communication.* Englewood Cliffs, NJ: Prentice-Hall.

Brown, H., Guskin, E., & Mitchell, A. (2012, November 28). The role of social media in the Arab uprisings. *Pew Research Center: Journalism & Media.* Retrieved from http://www.journalism.org/2012/11/28/role-social-media-arab-uprisings/

Bruhn, M., & Schnebelen, S. (2017). Integrated marketing communication—from an instrumental to a customer-centric perspective. *European Journal of Marketing, 51,* 464–489.

Buber, M. (1948). *Israel and the world.* New York, NY: Schocken.

Buber, M. (1955). *Between man and man* (R. G. Smith, Trans.). Boston, MA: Beacon Press.

Buber, M. (1958). *Paths in utopia.* Boston, MA: Beacon Hill.

Buber, M. (1966). *The origin and meaning of Hasidism* (M. Friedman, Trans.). New York, NY: Harper & Row.

Buber, M. (1970). *I and thou.* New York, NY: Touchstone Press.

Burke, K. (1954). *Permanence and change.* Berkeley: University of California Press.

Buzzanell, P. M. (Ed.). (2002). *Rethinking organizational and managerial communication from feminist perspectives* (3rd ed.). Thousand Oaks, CA: SAGE.

Callahan, D., & Bok, S. (1980). *The teaching of ethics in higher education.* Hastings-on-Hudson, NY: Institute of Society, Ethics, and the Life Sciences.

Carnegie, D. (1981). *How to win friends and influence people.* New York, NY: Simon & Schuster. (Original work published 1936)

Carr, C. E. (1906). *Lincoln at Gettysburg.* Chicago, IL: A. C. McClurg & Co.

Caygill, H. (1998). *Walter Benjamin: The color of experience.* New York, NY: Routledge.

Cheney, G. (2000). Interpreting interpretive research: Toward perspectives without relativism. In S. R. Corman & M. S. Poole (Eds.), *Perspectives on organizational communication: Finding common ground* (pp. 12–46). New York, NY: The Guilford Press.

Chesebro, J. W. (1969). A construct for assessing ethics in communication. *Central States Speech Journal, 20,* 104–114.

Chesebro, J. W. (1973). Cultures in conflict: A generic and axiological view. *Today's Speech, 21,* 11–20.

Chesebro, J. W. (1997). Communication ethics and sexual orientation. In J. Makau & R. C. Arnett (Eds.), *Communication ethics in an age of diversity* (pp. 126–154). Champaign: University of Illinois Press.

Christensen, L. T., & Cornelissen, J. (2011). Bridging corporate and organizational communication: Review, development and a look to the future. *Management Communication Quarterly, 25,* 383–414.

Christensen, L. T., Firat, A. F., & Cornelissen, J. (2009). New tensions and challenges in integrated communications. *Corporate Communications: An International Journal, 14,* 207–219.

Christensen, L. T., Firat, A. F., & Torp, S. (2008). The organisation of integrated communications: Toward flexible integration. *European Journal of Marketing, 42,* 423–452.

Christensen, L. T., Morsing, M., & Thyssen, O. (2017). License to critique: A communication perspective on sustainability standards. *Business Ethics Quarterly, 27,* 239–262.

Christians, C. G. (2002). The social ethics of Agnes Heller. In S. L. Bracci & C. G. Christians (Eds.), *Moral engagement in public life: Theorists for contemporary ethics* (pp. 53–73). New York, NY: Peter Lang.

Christians, C. G. (2004). Ubuntu and communitarianism in virtue ethics. *Ecquid Novi: African Journalism Studies, 25,* 235–256.

Christians, C. G. (2008a). Media ethics in education. *Journalism and Communication Monographs, 9,* 179–221.

Christians, C. G. (2008b). Media ethics on a higher order of magnitude. *Journal of Mass Media Ethics, 23,* 3–14.

Christians, C. G. (2010). The ethics of universal being. In S. J. A. Ward & H. Wasserman (Eds.), *Media ethics beyond borders: A global perspective* (pp. 6–23). New York, NY: Routledge.

Christians, C. G. (2011a). Journalism ethics in theory and in practice. In G. Cheney, S. May, & D. Munshi (Eds.), *The Handbook of Communication Ethics* (pp. 190–203). New York, NY: Routledge.

Christians, C. G. (2011b). The philosophy of technology: Globalization and ethical universals. *Journalism Studies, 12,* 727–737.

Christians, C. G. (2018). Truth, Al Jazeera, and crisis journalism. *International Journal of Crisis Communication, 1,* 79–91.

Christians, C. G., Ferré, J. P., & Fackler, P. M. (1993). *Good news: Social ethics and the press.* New York, NY: Oxford University Press.

Christians, C. G., & Traber, M. (Eds.). (1997). *Communication ethics and universal values.* Thousand Oaks, CA: SAGE.

Cissna, K. N. (Ed.). (1995). *Applied communication in the 21st century.* Mahwah, NJ: Lawrence Erlbaum.

Cissna, K. N., Eadie, W. F., & Hickson, M. (2009). The development of applied communication research. In L. R. Frey & K. N. Cissna (Eds.), *Routledge handbook of applied communication research* (pp. 3–25). New York, NY: Routledge.

Clark, B. R. (1972). The organizational saga in higher education. *Administrative Science Quarterly, 17,* 178–184.

Cleveland, H. (2006). The limits of cultural diversity. In L. A. Samovar & R. E. Porter (Eds.), *Intercultural communication: A reader* (11th ed., pp. 405–407). Boston, MA: Cengage Learning.

Cohen, H. (1994). *The history of speech communication: The emergence of a discipline, 1914–1945.* Annandale, VA: Speech Communication Association.

Cohen, R. A. (1998). Foreword. In E. Levinas, *Otherwise than being or beyond essence* (Trans. A. Lingis, pp. xi–xvi). Pittsburgh, PA: Duquesne University Press.

Collins, J. & Porras, J. I. (2004). *Built to last: Successful habits of visionary companies.* New York, NY: HarperCollins Publishers.

Commager, H. S. (1950). *The American mind.* New Haven, CT: Yale University Press.

Conrad, C. (1993). *The ethical nexus.* Norwood, NJ: Ablex.

Cook, M. (2005). *The scholarship and praxis of communication ethics: Rhetorical interruptions in historical narratives* (Unpublished doctoral dissertation). Duquesne University, Pittsburgh, PA.

Cooren, F., Kuhn, T., Cornelissen, J. P., & Clark, T. (2011). Communication, organizing, and organization: An overview and introduction to the special issue. *Organization Studies, 32,* 1149–1170.

Corman, S. R. (2005). Postpositivism. In S. May & D. K. Mumby (Eds.), *Engaging organizational communication theory and research: Multiple perspectives* (pp. 15–34). Thousand Oaks, CA: SAGE.

Corman, S. R., & Poole, M. S. (Eds.). (2000). *Perspectives on organizational communication: Finding common ground.* New York, NY: The Guilford Press.

Corporate Profile. (2017). *Chipotle Mexican Grill.* Retrieved from http://ir.chipotle.com/corporate-profile

Corradi Fiumara, G. (1990). *The other side of language: A philosophy of listening.* New York, NY: Routledge.

Couldry, N. (2010). Media ethics: Towards a framework for media producers and media consumers. In S. J. A. Ward & H. Wasserman (Eds.), *Media ethics beyond borders: A global perspective* (pp. 59–72). New York, NY: Routledge.

Couldry, N. (2013). Living well in and through media. In N. Couldry, M. Madianou, & A. Pinchevski (Eds.), *Ethics of media* (pp. 39–56). New York, NY: Palgrave-MacMillan.

Crasnow, S. (2009). Is standpoint theory a resource for feminist epistemology? An introduction. *Hypatia, 24,* 189–192.

Crichton, M. (1991). *Jurassic park.* New York, NY: Ballantine Books.

Crichton, M. (1999). *Timeline.* New York, NY: Alfred A. Knopf.

Crichton, M. (2006). *Next: A novel.* New York, NY: HarperCollins.

Cupach, W. R., & Spitzberg, B. H. (2004). *The dark side of relationship pursuit: From attraction to obsession and stalking.* Florence, KY: Lawrence Erlbaum.

Day, R. E. (2000). Tropes, history, and ethics in professional discourse and information science. *Journal of the American Society for Information Science, 51,* 469–475.

Deetz, S. A. (1992). *Democracy in an age of corporate colonization: Developments in communication and the politics of everyday life.* Albany: State University of New York Press.

Deetz, S. A. (1994). *Transforming communication, transforming business: Building responsive and responsible workplaces.* Cresskill, NJ: Hampton Press.

Deetz, S. A. (2001). Conceptual foundations. In M. F. Jablin & L. L. Putnam, L. L. (Eds.), *The new handbook of organizational communication: Advances in theory, research, and methods* (2nd ed., pp. 3–47). Thousand Oaks, CA: SAGE.

Deetz, S. A., & Mumby, D. (1990). *Power, discourse, and the workplace: Reclaiming the critical tradition in communication studies in organizations.* In J. Anderson (Ed.), *Communication yearbook 13* (pp. 18–47). Thousand Oaks, CA: SAGE.

Dewey, J. (1953). *Essays in experimental logic.* Mineola, NY: Dover Publications.

Dewey, J. (1969). The ethics of democracy. In J. A. Boydston (Ed.), *The early works of John Dewey* (Vol. 4, pp. 227–252). Carbondale: Southern Illinois University Press. (Original work published 1888).

Dickinson, G., Blair, C., & Ott, B. L. (2010). *Places of public memory: The rhetoric of museums and memorials.* Tuscaloosa: University of Alabama Press.

Disis, J. (2018, February 4). Why Super Bowl ads still matter. *CNN Money.* Retrieved from http://money.cnn.com/2018/02/01/news/companies/super-bowl-commercials/index.html

Dixon, T. L. (2015). Good guys are still always in white? Positive change and continued misrepresentation of race and crime on local television news. *Communication Research, 44,* 775–792.

Dorsey, A. M., Miller, K. I., Parrott, R., & Thompson, T. L. (Eds.). (2003). *The handbook of health communication.* Mahwah, NJ: Lawrence Erlbaum.

Dougherty, C. J. (1996). *Back to reform: Values, markets, and the health care system.* New York, NY: Oxford University Press.

du Pré, A. (2016). *Communicating about health: Current issues and perspectives* (5th ed.). New York, NY: Oxford University Press.

Duncan, R. (Ed.). (1972). *Gandhi: Selected writings.* New York, NY: Harper & Row.

Duran, R., Kelly, L. K., & Rotaru, T. (2011). Mobile phones in romantic relationships and the dialectical tension of autonomy versus connection. *Communication Quarterly, 59,* 19–36.

Dylan, B. (1979). Gotta serve somebody. On *Slow train coming* [Audio CD]. New York, NY: Special Rider Music.

Eason, D. L. (1986). On journalistic authority: The Janet Cooke scandal. *Critical Studies in Mass Communication, 3,* 429–447.

Eco, U. (2005). Books, texts and hypertexts. In M. Buccheri, E. Costa, & D. Holoch (Eds.), *The power of words: Literature and society in late modernity* (pp. 23–34). Ravenna, Italy: A. Longo Editore.

Egan, M. (2017, August 31). Wells Fargo uncovers up to 1.4 million more fake accounts. *CNN Money.* Retrieved from http://money.cnn.com/2017/08/31/investing/wells-fargo-fake-accounts/index.html

Eicher-Catt, D. (2017). A prelude to a semioethics of dialogue. *Language and Dialogue, 7,* 100–119.

Ellul, J. (1964). *The technological society* (J. Wilkinson, Trans.). New York, NY: Alfred A. Knopf. (Original work published 1954).

Ess, C. (2011). Ethical dimensions of new technology/media. In G. Cheney, S. May, & D. Munshi (Eds.), *The Handbook of Communication Ethics* (pp. 204–220). New York, NY: Routledge.

Fairhurst, G. T. (2001). Dualisms in leadership research. In F. M. Jablin & L. L. Putnam (Eds.), *The new handbook of organizational communication: Advances in theory, research, and methods* (2nd ed., pp. 379–439). Thousand Oaks, CA: SAGE.

Fairhurst, G. T. (2011). *The power of framing: Creating the language of leadership.* San Francisco, CA: Jossey-Bass.

Fay, M. J. (2012). Out of sight, out of . . . the loop? Relationship challenges for teleworkers and their co-located peers, managers, and organizations. In B. L. Omdahl & J. M. H. Fritz (Eds.), *Problematic relationships in the workplace, vol. 2* (pp. 125–144). New York, NY: Peter Lang.

Feiler, B. (2015, March 20). How to manage media in families. *New York Times.* Retrieved from https://www.nytimes.com/2015/03/22/style/how-to-manage-media-in-families.html

Felski, R. (1989). *Beyond feminist aesthetics: Feminist literature and social change.* Cambridge, MA: Harvard University Press.

Ferguson, A. (2004). *An essay on the history of civil society.* Kila, MT: Kessinger Publishing. (Original work published 1767).

Fisher, W. R. (1987). *Human communication as narration: Toward a philosophy of reason, value, and action.* Columbia: University of South Carolina Press.

Fisher, W. R. (2006, June). *Glimpses of hope.* Paper presented at the Bi-Annual National Communication Ethics Conference: Pittsburgh, PA.

Fortunati, L. (2005). Is body-to-body communication still the prototype? *The Information Society: An International Journal, 21,* 53–61.

Foster, N. (Producer). (1957). *Zorro* [Television series]. Burbank, CA: Walt Disney Productions.

Foucault, M. (1997). Self writing. In P. Rabinow (Ed.), *Ethics* (pp. 207–222). London: Penguin Books.

Fraleigh, D. M., & Tuman, J. S. (1996). *Freedom of speech in the marketplace of ideas.* New York, NY: Bedford/St. Martin's.

Frankl, V. E. (1963). *Man's search for meaning: An introduction to logotherapy* (I. Lasch, Trans.). New York, NY: Pocket Books.

Frankl, V. E. (1967). *Psychotherapy and existentialism: Selected papers on logotherapy.* New York, NY: Touchstone.

Fraser, N. (1990). Rethinking the public sphere: A contribution to the critique of actually existing democracy. *Social Text, 25/26,* 56–80.

Freed, R. C. (1993). Postmodern practices: Perspectives and prospects. In N. R. Blyler & C. Thralls (Eds.), *Professional communication: The social perspective* (pp. 196–214). Thousand Oaks, CA: SAGE.

Freimuth, V. S. (1995). Response: Applied health communication research. In K. N. Cissna (Ed.), *Applied communication in the 21st century* (pp. 39–47). Hillsdale, NJ: Lawrence Erlbaum.

Freire, P. (1972). *Pedagogy of the oppressed* (M. B. Ramos, Trans.). New York, NY: Herder & Herder.

Friedman, M. (1972). *Touchstones of reality: Existential trust and the community of peace.* New York, NY: E. P. Dutton.

Friedman, M. (1976). *Martin Buber: The life of dialogue.* Chicago: University of Chicago Press.

Fritz, J. M. H. (2013). *Professional civility: Communicative virtue at work.* New York, NY: Peter Lang.

Fritz, J. M. H. (2016). Interpersonal communication ethics. In C. R. Berger & M. E. Roloff (Eds.), *The international encyclopedia of interpersonal communication.* John Wiley & Sons, Inc. doi:10.1002/9781118540190.wbeic227

Fritz, J. M. H. (2018). Communication ethics. In N. Snow (Ed.), *Oxford handbook of virtue* (pp. 700–721). New York, NY: Oxford University Press.

Fritz, J. M. H., & Omdahl, B. L. (Eds.). (2006). *Problematic relationships in the workplace.* New York, NY: Peter Lang.

Fromm, E. (1994). *Escape from freedom.* Woodacre, CA: Owl Books.

Gadamer, H.-G. (1976). *Philosophical hermeneutics* (D. E. Linge, Trans. & Ed.). Berkeley: University of California Press.

Gadamer, H.-G. (1986). *Truth and method* (G. Barden & J. Cumming, Trans.). New York, NY: Crossroad Publishing. (Original work published 1960).

Geertz, C. (1973). *The interpretation of cultures.* New York, NY: Basic Books.

Gehrke, P. J. (2009). *The ethics and politics of speech: Communication and rhetoric in the twentieth century.* Carbondale: Southern Illinois University Press.

Geist-Martin, P., Ray, E. B., & Sharf, B. F. (2002). *Communicating health: Personal, cultural, and political complexities.* Belmont, CA: Wadsworth Publishing.

Glatzer, N. N. (Ed.). (1966). *The way of response: Martin Buber—selections from his writings.* New York, NY: Schocken Books.

Goffman, E. (1973). *The presentation of self in everyday life.* Woodstock, NY: Overlook.

Goodall, H. L. (2016). *A need to know: The clandestine history of a CIA family.* New York, NY: Taylor & Francis.

Grinberg, E., & Yan, H. (2018, March 16). A generation raised on gun violence sends a loud message to adults: Enough. *CNN.* Retrieved from https://www.cnn.com/2018/03/14/us/national-school-walkout-gun-violence-protests/index.html

Gudykunst, W. B. (2003). *Cross-cultural and intercultural communication.* Thousand Oaks, CA: SAGE.

Gudykunst, W. B. (2004). *Theorizing about intercultural communication.* Thousand Oaks, CA: SAGE.

Gueldenzoph, L. E., & May, G. L. (2002). Collaborative peer evaluation: Best practices for group member assessments. *Business Communication Quarterly, 65,* 9–21.

Gunther, D. F., & Diekema, D. S. (2006). Attenuating growth in children with profound developmental disability. *Archives of Pediatrics & Adolescent Medicine, 160,* 1013–1017.

Habermas, J. (1979). *Communication and the evolution of society* (T. McCarthy, Trans.). Boston, MA: Beacon Press.

Habermas, J. (1984). *The theory of communicative action: Vol 1. Reason and the rationalization of society* (T. McCarthy, Trans.). Boston, MA: Beacon Press.

Habermas, J. (1987). *The theory of communicative action: Vol. 2. Lifeworld and system: A critique of functionalist reason* (T. McCarthy, Trans.). Boston, MA: Beacon Press.

Habermas, J. (1996). *Between facts and norms: Contributions to a discourse theory of law and democracy.* Cambridge, MA: MIT Press.

Habermas, J. (2003). *The future of human nature*. Cambridge, UK: Polity Press.

Haiman, F. S. (1967). The rhetoric of the streets: Some legal and ethical considerations. *Quarterly Journal of Speech, 53*, 99–114.

Haiman, F. S. (1982). *Speech and law in a free society*. Chicago, IL: University of Chicago Press.

Haiman, F. S. (2002). Eternally vigilant: Free speech in the modern era. *Argumentation and advocacy, 39*, 141–143.

Hall, B. 'J' (2005). *Among cultures: The challenge of communication* (2nd ed.). Belmont, CA: Wadsworth.

Hall, E. T. (1973). *The silent language*. New York, NY: Anchor Books.

Hall, E. T. (1976). *Beyond culture*. New York, NY: Anchor Books/Doubleday.

Hall, E. T. (1990). *The hidden dimension*. New York, NY: Doubleday.

Hannan, J. (2011). Pragmatism, democracy, and communication: Three rival perspectives. *Review of Communication, 11*, 107–121.

Harding, S. (1991). *Whose science? Whose knowledge? Thinking from women's lives*. Ithaca, NY: Cornell University Press.

Harding, S. (2004). *The feminist standpoint theory reader: Intellectual and political controversies*. New York, NY: Routledge.

Harding, S. (2009). Standpoint theories: Productively controversial. *Hypatia, 24*, 192–200.

Harter, L. M., & Bochner, A. P. (2009). Healing through stories: A special issue on narrative medicine. *Journal of Applied Communication Research, 37*, 113–117.

Hartnett, S. J. (2017). Communication, globalization and the prospect of solidarity. [Public address.] *National Communication Association Presidential Address*. Dallas, TX. Retrieved from https://www.youtube.com/watch?v=5dOCxBHqedM

Hauerwas, S. (1981). *A community of character: Toward a constructive Christian social ethic*. Notre Dame, IN: Notre Dame University Press.

Hewlett, S. A., & Luce, C. B. (2006). *Extreme jobs: The dangerous allure of the 70-hour workweek*. Harvard Business Review, *84*(12), 49–59.

Homans, G. C. (1958). Social behavior as exchange. *American Journal of Sociology, 63*, 597–606.

Hotten, R. (2015, December 10). Volkswagen: The scandal explained. *BBC News*. Retrieved from http://www.bbc.com/news/business-34324772

Howells, W. S. (1986). *The empathic communicator*. Belmont, CA: Wadsworth Publishing Company.

Hugo, V. (1976). *Les miserables* (N. Denny, Trans.). New York, NY: Folio Press. (Original work published 1833).

Hyde, M. J. (2001). *The call of conscience*. Columbia: University of South Carolina Press.

Hyde, M. J. (Ed.). (2004). *The ethos of rhetoric*. Columbia: University of South Carolina Press.

Hyde, M. J. (2005). *The life-giving gift of acknowledgement*. West Lafayette, IN: Purdue University Press.

Hyde, M. J. (2010). *Perfection: Coming to terms with being human*. Waco, TX: Baylor University Press.

Hyde, M. J. (2012). *Openings: Acknowledging essential moments in human communication*. Waco, TX: Baylor University Press.

Hyde, M. J. (2016). *The interruption that we are: Communication ethics, the lived body, and our posthuman future.* Columbia: University of South Carolina Press.

Iltis, A. S. (Ed.). (2003). *Instituitional integrity in health care.* Dordrecht, Netherlands: Kluwer.

Intemann, K. (2010). 25 years of feminist empiricism and standpoint theory: Where are we now? *Hypatia, 25,* 778–796.

Jablin, F. M. (2001). Organizational entry, assimilation, and disengagement/exit. In F. M. Jablin & L. L. Putnam (Eds.), *The new handbook of organizational communication: Advances in theory, research, and methods* (2nd ed., pp. 732–819). Thousand Oaks, CA: SAGE.

Jackson, M. (2008). *Distracted: The erosion of attention and the coming Dark Age.* Amherst, NY: Prometheus Books.

Jackson, R. J., II (2000). So real illusions of black intellectualism: Exploring race, roles, and gender in the academy. *Communication Theory, 10,* 48–63.

Jackson, S. J., & Banaszczyk, S. (2016). Digital standpoints: Debating gendered violence and racial exclusions in the feminist counterpublic. *Journal of Communication Inquiry, 40,* 391–407.

Jaksa, J. A., & Pritchard, M. S. (1994). *Communication ethics: Methods of analysis* (2nd ed.). Belmont, CA: Wadsworth.

Jameson, D. A. (2001). Narrative discourse and management action. *Journal of Business Communication, 38,* 476–511.

Jameson, F. (1984). Postmodernism, or the cultural logic of late capitalism. *New Left Review, 146,* 53–93.

Jensen, J. V. (1991). Foreword. In K. J. Greenberg (Ed.), *Conversations on communication ethics* (pp. x–xii). Norwood, NJ: Ablex.

Jensen, J. V. (1997). *Ethical issues in the communication process.* Mahwah, NJ: Lawrence Erlbaum.

Jewison, N. (Director). (1971). *Fiddler on the roof* [Motion picture]. United States: Cartier Productions.

Johannesen, R. L., Valde, K. S., & Whedbee, K. E. (2008). *Ethics in human communication* (6th ed.) Prospect Heights, IL: Waveland.

Johnstone, C. L. (1981). Ethics, wisdom, and the mission of contemporary rhetoric. *Central States Speech Journal, 32,* 177–188.

Johnstone, H. W., Jr. (1981). Toward an ethics for rhetoric. *Communication, 6,* 305–314.

Jovanovic, S. (2012). *Democracy, dialogue, and community action: Truth and reconciliation in Greensboro.* Fayetteville: University of Arkansas Press.

Jovanovic, S., Steger, C., Symonds, S., & Nelson, D. (2007). Promoting deliberative democracy through dialogue. In L. R. Frey & K. M. Carragee (Eds.), *Communication activism, volume one: Communication for social change* (pp. 67–108). New York, NY: Hampton Press.

Kaldjian, L. C. (2017). Concepts of health, ethics, and communication in shared decision making. *Communication & Medicine, 14,* 83–95.

Kase, C., Rivera, N., & Hunt, M. G. (2016). The effects of sorority recruitment on psychological well-being and social support. *Oracle: The Research Journal of the Association of Fraternity/Sorority Advisors, 11*(1), 1–16.

Kazantzakis, N. (1996). *Zorba the Greek.* New York, NY: Simon & Schuster.

Kennedy, A. (2016). Landscapes of care: Feminist approaches in global public relations. *Journal of Media Ethics, 31*, 215–230.

Kim, Y. Y. (2005). Inquiry in intercultural and development communication. *Journal of Communication, 55*, 554–577.

Knapp, M. L., & Daly, J. A. (Eds.). (2011). *The SAGE handbook of interpersonal communication* (4th ed.). Thousand Oaks, CA: SAGE.

Kopf, D. A., Boje, D., & Torres, I. M. (2010). The good, the bad and the ugly: Dialogical ethics and market information. *Journal of Business Ethics, 94*, 285–297.

Kowalski, R. M., Giumetti, G. W., Schroeder, A. N., & Lattanner, M. R. (2014). Bullying in the digital age: A critical review and meta-analysis of cyberbullying research among youth. *Psychological Bulletin, 140*, 1073–1137.

Kramer, M. W. (2003). *Managing uncertainty in organizational communication.* Mahwah, NJ: Lawrence Erlbaum.

Kramer, M. W. (2010). *Organizational socialization: Joining and leaving organizations.* Malden, MA: Polity Press.

Kreps, G. L. (2006). Communication and racial inequities in health care. *The American Behavioral Scientist, 49*, 760–774.

Kreps, G. L., & Thornton, B. C. (1992). *Health communication: Theory and practice* (2nd ed.). Long Grove, IL: Waveland Press.

Landau, J. (2014, July 22). GoPro's viral video marketing campaign turns it into top YouTube brand in the world. *New York Daily News.* Retrieved from http://www.nydailynews.com/news/national/gopro-marketing-turns-top-youtube-brand-article-1.1875573

Lane, S. D. (2017). *Understanding everyday incivility: Why are they so rude?* Lanham, MD: Rowman & Littlefield.

Lanham, R. A. (2006). *The economics of attention: Style and substance in the age of information.* Chicago, IL: University of Chicago Press.

Lasch, C. (1991). *The true and only heaven: Progress and its critics.* New York, NY: W. W. Norton & Company.

Lauren, L. (2016, March 8). Respect and social media. *Huffington Post.* Retrieved from https://www.huffingtonpost.com/linda-lauren/respect-and-social-media_b_9315164.html

Lauterborn, R. (1990, October 1). New marketing litany: Four P's passe; C-words take over. *Advertising Age, 61*(41), 26.

Leeds-Hurwitz, W. (1995). *Social approaches to communication.* New York, NY: Guilford Press.

Levinas, E. (1969). *Totality and infinity: An essay on exteriority* (A. Lingis, Trans.). Pittsburgh, PA: Duquesne University Press.

Levinas, E. (1998). *Otherwise than being or beyond essence* (A. Lingis, Trans.). Pittsburgh, PA: Duquesne University Press.

Levinas, E. (2000). *Proper names.* London, UK: Athlone Press.

Lipari, L. (2004). Listening for the Other: Ethical implications of the Buber-Levinas encounter. *Communication Theory, 2*, 122–141.

Lipari, L. (2014). *Listening, thinking, being: Toward an ethics of attunement.* University Park: The Pennsylvania State University Press.

Lipari, L. (2017). The speech we do not speak: Dialogic mind, praxis, and ethics. *Language and Dialogue, 7*, 45–62.

Lyotard, J.-F. (1984). *The postmodern condition.* Manchester, IN: Manchester University Press.

MacIntyre, A. (1984). *After virtue.* Notre Dame, IN: Notre Dame University Press.

MacIntyre, A. (1989). *Whose justice? Which rationality?* Notre Dame, IN: Notre Dame University Press.

MacIntyre, A. (1998). *A short history of ethics: A history of moral philosophy from the Homeric Age to the twentieth century* (2nd ed.). Notre Dame, IN: University of Notre Dame Press.

MacIntyre, A. (2006). *Ethics and politics: Selected essays* (Volume 2). New York, NY: Cambridge University Press.

MacIntyre, A. (2016). *Ethics in the conflicts of modernity: An essay on desire, practical reasoning, and narrative.* Cambridge, UK: Cambridge University Press.

Macklin, R., & Mathison, K. (2017). Embedding ethics: Dialogic partnerships and communitarian business ethics. *Journal of Business Ethics* [Online first]. https://doi.org/10.1007/s10551-016-3431-0

Makau, J. M. (2002). Preface. In S. Bracci & C. G. Christians (Eds.), *Moral engagement in public life: Theorists for contemporary ethics* (pp. vii–x). New York, NY: Peter Lang.

Makau, J. M., & Arnett, R. C. (Eds.). (1997). *Communication ethics in an age of diversity.* Chicago: University of Illinois Press.

Makau, J. M., & Marty, D. L. (2001). *Cooperative argumentation: A model for deliberative community.* Prospect Heights, IL: Waveland Press.

Mandel, J. E. (1974). A strategy for selecting and phrasing questions in an interview. *Journal of Business Communication, 12,* 17–23.

Marks, M., & O'Connor, A. H. (2006). The round-robin mock interview: Maximum learning in minimum time. *Business Communication Quarterly, 69,* 264–275.

Martin, J. N., & Nakayama, T. K. (2004). *Experiencing intercultural communication: An introduction* (2nd ed.). New York, NY: McGraw-Hill Humanities/Social Sciences/Languages.

May, S., & Mumby, D. K. (2005). *Engaging organizational communication theory and research: Multiple perspectives.* Thousand Oaks, CA: SAGE.

McDonald, J. (2015). Organizational communication meets queer theory: Theorizing relations of "difference" differently. *Communication Theory, 25,* 310–329.

Mead, G. H. (1962). *Mind, self, and society: From the standpoint of a social behaviorist.* C. W. Morris (Ed.). Chicago, IL: University of Chicago Press.

Michaels, M. (2018, January 25). The price of a 30-second Super Bowl ad has exploded—but it may be worth it for companies. *Business Insider.* Retrieved from http://www.businessinsider.com/super-bowl-commercials-cost-more-than-eagles-quarterback-earns-2018-1

Miller, G. R. (1978). The current status of theory and research in interpersonal communication. *Human Communication Research, 4,* 164–178.

Miller, G. R., & Steinberg, M. (1975). *Between people: A new analysis of interpersonal communication.* Chicago, IL: Science Research Associates.

Miller, K. I. (2000). Common ground from the post-positivist perspective: From "straw person" argument to collaborative coexistence. In S. R. Corman & M. S. Poole (Eds.), *Perspectives on organizational communication: Finding common ground* (pp. 46–68). New York, NY: Guilford Press.

Miller, K. I. (2015). *Organizational communication: Approaches and processes* (7th ed.). Stamford, CT: Cengage.

Mitroff, I. (1978). *Methodological approaches to social science: Integrating divergent concepts and theories.* San Francisco, CA: Jossey-Bass.

Moroco, L. (2005). *Phenomenological distance in interpersonal relationships* (Unpublished doctoral dissertation). Duquesne University, Pittsburgh, PA.

Morris, C. E., III (2015). Context's critic, invisible traditions, and queering rhetorical history. *Quarterly Journal of Speech, 101,* 225–243.

Mumby, D. K. (2000). Common ground from the critical perspective: Overcoming binary opposition. In S. R. Corman & M. S. Poole (Eds.), *Perspectives on organizational communication: Finding common ground* (pp. 68–89). New York, NY: Guilford Press.

Mumby, D. K. (2015). Organizing power. *Review of Communication, 15,* 19–38.

Murray, J. C. (1960). *We hold these truths: Catholic reflections on the American proposition.* New York, NY: Sheed and Ward.

Myers, S. A., Goldman, Z. W., Atkinson, J., Ball, H., Carton, S. T., Tindage, M. F., & Anderson, A. O. (2016). Student civility in the college classroom: Exploring student use and effects of classroom citizenship behavior. *Communication Education, 65,* 64–82.

Nakayama, T. K., & Martin, J. N. (Eds.). (1998). *Whiteness: The communication of social identity.* London, UK: SAGE.

National Communication Association. (2017). *A code of professional ethics for the communication scholar/teacher* (rev. ed.). Retrieved from https://www.natcom.org/advocacy-public-engagement/public-policy/public-statements

Neher, W. W., & Sandin, P. (2007). *Communicating ethically.* Boston, MA: Allyn & Bacon.

Newton, M. (2002). *Savage girls and wild boys: A history of feral children.* London, UK: Faber and Faber.

Nicotera, A. M., & Cushman, D. P. (1992). Organizational ethics: A within-organization view. *Journal of Applied Communication Research, 20,* 437–462.

Noddings, N. (1984). *Caring: A feminine approach to ethics and moral education.* Berkeley: University of California Press.

Noddings, N. (2012). The caring relation in teaching. *Oxford Review of Education, 38,* 771–781.

Oetzel, J. G., & Ting-Toomey, S. (2011). Intercultural perspectives on interpersonal communication. In M. L. Knapp & J. A. Daly (Eds.), *The SAGE handbook of interpersonal communication* (4th ed., pp. 563–596). Thousand Oaks, CA: SAGE.

Oldenburg, R. (2001). *Celebrating the third place: Inspiring stories about the "great good places" at the heart of our communities.* New York, NY: Marlowe & Company.

Omdahl, B. L. (2006). Towards effective work relationships. In J. M. H. Fritz & B. L. Omdahl (Eds.), *Problematic relationships in the workplace* (pp. 279–294). New York, NY: Peter Lang.

Omdahl, B. L., & Fritz, J. M. H. (Eds.). (2012). *Problematic relationships in the workplace* (Vol. 2). New York, NY: Peter Lang.

Paine, T. (1984). *Common sense, the rights of man, and other essential writings of Thomas Paine.* New York, NY: Penguin Group. (Original work published 1776).

Paquette, M., Sommerfeldt, E. J., & Kent, M. L. (2015). Do the ends justify the means? Dialogue, development communication, and deontological ethics. *Public Relations Review, 41,* 30–39.

Paulsen, J. E. (2011). A narrative ethics of care. *Health Care Analysis, 19*, 28–40.

Pearce, W. B. (1989). *Communication and the human condition.* Carbondale: Southern Illinois University Press.

Pearce, W. B., & Cronen, V. E. (1980). *Communication, action, and meaning: The creation of social realities.* New York, NY: Praeger.

Persuit, J. M. (2013). *Social media and integrated marketing communication: A rhetorical approach.* Lanham, MD: Lexington Books.

Peters, M. (1995). Legitimation problems: Knowledge and education in the postmodern condition. In M. Peters (Ed.), *Education and the postmodern condition* (pp. 21–37). Westport, CT: Bergin & Garvey.

Petrilli, S. (2016). Semiotics and education, semioethic perspectives. *Semiotica, 213*, 247–279.

Petronio, S. (2003). *Boundaries of private disclosures.* New York: State University of New York Press.

Pinchevski, A. (2005). *By way of interruption: Levinas and the ethics of communication.* Pittsburgh, PA: Duquesne University Press.

Pirsig, R. (1974). *Zen and the art of motorcycle maintenance.* New York, NY: HarperCollins.

Plaisance, P. L. (2005). The mass media as discursive network: Building on the implications of libertarian and communitarian claims for news media ethics theory. *Communication Theory, 15*, 292–313.

Plaisance, P. L. (2013). Virtue ethics and digital "flourishing": An application of Philippa Foot to life online. *Journal of Mass Media Ethics, 28*, 91–102.

Plaisance, P. L. (2015). *Virtue in media: The moral psychology of excellence in news and public relations.* New York, NY: Routledge.

Plato. (1954). *The last days of Socrates* (3rd ed., H. Tredennick, Trans.). Middlesex, UK: Penguin Classics.

Polanyi, M. (1967). *The tacit dimension.* London, UK: Routledge & K. Paul.

Poole, M. S., & McPhee, R. D. (2005). Structuration theory. In S. May & D. K. Mumby (Eds.), *Engaging organizational communication theory and research: Multiple perspectives* (pp. 171–196). Thousand Oaks, CA: SAGE.

Popper, K. (1957). *The poverty of historicism.* Boston, MA: Beacon Press.

Poulos, C., Hamilton, C., Jovanovic, S., & Moretto, K. (2015). Our work is not done: Advancing democratic engagement as purpose and product of higher education. *Journal of Community Engagement and Higher Education, 7*(1), 34–46.

Proctor, T., & Kitchen, P. (2002). Communication in postmodern integrated marketing. *Corporate Communications: An International Journal, 7*, 144–154.

Putnam, L. L. (1983). The interpretive perspective: An alternative to functionalism. In L. L. Putnam & M. E. Pacanowsky (Eds.), *Communication and organizations: An interpretive approach* (pp. 31–54). Thousand Oaks, CA: SAGE.

Putnam, L. L., & D. K. Mumby (Eds.). (2014). *The SAGE handbook of organizational communication* (3rd ed.). Thousand Oaks, CA: SAGE.

Putnam, R. D. (2000). *Bowling alone: The collapse and revival of American community.* New York, NY: Touchstone.

Rapoport, A. (1967). Strategy and conscience. In F. W. Matson & A. Montagu (Eds.), *The human dialogue: Perspectives on communication* (pp. 79–96). New York, NY: Free Press.

Ray, E. B., & Donohew, L. (1990). *Communication & health: Systems & applications.* Hillsdale, NJ: Lawrence Erlbaum.

Reisberg, L. (2000, January 7). Fraternities in decline. *Chronicle of Higher Education,* *46*(18), A59–A62.

Ricoeur, P. (2000). *The rule of metaphor: Multidisciplinary studies of the creation of meaning in language* (R. Czerny, Trans.). Toronto, ON: University of Toronto Press. (Original work published 1975).

Roberts, K. G., & Arnett, R. C. (Eds.). (2008). *Communication ethics: Between cosmopolitanism and provinciality.* New York, NY: Peter Lang.

Rogers, E. M. (1997). *A history of communication: A biographical approach.* New York, NY: Free Press.

Roloff, M. E. (1981). Five approaches: Social exchange theory. In F. G. Kline & S. H. Evans (Eds.), *Interpersonal communication: The social exchange approach* (pp. 33–59). Beverly Hills, CA: SAGE.

Roloff, M. E., & Anastasiou, L. (2001). Interpersonal communication research: An overview. In W. B. Gudykunst (Ed.), *Communication Yearbook 24* (pp. 51–71). Thousand Oaks, CA: SAGE.

Roosevelt, F. D. (1946). *Nothing to fear: The selected addresses of Franklin Delano Roosevelt 1932–1945.* B. D. Zezin (Ed.). Freeport, NY: Books for Libraries Press.

Rorty, R. (1979). *Philosophy and the mirror of nature.* Princeton, NJ: Princeton University Press.

Rouse, J. (2009). Standpoint theories reconsidered. *Hypatia, 24,* 200–209.

Safronova, V. (2017, May 27). The rise and fall of Yik Yak, the anonymous messaging app. *New York Times.* Retrieved from https://www.nytimes.com/2017/05/27/style/yik-yak-bullying-mary-washington.html

Salo, K. (2010). Grab 'Em and keep 'Em: A guide to student organization recruitment and retention. *Campus Activities Programming, 42*(8), 6–9.

Sartre, J.-P. (1953). *Being and nothingness: An essay on phenomenological ontology* (H. E. Barnes, Trans.). New York, NY: Washington Square.

Schrag, C. (1986). *Communicative praxis and the space of subjectivity.* Bloomington: Indiana University Press.

Schultz, D. E., Tannenbaum, S. I., & Lauterborn, R. F. (1993). *Integrated marketing communications.* Chicago, IL: NTC Business Books.

Schwantes, M. (2018, January 9). Warren Buffett says if you hire people on intelligence but they lack this other trait, don't bother. *Inc.* Retrieved from https://www.inc.com/marcel-schwantes/warren-buffet-says-you-should-hire-people-based-on-these-3-traits-but-only-1-truly-matters.html

Seeger, M. W. (1997). *Ethics and organizational communication.* New York, NY: Hampton Press.

Seeger, M. W., & Griffin Padgett, D. R. (2010). From image restoration to renewal: Approaches to understanding postcrisis communication. *Review of Communication, 10,* 127–141.

Seeger, M. W., Sellnow, T. L., & Ulmer, R. L. (2007). *Crisis communication and the public health.* Cresskill, NJ: Hampton Press.

Seibold, D. R. (1995). *Theoria* and *praxis*: Means and ends in applied communication. In K. N. Cissna (Ed.), *Applied communication in the 21st century* (pp. 23–38). Mahwah, NJ: Lawrence Erlbaum.

Selby, G. S. (2001). Framing social protest: The exodus narrative in Martin Luther King's Montgomery bus boycott rhetoric. *Journal of Communication and Religion, 24,* 68–93.

Sennett, R. (1974). *The fall of public man: On the social psychology of capitalism.* New York, NY: Vintage Books.

Seymour, C. G. (2011). A place for the premodern: A review of modern and postmodern intimate interpersonal communication frames. *Review of Communication, 11,* 286–309.

Shelby, A. N. (1993). Organizational, business, management, and corporate communication: An analysis of boundaries and relationships. *Journal of Business Communication, 30,* 241–267.

Sias, P. M., Krone, K. K., & Jablin, F. M. (2002). An ecological systems perspective on workplace relationships. In J. Daly & M. L. Knapp (Eds.), *Handbook of interpersonal communication* (3rd ed., pp. 615–642). Newbury Park, CA: SAGE.

Simons, H. W. (Ed.) (1990). *The rhetorical turn: Invention and persuasion in the conduct of inquiry.* Chicago, IL: University of Chicago Press.

Smith, A. R., & Olmstead, K. (2018, April 30). Declining majority of online adults say the Internet has been good for society. *Pew Research Center.* Retrieved from http://www.pewinternet.org/2018/04/30/declining-majority-of-online-adults-say-the-internet-has-been-good-for-society/

Society of Professional Journalists. (2014, September 6). *SPJ Code of Ethics.* Retrieved from https://www.spj.org/ethicscode.asp

Sproule, M. (2007). The life of reason: Its contents and discontents. *Spectra, 43,* 3–4.

Stanek, S. (2005, July 31). Want to change your major? You're not alone. *Chicago Tribune,* 1.

Starosta, G., & Chen W. J. (Eds.). (2003). *Ferment in the intercultural field: Axiology/value/praxis.* Thousand Oaks, CA: SAGE.

Stephen, T. (1994). Communication in the shifting context of intimacy: Marriage, meaning, and modernity. *Communication Theory, 4,* 191–218.

Stewart, J. R. (2011). *Bridges not walls: A book about interpersonal communication* (11th ed.). Columbus, OH: McGraw-Hill.

Strate, L. (2017). *Media ecology: An approach to understanding the human condition.* New York, NY: Peter Lang.

Strom, W. (2013). Contractualism, committalism, and covenantalism: A worldview dimensional analysis of human relating. *Communication Studies, 64,* 353–373.

Stroud, S. R. (2016). Democracy, partisanship, and the meliorative value of sympathy in John Dewey's philosophy of communication. *Journal of Speculative Philosophy, 30,* 75–93.

Stroud, S. R. (2017). Rhetoric, ethics, and the principle of charity: Pragmatist clues to the democratic riddle. *Language and Dialogue, 7,* 26–44.

Swenson-Lepper, T. (2012). Teaching communication ethics and diversity: Using technology and community engagement to enhance learning. *Communication Teacher, 26,* 228–235.

Swenson-Lepper, T., Leavitt, M. A., Hoffer, M., Charron, L. N., Ballard, R. L., McManus, L. M. B., . . . Tompkins, P. S. (2015). Communication ethics in the communication curriculum: United States, Canada, and Puerto Rico. *Communication Education, 64,* 472–490.

Taylor, C. (1989). *Sources of the self: The making of the modern identity.* Cambridge, MA: Harvard University Press.

Taylor, C. (1991). *The ethics of authenticity.* Cambridge, MA: Harvard University Press.

Taylor, H. (2016, October 5). Most young terrorist recruitment is linked to social media, said DOJ official. *CNBC.* Retrieved from https://www.cnbc.com/2016/10/05/most-young-terrorist-recruitment-is-linked-to-social-media-said-doj-official.html

Tebeaux, E. (1999). Designing written business communication along the shifting cultural continuum: The new face of Mexico. *Journal of Business and Technical Communication, 13,* 49–85.

Thompson, T. L. (2009). The applicability of narrative ethics. *Journal of Applied Communication Research, 37,* 188–195.

Thompson, T. L. (2011). Hope and the act of informed dialogue: A delicate balance at end of life. *Journal of Language and Social Psychology, 30,* 177–192.

Ting-Toomey, S. (2011). Intercultural communication ethics: Multiple layered issues. In G. Cheney, S. May, & D. Munshi (Eds.), *Handbook of communication ethics* (pp. 335–352). London, UK: Routledge.

Ting-Toomey, S., & Dorjee, T. (2015). Intercultural and intergroup communication competence: Toward an integrative perspective. In A. F. Hannawa & B. H. Spitzberg (Eds.), *Handbook of communication science: Communication competence, volume 23* (pp. 503–538). Berlin, Germany: De Gruyter Mouton.

Ting-Toomey, S., & Korzenny, F. (Eds.). (2002). *Language, communication, and culture: Current directions.* Thousand Oaks, CA: SAGE.

Tocqueville, A. de (2000). *Democracy in America.* Chicago, IL: University of Chicago Press. (Original work published 1835 & 1840).

Toffler, A. (1970). *Future shock.* New York, NY: Random House.

Tolkien, J. R. R. (2004). *The lord of the rings* (50th Anniversary ed.). Boston, MA: Houghton Mifflin.

Tompkins, P. K., & Wanca-Thibault, M. (2001). Organizational communication: Prelude and prospects. In F. M. Jablin & L. L. Putnam (Eds.), *The new handbook of organizational communication: Advances in theory, research, and methods* (2nd ed., pp. xvii–xxxi). Thousand Oaks, CA: SAGE.

Tompkins, P. S. (2009). Rhetorical listening and moral sensitivity. *International Journal of Listening, 23,* 60–79.

Tompkins, P. S. (2015). Acknowledgment, justice, and communication ethics. *Review of Communication, 15,* 240–257.

Torp, S. (2009). Integrated communications: From one look to normative consistency. *Corporate Communications: An International Journal, 14,* 190–206.

Turkle, S. (2011). *Alone together: Why we expect more from technology and less from each other.* New York, NY: Basic Books.

Ulmer, R. R., Sellnow, T. L., & Seeger, M. W. (2007). *Effective crisis communication: Moving from crisis to opportunity.* Thousand Oaks, CA: SAGE.

Vilhauer, M. (2009). Beyond the "fusion of horizons": Gadamer's notion of understanding as "play." *Philosophy Today, 53,* 359–364.

Waldron, V. R., & Kelley, D. L. (2008). *Communicating forgiveness.* Thousand Oaks, CA: SAGE.

Wall, S. V. (2004). Writing the "self" in teacher research: The potential powers of a new professional discourse. *English Education, 36,* 289–317.

Wallace, K. R. (1955). An ethical basis of communication. *Speech Teacher, 4,* 1–9.

Ward, S. J. A. (2011). Ethical flourishing as aim of global media ethics. *Journalism Studies*, *12*, 738–746.

Watt, I. (2002). *Myths of modern individualism.* West Nyack, NY: Cambridge University Press.

Weaver, R. M. (1970). *Language is sermonic.* Baton Rouge: Louisiana State University Press.

Weaver, R. M. (1984). *Ideas have consequences.* Chicago, IL: University of Chicago Press.

Willard, N. E. (2007). *Cyberbullying and cyberthreats: Responding to the challenge of online social aggression, threats, and distress.* Champaign, IL: Research Press.

Wilmot, W. (1995). *Relational communication.* New York, NY: McGraw Hill.

Witte, K., Meyer, G., & Martell, D. (2001). *Effective health risk messages: A step-by-step guide.* Thousand Oaks, CA: SAGE.

Wood, J. T. (1992). *Spinning the symbolic web: Human communication and symbolic interaction.* Norwood, NJ: Ablex.

Wood, J. T. (1994). *Who cares? Women, care, and culture.* Carbondale: Southern Illinois University Press.

Wood, J. T. (1996). *Everyday encounters: An introduction to interpersonal communication.* Belmont, CA: Wadsworth.

Wood, J. T. (2004). *Interpersonal communication: Everyday encounters* (4th ed.). Belmont, CA: Wadsworth/Thomson Learning.

Wood, J. T., & Gregg, R. B. (Eds.). (1995). *Toward the 21st century: The future of speech communication.* Cresskill, NJ: Hampton Press.

Wyatt, W. N. (Ed.). (2014). *The ethics of journalism: Individual, institutional and cultural influences.* New York, NY: I. B. Tauris & Co.

Yancy, G. (2012). *Look, a white! Philosophical essays on whiteness.* Philadelphia, PA: Temple University Press.

Yancy, G. (2013). Performing philosophical dialogue as a space for *dwelling near. Philosophia Africana*, *15*, 99–105.

Yancy, G. (2015). Through the crucible of pain and suffering: African-American philosophy as a gift and the countering of the western philosophical metanarrative. *Educational Philosophy and Theory*, *47*, 1143–1159.

Yancy, G. (2016). *Black bodies, white gazes: The continuing significance of race in America.* Lanham, MD: Rowman & Littlefield.

Yancy, G. (2018). *Backlash: What happens when we talk honestly about racism in America.* Lanham, MD: Rowman & Littlefield.

Zarefsky, D. (1995). On defining the communication discipline. In J. T. Wood & R. B. Gregg (Eds.), *Toward the twenty-first century: The future of speech communication* (pp. 103–112). Cresskill, NJ: Hampton Press.

Zion, L., & Craig, D. (Eds.) (2015). *Ethics for digital journalists.* New York, NY: Routledge.